T0287744

THE FALL OF EMPIRES

THE FALL OF
EMPIRES

A Brief History of Imperial Collapse

CHAD DENTON

WESTHOLME
Yardley

Facing title page: The Alexander Mosaic, House of Faun, Pompeii, c. 100 BCE (detail). (*Berthold Werner*)

Westholme Publishing, LLC
904 Edgewood Road
Yardley, Pennsylvania 19067
Visit our Web site at www.westholmepublishing.com

ISBN: 978-1-59416-334-0
Also available as an eBook.

Printed in the United States of America.

CONTENTS

List of Maps

INTRODUCTION

The Lifespan of Empires

E mpire is a dirty word in politics. Few today would call their nation an empire and mean it as a compliment or perhaps a bit of historic nostalgia. Also, in name at least, there are no empires left. There is still one remaining emperor in the world today, the emperor of Japan, and even that is based on a clumsy Western translation of the name for a uniquely Japanese position. True, part of the disappearance of *de jure* empires and emperors is the dramatic decline of monarchy as the preferred form of government on a global scale in favor of national republics, but it is also obvious that after the twentieth century, with its worldwide wave of decolonizing and liberation movements, the very word empire has come to conjure images of slavery, war, repression, and colonialism.

There are, of course, still dissenters. Popular British historian Niall Ferguson in particular has been an unashamed apologist of empire. "Did Senegal ultimately benefit from French rule?" Niall asks himself in an interview with *The Guardian*. His answer cuts clean. "Yes, it's clear."[1] An economist, Deepak Lal, wrote the provocatively titled *In Praise of Empire*, in which he defends not only American imperialism but most empires since the Roman Empire: "The order provided by empires has been essential for globalization, which promotes prosperity."[2]

Such defenses of empire, of course, always—and, to be blunt, have to—refuse to even acknowledge the humanitarian ugliness. After all, empires are inevitably built through the hardship and displacement of entire peoples or at the very least economic exploitation of entire societies. Further, only the most callous would fail to be moved if they really meditated on how many lost cultures there are, absorbed and digested into nothing except a memory by expanding empires. Thanks to the Roman Empire, there is much that will never be known about the Etruscans, the Gauls, the Carthaginians, and the Dacians, while the wholesale destruction of Mayan codices and artifacts by seventeenth-century Spanish zealots erased a precious record of their religion, culture, history, and writing system.

Even the cool, rationalist praises of economic stability and growth under imperialism cannot be taken for granted. John A. Hobson, who lived at the time the British Empire was at its apex and still remains one of the great critics of empire, had a simple but devastating diagnosis for the seemingly prosperous British Empire of his day: "Although the new Imperialism has been bad business for the nation, it has been good business for certain classes and certain trades within the nation."[3] Whatever one gets out of this debate—which no matter where one stands can only bring to mind the Jewish rebel leader in *The Life of Brian* who has to grudgingly admit that the Romans at least brought roads, aqueducts, sanitation, medicine, education, law and order, and wine—it is hard to deny that the word empire, in our fiction as well as our politics, has become tainted. Even to some of those inclined to agree with him, Niall Ferguson's rough claim that Africans were better off under European rule would strike many as obscenely heartless at worst or willfully contrarian at best, especially if thoughts of the atrocities committed in the Congo under Belgian rule come to mind.

None of this is to say that empires are confined to the past, and that entities that are empires by at least some reasonable definitions don't exist today. The countless articles and books speaking at least briefly of the decline of the American Empire, or comparing the United States' history to that of Rome or the British Empire, say as much, as do the independence movements from Basque Country to Tibet that would without a doubt not hesitate to deploy the adjective "imperial" to help describe their plights. But it is hard to imagine even the most hawkish United States senator speaking candidly of America's imperial interests in the Middle East or just using the word "empire" in open discussions of the nation's future the same way British politicians did in the last century.

As with so many things, definitions are a conundrum. Most would agree, however, that empires don't have to fit the classical Roman mold, with thousands of soldiers marching in to occupy foreign climes. There are multiple species of empire and varieties of imperialism, such as cultural imperialism and economic imperialism. There are even empires that are paradoxically based on a promise of liberation, like the Enlightenment-spawned empire of Napoleon Bonaparte. Even in the face of so many variations, one may think, like Alexander J. Motyl, of empire as a system relying on separate parts working in balance, keeping one society in a dominant spot with two or more societies stranded in a subordinate position.[4] What is important to wrestle out of the jumble of semantics is that empires can be subtle things, and that even countries that appear at a glance to be autonomous can be argued to be, at least in part, imperial subjects.

Whatever quibbles one might have in how to define empires, there are interesting consistencies across time and cultures. Empires are always almost organic things, born out of conflict, enjoying a healthy youth, navigating through times of crisis and recovery, enduring a debilitating old age, and finally facing a definite end. An army officer, Sir John Glubb, saw the British Empire at work firsthand in the Middle East and was inspired to write an essay titled *The Fate of Empires and Search for Survival.*[5] Although admittedly only looking at empires from the history of Europe and the Middle East, Glubb theorized that empires usually have, at most, lifespans with an average of 250 years. However, Glubb at least concedes that the ways empires die vary, plagued by a plethora of outside pressures and internal illnesses.

Admittedly, as fascinating as the question of what causes empires to collapse and whether or not they have common factors that breach the barriers of time and geography, this book is no attempt to assess Sir John Glubb's hypothesis. Instead it is an exploration into the drama of imperial collapse through a series of vignettes. While I do not dare even try to fashion a universal theory of imperial decline, through this series of episodes of collapse I hope to at least delve into the many recurring ways an empire can falter: military hubris (Athens and Britain), destruction of a capital (Persia), alienating its subjects through oppression (Qin China and the Russian Empire), being dismantled by a rising power (Carthage), corruption in its heart (Han China), dynastic squabbles (the Carolingians), political disintegration followed by a sudden invasion (the Abbasid Caliphate), the marriage of sectarian conflict with cynical power politics (Byzantium), ecological catastrophe (Khmer), colonial exploitation (the Aztecs), the failure to achieve unity (Rome and the Mughals), and nationalist awakenings (the Ottomans and the Soviet Union).

Of course, none of these events alone explain why any of the empires fell. But they do provide a glimpse into the often-unpredictable currents of history, which have so far spared no empire. At the very least, I want to take a topic that has so often been the subject of sweeping political, military, and economic history, and instead put a spotlight on the personalities involved. These are people who did not enjoy our hindsight, who acted in sometimes understandable and rational or sometimes frustratingly baffling and self-serving ways, but who in most cases had little if any idea that the world was shifting around them. Ultimately, they, not the systems they serve, are the ones that make history.

1.

THE ATHENIAN EMPIRE

The Grand Expedition

Standing firm before the general assembly of Athens, the celebrity-general Alkibiades appealed to all the citizens of the city to stay the course for war. From the start, the war was un-abashedly for profit, to be fought on the far-off island of Sicily through a sixty-ship armada. Meticulously recording these events for his *History of the Peloponnesian War*, the pioneering historian Thucydides recorded that, with promises of a quick and easy victory, Alkibiades lured the votes of the young and the old alike. "And so," Thucydides writes, "because of the extremes of eagerness among the majority, if anyone felt at all unhappy he was afraid of seeming un-patriotic by an opposing vote, and he kept quiet."[1]

The whole debate was over whether or not to take back the deci-sion to answer the call of a native Sicilian city, Egesta (or Segesta), which had been at war with a nearby Greek colony, Selinous. Egesta fell into a serious disadvantage once Syracuse, easily the most power-ful city in Sicily, sided with Selinous. Although, like their Sicilian neighbors, the people of Egesta feared with good reason that the Athe-nians once invited would never leave, desperation pushed them into begging for a military intervention. In 415, Athenian envoys arrived in Egesta, where the locals treated them to a tour of the city's temple of the goddess Aphrodite, which had been decked with silver bowls and gilded incense burners and lavish offerings, all carefully laid out to give the visitors a mistaken impression of Egesta's wealth.

Even without the deception, Sicily was an alluring prize. If Athens could dominate there, they would have at their disposal all the trade between Greece and the wealthy network of Greek colonies in southern Italy. This was even more enticing since Athens had in 421 made a fragile peace treaty with its nemesis Sparta. If the peace ever fell apart supplies of wood and grain from Sicily might give them an essential edge, particularly since most of mainland Greece was not known for the quality of its farmland. Finally, there was the question of Syracuse, which was becoming so powerful the city's tendrils were reaching out of Sicily and elsewhere into the Mediterranean. Like all states drunk on their own supremacy, Athens tolerated no rivals, actual or potential, and it was a juicy opportunity to humble Syracuse before it had even a chance to become a threat.

There were skeptics, naturally. The most important among them was the politician and general Nikias, who had negotiated the last peace treaty with Sparta. Nikias denounced the plan for a Sicilian expedition as a stupid and worthless adventure, amounting to Athens turning its back to a Sparta that was ready to pounce. Also Nikias, who was appointed to lead the expedition alongside Alkibiades and another general named Lamakhos, was by then in his sixties and suffering every day from a disease of the kidneys. Just the prospect of personally taking on the responsibility for a massive fiasco must have made his illness look like a little distraction.

The assembly gathered again to discuss how to arm the expedition. The lingering doubts were serious enough that Nikias had usurped the debate and steered it once again toward the topic of whether or not the entire expedition should be canceled. Alkibiades, irresistibly charismatic as always, assured skeptics that "hatred of the Syracusians will bring in many barbarians to join us in attacking them, and the situation here will be no obstacle if you consider it correctly."[2] Likely enough, only a few worldly merchants in the assembly knew or cared anything about Sicily's local politics, or even had a real grasp on the size and the scope of its population. Alkibiades's supporters won the day, but there are still hints fossilized in ancient reports that Nikias was far from the only one not convinced. One of these skeptics was a young philosopher named Socrates who was already attracting a following among aristocrats and craftsmen alike. Another was a fa-

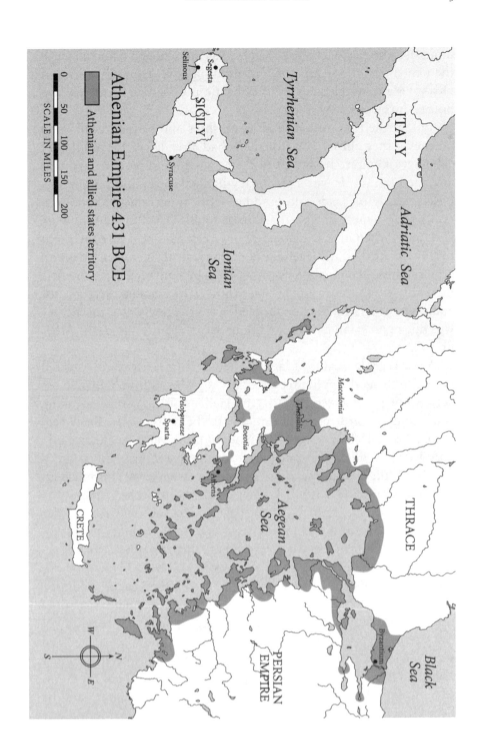

Athenian Empire 431 BCE

Athenian and allied states territory

0   50   100   150   200
SCALE IN MILES

ITALY

Adriatic Sea

Tyrrhenian Sea

Ionian
Sea

SICILY

Segesta
Selinous

Syracuse

Macedonia

Thessalia

Peloponnese

Boeotia

Sparta

Athens

CRETE

Aegean
Sea

THRACE

Byzantium

PERSIAN
EMPIRE

Black
Sea

mous astronomer, Metron. When he was appointed a commander in the expedition, he seized some inspiration from Homer's stories of Odysseus and wiggled out of his obligations by setting fire to his own house, "proving" his insanity.

Still, at the time Athens had many ships and forces to call upon whenever they chose. The Athenians had already crafted a different category of empire from that of their contemporaries the Egyptians and the Persians. It was a less heavy-handed incarnation of empire, based mostly on trade and binding political agreements and given the shallow veneer of a partnership of equals. The foundations were laid down when in 490 an alliance of Greek cities, led by Athens but totally unaided by the legendarily militaristic Spartans, drove off an attack by the seemingly irresistible Persian Empire. It was the first time any Greek army won an important battle against the Persians, and even the Spartans acknowledged, just grudgingly, that the victory was due in no small part to the resources and leadership of the Athenians.

A few years later at the island of Delos, neutral territory considered sacred to the god Apollo, representatives gathered from many places across not just Greece but all "the Hellenes," the Greek-speaking communities that stretched from Italy to the shores of the Black Sea. Dubbed the "Delian League" by modern historians, the alliance was founded to eventually liberate the Greek colonies in Asia Minor (modern-day Turkey) from Persian rule and to guarantee the continued independence of Greece itself. As the richest city in Greece, Athens was elected the leader, *hegemon*, of the new alliance, agreeing to shoulder most of the cost and responsibility for any future military undertaking. The other members would contribute through tributes of money and by sending their own ships and troops. All would vow to "have the same friends and enemies." Any policy of the League would be decided at conferences held at Delos, and Athens would have only one vote. Athens was to be the first among equals—in theory.

Gaps in the historical accounts make it unclear how Athens molded such a friendly alliance into what some modern historians call the Athenian Empire. It must have helped Athens's cynical bid for domination that tensions between the Delian League and Sparta and its own group of allies, the Peloponnesian League, escalated into a war that would last on and off for generations. However it was done, Athens had been slowly whittling away at the independence of its "equals." On some forgotten excuse, the treasury of the League was moved from Delos to Athens itself. Members of the League were compelled to adopt Athens's currency and its system of weights and measures. Delegates from member cities had to be present for Athens's annual festivities honoring the wine god Dionysus. Most ominous of all, garrisons staffed entirely by Athenian troops were stationed in every city of the Delian League. No wonder historians like to refer to the members of the Delian League as Athens's "subject-allies," a beautifully Orwellian term.

The tiny but strategically valuable island of Melos was witness to the most unmistakable and savage demonstration of Athens's new imperial attitude. Even though Melos had declared itself neutral, Athens submitted to its leaders a simple deal: submit or be destroyed. In Thucydides's famous—or infamous—account of the debate between Athenian ambassadors and the leaders of Melos, the Melesians warned that the gods will defend them since Athens was in the wrong by all the moral laws the Greek people hold sacred. The Athenians flatly replied that both the gods and humanity ultimately only respect power. Ultimately concerns about morality only matter when both sides are on a level playing field. Otherwise "the strong do as they can and the weak suffer what they must."[3] In the end, might did indeed make right. Melos fell and the Athenian assembly voted to have all the men old enough to fight massacred and to sell all the women and children into slavery.

If the massacre of the men of Melos, which did strain the normal Greek ethics of warfare (the Melesians were right in that sense, for all the good it did them), excited any real outrage in Athens, we do not know. However, there were those who were tired of the constant warfare required to fuel Athens's supremacy. Aristophanes's play *The Peace* was staged at the festival of Dionysus, just after the Peace of Nikias was signed. In the play, a grape farmer Trygaeus, whose livelihood had been ruined by all of Athens's wars, flies to heaven on a giant dung beetle in search of the missing goddess of peace, but he only meets the god Hermes. All the other gods have deserted Mount Olympus to protest in vain the unending wars between the Greeks except the god of war Ares, who is busy personally keeping the goddess of peace imprisoned in a cave.

While there probably were many real-life Trygaeuses, there were also many other Athenians who could sleep easily, since their empire did bring them into a golden age, when Athens was the richest city in Greece with some benefits even for those outside the upper classes. Even less wealthy Athenians had their pick of luxuries—incense, cloth, jewels, and metals—from as far as Libya, Italy, and Mesopotamia in the marketplace. If Aristophanes's descriptions of Athenian life are any indication, someone could stroll down the streets of Athens and purchase pumpkins, grapes, flowers, and cucumbers from vendors even in the dead of winter.[4]

No wonder there was a chorus of voices calling out for an expedition in Sicily. Those who voted in favor could expect to profit directly, either by sharing in the usual spoils of victory, being allotted land in Sicily, or just receiving special trade privileges. Unfortunately, a summer morning on the day before the armada was supposed to set sail, the citizens of Athens woke up to find that their sacred *hermai*, holy statues built all across Athens and sanctified to the god Hermes, had been vandalized. The *hermai* look absolutely avant-garde to modern eyes: a bearded head sits atop a rectangular block with two square bumps where the shoulders would be and with fully erect genitals at the base. These statues stood guard at the entrances of homes and temples all throughout the city. Over the course of that night, a group, or perhaps even just one person, had moved through the entire city, mutilating the faces and breaking off the genitals as they went. That Hermes was among other things the patron god of travelers only sharpened the bad omen. In modern terms, it was almost as if the statue of Abraham Lincoln at the Lincoln Memorial had been decapitated on the eve of the invasion of Iraq, although even this allegory does not capture that, for the Athenians, the act carried as much blasphemous weight as burning down St. Peter's Basilica.

Apparently few people thought this was just some drunken prank by the ancient world's equivalent of frat boys. Rumors started flying that it was sabotage by spies working for Athens's then-rival Corinth or that it was some conspiracy to overthrow the democracy. Perhaps it was even the earliest anti-war protest in recorded history, which Aristophanes himself may have thought when he was inspired to write *Lysistrata*, about women withholding sex as an anti-war protest, but it is impossible to know anything for sure about this coldest of cases. What can be said for sure is that so much blame went toward the one figure who nonetheless seemed poised to obtain loot and glory from the venture: Alkibiades himself.

It might seem Alkibiades would be the last reasonable suspect, but he was an eccentric, even demonic figure who had a knack for attracting people's admiration and contempt in equal measure. In fact, he made himself impossible to ignore. For starters, his references were impeccable. Not only was he a direct descendant of the old Athenian royal family and a nephew of the best politician the democracy of ancient Athens ever produced, Perikles, he was also a favorite pupil and possible lover of Socrates. One part ancient Greek soldier-politician and one part distant prototype of the modern pop star, the athletic and handsome Alkibiades often appeared in public wearing lavish robes and with defiantly unfashionable long hair, like a barbarian or a warrior of Homer's times.

Anecdotes about Alkibiades abound and reached even Plutarch, writing centuries after Alkibiades's death in the days of the Roman Empire. One day Alkibiades purchased an expensive and exquisite-looking dog, only to cut off its tail. A friend asked why he would do such a thing and Alkibiades earnestly replied that it was just to get people talking. When a painter charged him too much, Alkibiades locked him in for days until he finished painting the entire house. His wife, Hipparete, an extremely rich heiress, once tried to divorce him for his many, many infidelities, but Alkibiades simply stormed into the court, flung her over his shoulder, and carried her off. Finally, despite having been one of the strongest advocates in the assembly for the massacre at Melos, Alkibiades purchased one of the enslaved Melasian women, fell in love, and had children with her. A contemporary claimed that if such a thing happened in a play, the public would have been disgusted, but since it was real and it was just Alkibiades, they shrugged it off.[5] Plutarch in his biography of Alkibiades makes much the same diagnosis:

> The truth is, his liberalities, his public shows, and other munificence to the people, which were such as nothing could exceed, the glory of his ancestors, the force of his eloquence, the grace of his person, his strength of body, joined with his great courage and knowledge in military affairs, prevailed upon the Athenians to endure patiently his excesses, to indulge many things to him, and, according to their habit, to give the softest names to his faults, attributing them to youth and good nature.[6]

Like almost any celebrity, Alkibiades had his own enemies and critics, who were ready and willing to exploit any scrap of proof of his
guilt. Slaves stepped forward to testify that Alkibiades and his young
entourage had hosted parties where the most sacred and widely practiced religious initiation ceremonies in all of Greece, the Eleusian mys-
teries, were mockingly imitated by both party-goers and paid actors.
Maybe he had a political motive to ridicule the influential Eleusian
priesthood or maybe his motives were no more complex than those
of college students who steal a miniature statue of the Virgin Mary
from a manger scene on a dare. Either way, the testimonies fit the portrait Alkibiades's enemies were painting of him: an unstable extremist
with a pathological need to undermine everything Athens held sacred
and who posed a danger to the democratic traditions of the city itself.

Even with the superstitious fears the desecration of the *hermai* excited, and with Alkibiades officially accused of the act, the expedition
went ahead as planned. Alkibiades's own pleas that he be formally
tried before the armada departed from Greece fell on deaf ears. He
knew very well it was an opportunity for his rivals to have free reign.
However, such unpleasantness could not be allowed to sully the glory
of the departure of the largest armada any Greek had ever seen in
415. The force boasted 134 ships and 5,100 soldiers, many supplied
by Athens's dear "subject-allies."[7] Thucydides, who likely did watch
the armada leave port in person, remarked, "For taken as a force
launched from a single city from the might of Hellas, this was indeed
the first to be more costly and splendid than any up to that time. . . .
And what resulted . . . was something resembling an exhibition of
might and wealth, so far as the rest of Hellas was concerned, rather
than an army directed against enemies."[8] This magnificent, unprecedented exhibition, the embodiment of both Athens's might in the present and its hopes for the future, was doomed the second it set sail.

Once they reached Sicily, the three generals in charge—Alkibiades,
Nikias, and Lamakhos— found that Egesta was not nearly as rich as
its leaders claimed it was. Right then the option to return to Athens
immediately was put on the table, but Alkibiades sweet-talked his
comrades into searching for other allies among the city-states of Sicily.
There were a few who at least offered supplies to the Athenians or allowed them to trade in their markets, but the great city of Rhegium,
which at one time had pledged itself as the "eternal ally" of the Delian
League, refused to even let the Athenians set one foot past the city

An Attic red-figured stamnos (container for liquids) from the fifth century showing an Attic/Athenian warrior, left, fighting another warrior. (*National Gallery of Victoria, Melbourne. Purchased through The Art Foundation of Victoria with the assistance of the National Bank of Australasia Limited, 1980*)

gates. Discouraged, Alkibiades set sail for Greece alone, leaving the entire expedition in the hands of Lamakhos and Nikias. Perhaps the reputation Alkibiades had for waging war was puffed up by his charisma, but nonetheless the expedition had been dealt a blow by losing its most popular champion. Worse, just before his departure Alkibiades had made the fateful choice to throw his lot against the city that had been his home but was now persecuting him. To that end, he had dispatched a secret message to the city of Messina, revealing every detail of a plot planned by a pro-Athens faction to take over the city government and throw open their city and its wealth to the expedition.[9]

Back in Athens, Alkibiades's opponents in the assembly had turned political opinion in their favor and managed to wring out a death sentence *in absentia* on charges of sacrilege. On top of such a fatal condemnation, Alkibiades's property was to be confiscated, his name inscribed on a stile of disgrace right on the Acropolis at the heart of the city, a bounty was offered to anyone who killed him, and his name was to be cursed forever by the Eleusinian priests. When he heard of what the assembly had done, Alkibiades vowed, "I will show them I am alive."[10] Instead of Athens, he sailed to Sparta, although he must have already had Sparta in mind since he decided to betray the expedition in Sicily. However much Alkibiades was actually committed to Sparta before he found out about the aftermath of his trial, he was still welcomed by the Spartans as a prestigious defector. Sparta's new favorite child urged his benefactors to finally break the peace and step in against Athens in Sicily. Sparta would send only a small force to fight for Syracuse in Sicily, but they were more than willing to officially reopen hostilities with the Delian League.

Back in Sicily, the Athenians decided to risk a confrontation with Syracuse, even though morale was plummeting. Under the command of Nikias, the Athenians tried to take the fight right into Syracuse's territory and won an early victory, but they were not able to press the advantage. In the spring of 414, the Athenians finally besieged Syracuse, just as war once more broke out between Sparta and Athens. From the Athenian perspective, this only made a sure victory in Sicily even more paramount, and the assembly promptly voted to send reinforcements. Even with fresh bodies, the campaign collapsed, with the navy being almost completely wiped out and Syracuse's land forces crushing the Athenian army. As one modern historian remarked, "There was no longer any question of victory, the only thought now was of escape."[11]

The Syracusans had been on the defensive, but this time they pursued the surviving Athenians with a vengeance. The Athenians had to flee with their dead unburied, which under normal circumstances for Greek soldiers would have been an unthinkable act of disrespect. According to Thucydides:

> For since the dead were unburied, whenever anyone saw one of his close friends lying there he was stricken with grief along with fear, and those who were being left behind while alive, the wounded and the sick, made the living feel far more grief than they felt for the dead and far more pity than they felt for the departed. In turning to entreaties and lamentations, they drove the men to distraction, begging them to take them along, crying out to each of them whenever anyone saw a friend or kinsman, hanging on to tentmates who were now departing, following along as far as they could, and, whenever spirit or flesh failed any of them, never dropping behind without many wails and appeals to the gods, so that the whole army, filled with tears and in this dis-

tracted mood, found it not easy to set out, even from a hostile land and after they had already experienced suffering too great for tears, while fearing what unknown suffering may lie ahead.[12]

One of the Athenian armies surrendered. Even with the Syracusans nipping at their heels, however, Nikias's army continued their grim march, trying desperately to reach friendly land. The soldiers were exhausted, dehydrated, and as broken in spirit as in body. Eventually the soldiers came within sight of a river, but even this bit of good fortune was a mirage. Syracusan forces already blocked the bridge and a ford within sight. Drawing on Thucydides, the modern historian Peter Green paints a picture of the precise moment when the hopes of an empire actually died:

> They forgot order and discipline, they forgot the Syracusans, they forgot everything save their torturing and insupportable thirst. The men at the head of the column broke ranks, and went scrambling down the river-bank in a blind, frenzied stampede. As they did so there came a peal of thunder from overhead, and the rain, too long delayed, came sluicing down in torrents. [. . .] The Syracusans quickly . . . began to slaughter the hysterical mob in the river-bed, with every weapon they could lay hands on. Arrows and javelins discharged at point-blank range were reinforced by rocks from the bank itself. The Athenians fought and clawed for space, trampling each other underfoot, gulping greedily at the fouled and bloody water.[13]

There were still many survivors, seven thousand of them in Thucydides's estimation. These men were forced to work in the stone quarries near Syracuse, where they were given about a half-pint of water and a pint of food for each day of backbreaking work. Many died from illness or malnutrition, and their corpses were simply piled together at the site. Those who survived that last ordeal fared somewhat better. They were sold into slavery, but luckily at the time Athenian slaves were in high demand in Sicily and around the Mediterranean as tutors in wealthy households. Because of that, when information about a missing man in Athens was sought a popular macabre joke was "he's either dead or teaching school."[14] As for Nikias, the general whose support for the expedition had been at best lukewarm, the Syracusans promptly executed him.

The catastrophe of the Sicilian expedition was only a prelude. Athens would lose to Sparta in 404. Far from continuing to lead a formidable confederation of Greek cities and colonies, the future of Athens itself hung on a whim. Sparta's allies Thebes and Corinth demanded to see Athens razed and its population enslaved, but perhaps out of a genuine respect for its fallen adversary Sparta was far kinder to Athens than Athens had been to Menos and staunchly refused. Still, the peace imposed on Athens was hardly a slap on the wrist. The Athenians were forced to tear down their city's own fortifications and to surrender all but twelve of their ships. Even their foreign policy was to be decided in Sparta.

Athens's fabled democracy was also ripped away, replaced by a brutal pro-Sparta puppet regime remembered not too fondly in Greek history as the "Thirty Tyrants." As for Alkibiades, he had returned to Athens to try to support the war effort against his former benefactors, the Spartans. Unsurprisingly resentment against this double traitor chased him to the Persian Empire where he tried this time to solicit Persian aid against Sparta. Appropriately enough for a person who led such a bizarre life, Alkibiades's death is a mystery, but the most exciting account asserts that he perished in a hail of arrows, courtesy of assassins working for a vengeful Sparta.

As for Athens, the final years of its empire and even the time following its fall were still vastly important for Athens, and in fact all of ancient Greece. Before and after the Sicilian expedition, the golden age of classical Greek literature was still unfolding, with Thucydides's *History of the Peloponnesian War*, which would define the genre of history for Western civilization, yet to be written. Also a young disciple of Socrates named Plato, while devastated by the trial and execution of his exalted teacher by a paranoid new democracy of Athens erected after the fall of the Thirty Tyrants, would write a series of books featuring his late mentor that would form the very foundations of intellectual thought for Europe. Maybe this all proves that the Athenian ambassadors at Menos, consumed with imperial hubris, were completely wrong after all. In the end, the real enduring legacy of Athens was not in the power of wealth and brute force but in the ideas that their society left behind.

2.

THE PERSIAN EMPIRE

Persepolis Burns

N o one really lives on the site of Persepolis today. The nearest
city, Shiraz, lies just a little over forty miles to the southwest.
Only the ancient ruins of Persepolis itself and a nearby hotel
that caters to historically minded tourists testify to the existence of
what was long ago one of the greatest capitals of the ancient Mediterranean world, where once ambassadors from North Africa to India
came personally to lay their tributes before the throne of the *shahan-
shah*, King of Kings. More than a nation's capital in the modern sense,
it had been the actual soul of the Persian Empire, boasting an importance that transcended mere politics. For all that, it only took one
night for the city to be all but destroyed.

Under the Achaemenid dynasty, the Persian Empire engulfed all
the territories of all the old superpowers of the ancient Middle East—
the Hittites, Assyria, Babylon, and Egypt—and became the largest
empire yet known west of China. Its rise amazingly happened in just
one lifetime. In 550 BCE, under the leadership of Kurush "the Great"
(still usually remembered by the Greek transliteration of his name,
"Cyrus"), the Persians revolted against and then subdued their former
overlords, the Medians. Then, within three decades, the Persians
would conquer the proverbially wealthy kingdom of the Lydians in
modern-day Turkey, the seemingly timeless city of Babylon, and the

empire of the Egyptian pharaohs. East of Persepolis, the word of the King of Kings had weight as far as the Indus River. Westward, after reaching into the Balkans, the march of the Persians would only be stopped by a confederation of Greek cities led by Athens.

One advantage the Greeks have even today is that the Persians cannot speak for themselves. Like most of their neighbors (and, unfortunately for the author of this book, many imperial peoples across the world), the Achaemenids left behind lists of kings, proclamations of their victories, and imperial decrees but no histories like those of the Greeks. "To ride, to shoot the bow, to tell the truth—but not to write it," as Michael Axworthy puts it.[1] Luckily for future historians, however, the Greeks were endlessly intrigued by their own would-be conquerors. The Athenian philosopher Xenophon even wrote a reverent biography of Kurush the Great, praising "Cyrus" as both the ideal general and an exceptional human being in every possible respect but ending his story by assuring his Greek readers that the Persians of the present day are obviously "now much more effeminate than they were in Cyrus' day."[2]

However, to manage such a leviathan empire with just Iron Age technology the Persians had to be much more than just excellent warriors. A meticulously maintained highway stretched over 1,600 miles from one of the old imperial capitals, Susa, to Sardis, the westernmost center of the empire. There was a postal service centered around relay stations that were all only one day apart. The speed of Persian couriers became the stuff of bureaucratic legend. One Greek historian, Herodotus, actually sounds like a Persian spokesperson: "No mortal thing travels faster than these Persian courtiers."[3] Meanwhile a series of reforms under the Shah Darayavahush I (Darius I) set up an elaborate system of self-monitoring among the empire's governors, promoting an admirable administrative ethic that prized "truth," *arta*.

Maintaining *arta* was not just a political virtue but a tenet of the Archaemenids' faith, Zoroastrianism, the first of the revealed monotheistic faiths. There are very few sure facts today about the religion's founder, Zoroaster, who may have lived as far back as the 11th century BCE. What the legends about him are clear on is that he braved hostility for teaching there was one supreme god, Ahura Mazda, and that his teachings on proper worship of Ahura Mazda and how to resist the temptations of the spirit of chaos and evil, Angra Mainyu, were preserved in a collection of sacred texts, the Avesta.

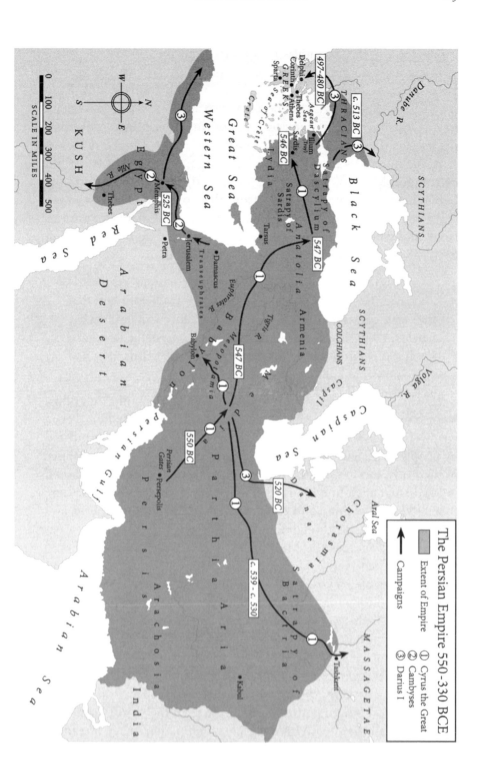

The Persian Empire 550-330 BCE

Extent of Empire
Campaigns

① Cyrus the Great
② Cambyses
③ Darius I

Unlike some of the monotheistic faiths to come, the Zoroastrian rulers of Persia felt no compulsion to impose their beliefs. The Persian people were still allowed to worship their ancestral Iranian gods. Even the societies the Persians conquered were permitted, even encouraged, to stay loyal to their native deities. Surviving inscriptions prove that Kurush justified his conquest of Babylon in part by accusing its last king, Nabu-na'id, of maliciously neglecting the worship of Babylon's patron god Marduk. Among the Jews, whom the Assyrians and the Babylonians had forcibly exiled from their own homeland, Kurush was immortalized as their champion who allowed them to return to Israel and who rebuilt the Temple in Jerusalem. The Book of Isaiah praises Kurush as God's "anointed," whom God:

> . . . has taken by his right hand to subdue nations before him and strip the loins of kings, to force gateways before him that their gates be closed no more: I will go before you leveling the heights. I will shatter the bronze gateways, smash the iron bars. I will give you the hidden treasures, the secret hoards, that you may know that I am the Lord.[4]

If you accused him of just indulging in good public relations, Karush would most likely just shrug his shoulders. The shahs of Persia were very much aware of how they were heading an empire populated by peoples who had long, proud histories and even once had empires of their own in their names. Decrees and inscriptions were published in local languages, and images survive showing the shahs presenting themselves in the dress and ritual stylings of Egyptian pharaohs and Babylonian kings. Although they were without a doubt the most determined conquerors the Middle East had yet seen, they presented what the United Nations today claims to have been the world's first human rights charter, dating from sometime between 539 and 530 BCE. Housed today in the British Museum, the "Cyrus Cylinder," a nine-by-four-inch column, promises freedom of religious worship and to allow any populations deported under the old regimes to return to their homelands if they choose. Of course, to modern Westerners' ears it is a contradiction that a ruler who decrees himself the "king of the world, the great king, the powerful king, king of Babylon, king of Sumer and Akkad, king of the four quarters of the world" can have anything at all to do with human rights, and perhaps such a reading is anachronistic as its critics say, but at the very least it does show that the Persian Empire was built on the power of public outreach almost as much as it was built through the sword.

When Persepolis was built by Shah Darayavahush I on a plateau in the shadow of the Kuh-i Rahmat Mountain, it was in its own way meant to be as much of a declaration as the Cyrus Cylinder. A visitor to Persepolis would have passed through the "Gateway of Nations," where two winged bulls with human heads stood guard against evil spirits. If on official diplomatic business, one would likely be conducted to the *apadana*, the massive reception hall where the shah received all visitors. It was over half the length of an American football field and half the height of the Arc de Triomphe (60.5 meters long and 25 meters high, to be precise) and could probably house up to ten thousand people.[5] Among the ruins, one can still see an engraving where under the sacred emblem of Ahura Mazda "Darius himself steps out with scepter and lotus to welcome his guests and to review the Immortals [elite Persian soldiers]; two smaller attendants follow to hold over his head the golden parasol and fly-flapper and to carry the napkin which Assyrian practice had dedicated to royal usage."[6] Although the Greeks overestimated its spiritual significance—the claim that Greeks were barred from setting foot in the city is almost definitely false—Persepolis was from the start consecrated as one giant temple to Ahura Mazda:

> I, Darius, the Great King, king of kings, king of countries, king on this earth, son of Hystapes the Achaemenid says: 'On this site where this fortress was built, previously no fortress had been built there. By the grace of Ahura Mazda, this fortress, I constructed it according to the plan of Ahura Mazda, all the gods [being] with him, [namely] that this fortress be built. And I built it, completed it, and made it beautiful and impervious, just as had been ordained of me.[7]

Persepolis was in the end actually not impervious, nor was the empire founded by Kurush. Its destruction was designed and executed for the sake of the ambitions of one person, Alexander the Great.

Although Alexander was born the hereditary heir to Macedonia, a kingdom on the fringe of the Greek-speaking world that Greeks sneered at as barbaric at worst and quasi-Greek at best, he advertised himself as the avenger of the Greeks against the humiliations and fears they endured because of the Persians in centuries past. Luckily, by

Alexander's time, the Persian Empire had already been sickened by internal bickering. A vizier Bagoas had poisoned Shah Artaxsaca III (Artaxerses III) and had his sons assassinated except for a young prince, Arses. When Arses too began to show unacceptable signs of independent thought, Bagoas arranged to have him murdered and replaced with a cousin in 336, who adopted the regal name Darayavahush III. Bagoas was about to start the bloody process all over again, but Darayavahush III seized the initiative and had Bagoas killed first.

Unfortunately, Darayavahush III only had a chance to peacefully be shah for two years before Alexander, already flush with victories over his Greek rivals and now at the head of a powerful alliance of Greek cities, launched his grand and holy crusade against the Persian Empire. After a series of victories in Asia Minor, Syria, Palestine, and Egypt, not just the course of the war but the fate of the entire Mediterranean world was decided at the Battle of Gaugamela, which most likely took place in the highlands of northern Iraq. There Alexander's tightly organized forces shattered a larger Persian army and sent Darayavahush III scrambling for help. The last Achaemenid to truly rule was casually murdered by his own nobles, left to bleed to death in a wagon. As magnanimous in triumph as he was ruthless in the pursuit of it as always, Alexander tenderly covered the blood-soaked corpse of the shah with his own cloak.

The far more vicious and fickle side of Alexander's persona would quickly manifest itself. Alexander easily captured Persepolis itself and he had plans for the city very unlike his kinder intentions for Babylon, the capital of his new, grand Asiatic empire. "The private homes of the Persian nobility were sacked without mercy, the men cut down and the women enslaved," a modern biographer of Alexander writes. "It was an act of outrage on a helpless populace and was coldly calculated."[8] A much more ancient observer, the first century BCE geographer and historian Diodorus Siculus, exclaimed, "As Persepolis had exceeded all other cities in prosperity, so in the same measure it now exceeded all others in misery."[9] While Alexander wished to pass himself off as the successor of the shahs, he also wanted and perhaps needed to be the righteous and merciless settler of Greek scores against the empire of Xsayarsa (Xerxes), the shah who first attempted to invade Greece and who had burned down the sacred Acropolis of Athens.

A sixteenth-century Italian earthenware plate with an illustration intepreted as Alexander ordering the burning of Persepolis. (*Walters Art Museum*)

The sources disagree on what exactly happened next. The only thing they synchronize over is that in just one night Alexander and his men set fire to the luxurious imperial palace at Persepolis. Evidence that such a fire broke out is still etched on the ruins. A Roman biographer of Alexander named Arrian[10] believed that it was a deliberate decision but admits that even writings from people who were alive at the time (accounts that, sadly, have not survived to our time) disagreed and claimed quite simply that Alexander got drunk. According to this version, at a banquet where Alexander and his generals celebrated finally bringing the Persian Empire to an end, Thaïs, the general Ptolemy's mistress, loudly spoke up over the din of the party. She goaded Alexander to take a city for a city and avenge what Xerxes did to Athens by putting Persepolis to the torch. Plutarch takes up the story:

> As soon as she had thus spoken, tumultuous applause arose, and the companions of the king eagerly urged him on, so that he yielded to their desires, and leaping to his feet, with a garland on his head and a torch in his hand, led them the way. The company

followed with shouts and revelry and surrounded the palace, while the rest of the Macedonians who learned about it ran thither with torches and were full of joy. For they hoped that the burning and destruction of the palace was the act of one who had fixed his thoughts on home, and did not intend to dwell among Barbarians. This is the way the deed was done, according to some writers; but others say it was premeditated. However, it is agreed that Alexander speedily repented and gave orders to put out the fire.[11]

The fire did not spread to the entire city, and apparently Persepolis remained inhabited for some years yet. However, the devastation had consumed many valuables, including the original holy text of the Avesta, and the city would never recover, instead entering into a terminal decline.

The Zoroastrians never forgave Alexander for his actions. For his book and TV series *In The Footsteps of Alexander the Great,* the historian Michael Wood interviewed a member of a thriving Zoroastrian community in the Iranian city of Yazd:

> He may be Great to the Greeks, and to you Europeans, but we call him a devil. This is because he burned down our temples, killed our priests; he forcibly made our children marry Greeks to make them lose their identity; he destroyed our most precious holy book, our Bible, the Avesta, which was written on 12,000 calf skins in letters of gold. So why should we call him the Great? To us he is a devil. For this reason we call him Iskander Gujaste. Alexander the Accursed.[12]

In a village just north of Yazd, what is claimed to be the very same sacred flame that once burned in a fire temple in Persepolis lives on. It is kept in a locked room inside a temple with no windows. No one can even look at it except purified priests who over the flame still chant the same sacred hymns that were recited even before the days of the Achaemenids, centuries before an upstart king from some small mountain country had ripped apart the flame's original home.

Of course, Zoroastrianism did survive, as it does to this day even in the shadow of Iran's theocratic Islamic government, and it had been the faith of another thriving empire, the Sassanids of medieval Iran. Yet the ravaging of the great city once consecrated to Ahura Mazda and the destruction of the glorious empire that made its holy principles the basis of law will always be a stinging wound. Those who call Alexander "the Accursed" are all too aware that Alexander had not only brought an end to an empire but very nearly destroyed an entire way of life.

3.

THE QIN EMPIRE

*The Ten-Thousand-Year Empire that Lasted
Two Generations*

In 1974, farmers who were digging wells not far from the city of
Xi'an in China accidentally began one of the great archaeological
excavations of the twentieth century when they unearthed a soldier in full regalia made of terracotta. As of this writing, the dig is
still incomplete. Over the years, as archaeologists from across the
world followed up on this unexpected discovery, they began to un-
cover a royal tomb large enough to be a city of the dead. It was a
monument to imperial hubris even modern governments would be
daunted to imitate even with current technology, yet it was all built
in the second century BCE. This impressive site was the mausoleum
of the First Emperor, Qin Shi Huangdi, whose dynastic name of Qin
may have been the origin of the name for China in English and other
European languages.

The tomb was modeled after the First Emperor's capital, Xianyang,
imitating with pathological precision the world that the emperor
would have known in life. According to *The Records of the Grand
Historian*, composed by Sima Qian during the Han dynasty that eventually replaced that of the First Emperor, "Mercury was used to fashion imitations of the hundred rivers, the Yellow River and the
Yangtze, and the seas, constructed in such a way that they seemed to

flow. Above were representations of all the heavenly bodies, below, the features of the earth."[1] Such exquisite craftsmanship had a heavy price. The artisans who helped plan and build the tomb and who designed statues carrying automatic crossbows intended to protect the tomb from robbers were all killed. Buried alongside the emperor were the bodies of his faithful servants, administrators, and concubines. All of them were protected by the now famous terracotta army, staffed with over eight thousand soldiers and a hundred chariots and equipped with horses and carrying authentic weapons and armor.[2]

It was naturally an epic undertaking, rivaling the construction of the Great Wall, which was being built about the same time. The historian Sima Qian estimated that seven hundred thousand men built the tomb, most if not all of them were convicts who had been condemned to hard labor under the empire's laws. In that sense, the tomb of the First Emperor was not only a monument to the man himself but to the harsh philosophy that bound his vast empire together, Legalism. An ideology centered around the basic assumption that only a strict law code backed by a strong, autocratic government can guarantee order, Legalism gave the First Emperor one of the greatest administrative engines of preindustrial civilization and countless bodies to help realize his projects. However, such a philosophy also gave rise to the resentments that would one day tear the empire apart.

Traditional Chinese historiography insisted quite a bit that, before the republicans and then the communists came to power, there always had been an empire, beginning with the Three Sovereigns and Five Emperors who were said to have reigned during a blessed time when the gods freely mingled with humanity and people's lifespans lasted for centuries. The exact names of these legendary monarchs vary, but the myths agree the last of them was Shun, who chose as his successor not a great warrior as might be expected but a brilliant hydraulics engineer, Yu. Despite Yu's own appointment based on merit, legend claims he became the first monarch to introduce the principle of hereditary succession, inaugurating the first of China's imperial dynasties, the Xia, who would rule from the end of the third millennium BCE toward the middle of the second.

Archaeological research has spoiled parts of this clean, orderly account, mainly by pointing out that China was not nearly as politically and culturally unified in the darkest depths of antiquity as the stories like to assume. At the same time, excavations have recently shown that the Xia dynasty, once believed to have been completely mythical, actually may have existed in one form or another. Whoever they were, traditional Chinese history says they were eventually dislodged by a new dynasty, the Shang, who were in turn deposed by the Zhou. With plenty of hindsight, later Chinese commentators would say this proved the idea of *tian ming*, the "Mandate of Heaven." If a ruler proved corrupt and incompetent, then heaven would withdraw its blessings from that ruler and his family and extend it to some other dynasty that would be justified in violently replacing the old. The use of the term can be traced all the way back to 1043 BCE, and it, as well as the concept that dynasties appear and disappear in cycles of ascendancy and decadence, would shape how the history of China would be told for thousands of years.[3] However, these early dynasties did not rule anything close to the size of modern China, and the Shang and Zhou rulers were actually just known under the title *wang*, often translated into English as king.

The Zhou would last longer than any of the other "official" Chinese dynasties, from sometime in the middle of the eleventh century BCE to 256 BCE, but their decline was agonizingly slow. The government of the Zhou had been based on entrusting the administration of lands to dukes and marquises and their descendants, and over the centuries these vassals became increasingly independent until, finally in the fourth century, these nobles promoted themselves into being kings, throwing open the floodgates for the many struggles of the Warring States era. Eventually the Zhou kings effectively ruled only a small strip of territory around their old capital Chengzou (modern-day Luoyang). There among the luxuries of Chengzou they presided over a ghostly court where ancient rituals perfected in far better times were meticulously carried out by the king, who could only buy favors and respect by offering sacred endorsements to his increasingly apathetic ex-vassals.

It was perhaps only a matter of time until the royal families of one of the other states declared that heaven now favored them, but luckily for the Zhou the upstart kings all kept each other in check. For all the bloody wars and cutthroat intrigues between them, the Warring States were unified by a shared culture and a reverence for Kong Fuzi, far better known to English language readers by the name "Confucius." Despite dying as an underpaid and virtually unknown bureaucrat in 479 BCE, just a couple of generations later his teachings would

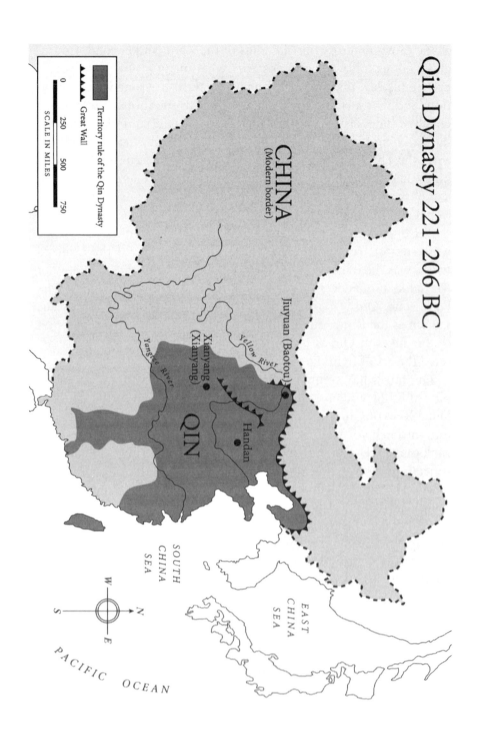

shape thought across the old lands of the Zhou and beyond. Confucius told his followers and posterity what many probably suspected
even in his day; that something had gone terribly wrong with civilization, and that a stable society unified under one revered ruler, not a
clutch of states clawing against each other, was the natural order. Only
by searching for "the Way" through a meticulous study of tradition
from the Three Sovereigns and Five Emperors to the last great Zhou
kings, and through education and etiquette and adherence to ritual,
can both an individual be made virtuous and society rendered func-
tional and moral.

Yet one of the Warring States took a very different path. On the
westernmost frontier of what the Chinese considered the civilized
world was the duchy of Qin. Like Alexander the Great's kingdom of
Macedonia, outsiders saw Qin as mired in a half-civilized, half-bar-
baric state. Qin was in a perpetual war with a group of barbarians
known as the Rong, an unending conflict that refined the reputation
of the dukes of Qin as brilliant but uncouth warriors who had mas-
tered the art of fighting on horseback.

Qin might have remained a tough frontier backwater if an unem-
ployed scholar named Shang Yang had not arrived at the court of
Duke Xiao of Qin sometime in 361 BCE. Shang Yang had been born
into the duchy of Wey's ruling family, but after never rising above the
rank of a lowly-paid bureaucrat he, like countless other scholars and
officials in the Warring States era, left home to find a better job elsewhere. He found it with Duke Xiao, who was an eager pupil to Shang
Yang's new and decisively un-Confucian ideas.

Rather than believing that people, and through them society, could
be improved through a good education and adherence to tradition,
Shang Yang preached a far more cynical doctrine. The morality and
loyalty of people, even or perhaps especially those born with high
rank and with their every need normally fulfilled, cannot be trusted.
Only hope for promotions and terror of the law can reliably steer
human behavior toward the greater good. Guided by that one principle and with Duke Xiao's full support, Shang Yang reorganized Qin
into an administrative powerhouse. Weights and measures were stan-
dardized, the entire populace was universally registered and con-
scripted either into the armies or toward public works projects, and
laziness itself was criminalized on pain of enslavement. Other misde-
meanors could be punished severely, while family members, spouses,

and fellow soldiers were given incentives and threatened with shared punishments to encourage them to turn in a relative, spouse, or comrade who was a known offender. Households, which were legally grouped together in fives or tens, were held legally responsible if any of their members committed a crime. If they failed to report the crime, all of the members would share in the offender's punishment. The impact of this on Qin society did not go unremarked. When the scholar Xunzi visited Qin's capital Xianyang in 263 BCE, he admired the orderliness of even the day-to-day life of the citizens but was appalled by how the entire country appeared "living in constant terror and apprehension lest the rest of the world should someday unite and strike it down."[4]

In a cruel but poetic irony, Shang Yang himself was ground up by the very machine he built. When Duke Xiao's teenage heir lived a lifestyle less than appropriate for a duke's son, Shang Yang personally ordered that the heir's tutors have their noses cut off as punishment for failing to correctly educate and discipline the young man. Once Xiao died, the young man succeeded him as Duke Huwein and proved less than appreciative of Shang Yang's tender concerns. Trying to flee the country, Shang Yang stopped at an inn, but the innkeeper refused to allow him to stay because one of the very laws Shang Yang had instituted decreed that no one could spend a night at an inn without proper identification papers. Shang Yang was eventually arrested on trumped-up charges of treason, torn apart by chariots, and his entire family executed. However, his philosophy Legalism survived him. In fact, Huwein, who like his eastward neighbors ditched the title of duke and took on the grander title of king, tapped into Legalism in order to turn his entire country into a war machine directed not toward the barbarians of the west but his civilized rivals in the east. It would be a king of Qin, Zhaoxiang, the grandfather of the First Emperor, who would in 256 BCE finally end the stalemate that had shaped the Warring States era by overrunning the city of Chengzou and deposing the Zhou, the last of whom would live off a pension from the king of Qin for six years before being executed on suspicion that he was scheming against his "benefactor."

Even after bringing about the finale of the centuries-long reign of the Zhou dynasty, there was still nothing inevitable about Qin beating out the other states. The king who would become the First Emperor, Ying Zheng, succeeded to the throne as a child trapped under the self-interested "guidance" of his mother Zhaoji and his chief minister, the former merchant Lü Buwei. At the heart of the new regime was a scandal that threatened to unravel the entire monarchy. Zhaoji had a secret lover, Lao Ai, with whom she had two very young sons. Lao Ai and Zhaoji allegedly met through fairly extraordinary circumstances. Allegedly at a party Lao Ai showed off his natural talents by holding a cartwheel at the end of his erect penis, and when the story reached Zhaoji she insisted on meeting him. Seeing a chance to keep the queen mother's favor, Lü Buwei obligingly arranged to have Lao Ai accused and convicted of a crime that was punished with castration. As a eunuch, there was nothing improper with Lao Ai being retained at Zhaoji's isolated residence away from the royal court, but the punishing operation was of course faked so Lao Ai's assets would not go to waste.

Lao Ai was made a marquis and, in Sima Qian's account, "had a free hand in . . . all affairs of state great and small."[5] The fake eunuch had even learned how to forge the official seals of the queen mother and the king himself. Even this was not enough, and Lao Ai and his inner circle began to scheme to get rid of Ying Zheng. Lao Ai himself might have had the ambition to secretly replace the king with his own descendants by Zhaoji, but Lü Buwei, Lao Ai, and even Zhaoji herself might have just been hoping to stay in power by replacing the now twenty-year-old monarch with another compliant boy king.[6] Lao Ai tried to bluster his way into launching a coup, and he may have come close to winning, but in the end he was captured by those who were either loyal to the king or enticed by the massive bounty placed on his head. According to the law as laid down by Legalism, Lao Ai was ripped apart by four chariots and his entire family down to his first cousins were slaughtered. Ying Zheng did not hesitate to sign off on the deaths of his own two half-brothers, although he did spare their mother, who was sentenced to a lifetime of home imprisonment. Her son ordered that no one, not even ministers, could dare talk to him about her guilt, much less the need for a more dramatic punishment, on pain of being killed, the flesh melted from their bones, and "their limbs piled around the city gates like a curb around a well."[7] Apparently twenty-seven officials underestimated the seriousness of this request. As for Lü Buwei, whether or not he was complicit in the coup attempt, he would be banished from the court and exiled to the unpleasant southernmost territory of Qin. Taking the hint, Lü Buwei performed one last service to the government he once helped head and downed some poison.

Perhaps the young Ying Zheng, brooding on how close he came to being assassinated and replaced by a cipher, appreciated the necessity of a cold head at the helm of his kingdom. Luckily Ying Zheng had found an ideal ally in the form of one of his tutors, Li Si, who specifically sought employment with the kings of Qin because he predicted correctly that they would be the ones to unify the Warring States under one monarch.[8] Another Legalism-minded foreign scholar whom Ying Zheng admired and offered employment to was Han Fei. His writing spelled out the proper philosophy of a king: "Therefore in the state of an enlightened ruler there are no books written on bamboo strips; law supplies the only instruction. There are no sermons on the former kings: the officials serve as the only teachers."[9] Nonetheless, for whatever reason Li Si soon had Han Fei pegged as a serious rival and convinced Ying Zheng to reluctantly order his idol's death by accusing him of secretly lending support to his home country of Hán.

If Li Si truly anticipated that Ying Zheng would make Qin the last kingdom standing, then he took a gamble that paid off exceptionally well. Under Ying Zheng's rule, Qin conquered no less than seven of its rivals, including their eastern neighbor Chu. Not only was Chu larger than Qin, but it also controlled some of the most populated and prosperous regions of central and southern China. Despite these natural advantages, by 224 the armies of Qin had captured Chu's capital, Shouchun. Three years later, the Qin would finally liquidate the last of their rivals. As far as Ying Zheng's contemporaries were concerned, the Qin now presided over the entire world.

It was an unprecedented situation, and Ying Zheng boasted that the dominion of the Qin now encompassed more land than not only that of the Zhou kings but even that of the Three Sovereigns and Five Emperors of myth. In an inscription, the new government would dismiss even those fantastic rulers of legend as charlatans who "posed as divine beings to deceive and frighten their different subjects, but their deeds did not live up to their boasts, and so their reigns did not endure."[10] Such an incredible claim to be better than even the godlike monarchs of the distant past demanded a change in the king's title. When asked to devise a title that suitably reflected his newly minted status, Ying Zheng's advisers combined a term denoting heavenly or all-highest (*huang*) and the archaic title reserved for each of the Three

Sovereigns and Five Emperors, *di. Huangdi* would become the standard title for all future Chinese emperors. However, Ying Zheng went one step further, revealing ambitions that would extend far beyond his own death, when he addressed the old custom of dukes and kings being able to bestow posthumous titles on their predecessors:

> This results in the son passing judgment on the father, and subjects passing judgment on their ruler. Such a procedure is highly improper and we will have none of it! From now on, this manner of assigning posthumous names shall be abolished. We ourselves shall be called First Emperor, and successive generations of ruler shall be numbered consecutively, Second, Third, and so on for 1,000 or 10,000 generations, the succession passing down without end.[11]

Thus Ying Zheng became with literal high-mindedness Qin Shi Huangdi, "First Emperor of the Qin."

All Chinese would now have to cope with life under Qin principles. Since the Legalist penal code allowed for the punishment of even minor crimes like petty theft with forced labor, Qin Shi Huangdi had at his disposal the human resources for massive construction projects. Besides being sentenced to work on one of the emperor's tombs, the worst punishment a criminal could receive was embodied in one word found over and over again in judicial records from the time: wall. Although only a little of the original Great Wall built under Qin Shi Huangdi survives today, it was the basis for today's wall. The wall that was constructed from 220 to 214 BCE linked two existing wall structures and was designed to defend China's northern border from excursions by barbarians. Today no one knows how long the original Great Wall stretched; the undertaking must have been massive. The folklorist William Edgar Geil published in 1909 a collection of folktales from villages near the wall that existed since the First Emperor's lifetime. The tellers of the tales claimed that the First Emperor had a giant shovel that could flip up an entire stretch of wall in a day or that workers were bound together by a rope sent from heaven that gave them superhuman strength. In the words of the First Emperor's modern biographer Jonathan Clements, these stories "spoke of magic because they could not comprehend the organizational alternative."[12]

While the First Emperor may have been the originator of one of the great surviving marvels of the world, he also instigated one of the

A view of several of the more than six thousand terracotta figures in Pit 1 in the mausoleum of Qin Shi Huangdi, Xi'an, China. (*Maros/Creative Commons*)

greatest crimes ever committed against posterity. At a banquet, a scholar, Chunyu Yue, stood up and began berating the First Emperor for not following the model of the Zhou by entrusting his brothers and sons with territories. In spite of his fierce reputation, this was not unprecedented since the First Emperor likely did tolerate open debate among his advisers and scholars. What was new was Li Si's dramatic counterproposal. Seizing the gauntlet Yue had thrown, Li Si fired back that he was nothing but a "stupid Confucianist." The dynasties of the past were obviously no fit model for the present. "In other times the feudal rulers vied with one another in inviting wandering scholars to their courts and treating them generously," Li Si argued before the emperor. "But now all under heaven have been pacified and laws and ordinances proceed from a single source." Li Si denounced scholars (except himself, of course) because they only wanted to "study antiquity in order to criticize their own age, misleading and confusing the black-headed people [a traditional term for the Chinese]." Therefore Li Si proposed that all past literature not approved by the government be tracked down and destroyed. Only old books on divination, medicine, and agriculture should be exempted. The First Emperor approved of Li Si's logic and the Burning of the Books was carried out, with the only surviving copies of the forbidden books reserved for the First Emperor's own private library.[13] To call the atmosphere the First Emperor cultivated for his empire totalitarian might seem carelessly anachronistic, but such cavalier destruction of centuries of thought, such an unapologetic determination to exterminate the past in favor of a present designed under the direction of one living man instead of by past generations, begs for no other term in English.

The First Emperor was absolutely confident that he really had single-handedly designed a new world order. At each of the empire's borders, an inscribed stone was erected. One such stone declared:

> In his twenty-eighth year the August Emperor made a new beginning. He adjusted the laws and regulations, standards for the ten thousand things. He clarified human concerns, bringing concord to father and son, sage, wise, benevolent and righteous, making plain the principle of the Way. In the east he toured the eastern lands, inspecting their officers and men, and when his tasks were grandly completed, he gazed down on the sea. The merit of the August Emperor lies in diligently fostering basic concerns, exalting agriculture, abolishing lesser occupations, so the black-headed people may be rich. All under heaven are of one mind, single in will. Weights and measures have a single standard, words are written in a uniform way. [. . .] He pities the black-headed people, morning and evening never neglectful. He erases doubt and establishes laws, so all will know what to shun. [. . .] The August Emperor in his enlightenment scrutinizes the four quarters. Exalted, lowly, eminent, or humble never overstep their proper course. Evil and wrongdoing are not permitted; all practice goodness and integrity.[14]

Like in a fable about the perils of achieving absolute power, the First Emperor did not live easily despite having such awe-inspiring power at his beck and call. He did everything possible to ensure that he kept the favor of destiny. Believing that the Five Phases (wood, fire, earth, metal, and water) succeed each other in an ending cycle and that the Zhou dynasty, which had red as its color, was ruled by fire, the First Emperor declared that since the Qin had replaced the Zhou, Qin should represent the phase that overwhelms fire, water. The color traditionally associated with water, black, would be the official color of the Qin. The associated number, six, was made the standard measurement. For example, official caps were six inches while carriages were six feet tall and drawn by six horses.

However, there was one problem that the First Emperor turned his formidable resources toward that could not be resolved: the emperor's own mortality. "The First Emperor hated any talk of dying, and none of his officials dared even allude to the matter of death," Sima Qian claimed.[15] On the advice of a magician, the First Emperor sent an expedition of a thousand virgin girls and boys led by Xu Fu to find some fabled islands whose inhabitants had discovered the medical antidote to death itself. Much later, while on a tour of his eastern provinces the emperor stumbled across Xu Fu, who was apparently just quietly living off the money meant to fund the expedition. Saved by his own wit, Xu Fu claimed that he really had singled out the location of the islands of the immortals but fierce sea monsters impeded the voyage. Since this was verified by a dream he recently had, the emperor ordered a fishing party to set out into the sea, led by the First Emperor himself, clutching a crossbow. Days later they found a "large fish," which could have been a dolphin or a shark. Whatever it was, the emperor to his own delight killed one himself, and they returned to Xu Fu to proudly report that the way had been cleared. Xu Fu set out again and wisely vanished for good this time. Legend would claim that he ended up in Japan, secure from even his master's reach.

Modern historians often admit the fact that Sima Qian, whose book records most of the known details about the First Emperor's life, was an official under the Han dynasty that replaced the Qin, and as such he may have felt obligated to cast the First Emperor in as poor a light as possible. Then again, Sima Qian would compliment the Qin on the order they imposed on a fractured and feuding China and took seriously his role as a transmitter of past knowledge.[16] Even if Sima Qian exaggerated some accounts, one does get the impression that it was less the inherent qualities of Legalism and more the sheer force of the First Emperor's steel personality that kept the Qin empire running smoothly.

So the real test inevitably came when, while returning from his tour of the eastern provinces (the same one where he stumbled across Xu Fu and his "expedition" in 210), the First Emperor suddenly collapsed from illness and soon died. He was still only in his forties. Sima Qian does not speculate on what killed him, but modern historians think the First Emperor may have been ingesting toxic amounts of cinnabar, a key ingredient in the immortality potions his alchemists prescribed for him.[17] Whatever the cause, ironic or not, the timing would prove to be disastrous for the ten-thousand-year empire. The First Emperor's will ordered that his son Fusu be recalled and appointed emperor. However, the only people who knew of the will—and, indeed, about the First Emperor's sudden demise—were Li Si, the First Emperor's youngest and favorite son Huhai, and Zhao Gao, a palace eunuch and a prominent minister. The nomination of Fusu horrified Zhao Gao, who was bitter rivals with the Meng family, one of whom was Meng Tian, a general who happened to be Fusu's friend and comrade on the northern frontier. With reason, he became convinced that the crowning of Fusu would mean a gruesome death sentence for him.

It is easy to imagine Zhao Gao acting with haste, holding clandestine meetings in whispers while the lavishly adorned corpse of the First Emperor silently decayed nearby. His first target was Huhai, who may have been as young as fourteen at the time. Why shouldn't the emperor's most beloved son, Zhao Gao urged, succeed him? Sima Qian suggests that Huhai was understandably terrified at the idea of taking over his father's tremendous role and having to live his entire existence in terror of assassination attempts and revolts, but he was even more afraid of the consequences of failure. Still, Zhao Gao eventually persuaded him, likely by simply overawing the all-too-young man. A tougher sell was Li Si, whose compliance was just as mandatory. Zhao Gao played on his fears, arguing that, as a man in his sixties, Fusu would only force him to retire to make way for his own friends. If that happened, the best he could hope for was being allowed to commit suicide in the comfort of his home surrounded by loved ones, since under the very principles of Legalism he promoted valuable intellectual talent must never be allowed a chance to seek other employment.

The three agreed to pretend that the emperor was still alive in his private wagon until they could reach the safety of the capital. The fact that it was the middle of summer posed an odious logistical challenge, but Zhao Gao had a fish cart placed next to the emperor's wagon to disguise the smell of rotting human flesh. In the meantime, Li Si and Zhao Gao had forged a letter from the emperor that was promptly sent to the northern frontier. "The emperor" accused Fusu of treason and Meng Tian of willfully refusing to report it. The letter concluded by commanding that Fusu and Meng Tian kill themselves. Weeping, Fusu impaled himself on a sword. Meng Tian, on the other hand, was skeptical and refused, but in the end, he would be imprisoned and forced to join his friend in death.

Arriving in Xianyang, the three conspirators must have been relieved they were not greeted by an army led by Meng Tian. Instead Huhai was promptly given a coronation as Er Shi Huangdi ("Second Emperor"). Yet Zhao Gao's hands stayed firmly at the wheel, and like so many people throughout history whose grip on power was shaky he became obsessed with striking down any and all possible threats. Instituting a reign of terror that must have made even the most deranged and arbitrary excesses of the First Emperor seem like mild inconveniences, Zhao Gao convinced the Second Emperor to purge his government and "examine" the governors and generals of the empire while cracking down on the populace as a whole. Sima Qian records Zhao Gao advised all this to the Second Emperor with perfect candor: "By doing so you can strike terror into the empire as a whole, and at the same time do away with those who disapprove of your actions."[18]

The worst victims were the Second Emperor's own family. Six of the First Emperor's sons and all ten of his daughters were killed in the days following the Second Emperor's ascension, with only Jianglü and two other brothers left alive but kept under close watch. Then suddenly they received a written decree declaring that they had "failed to act as proper subjects" and ordering them to commit suicide. Jianglü fired back to the official tasked with delivering the news that they always followed court ritual and never failed to observe protocol. The messenger simply replied that he was following orders. Jianglü screamed, "This is Heaven's doing! I have committed no crime!" (an ominous declaration, invoking the Mandate of Heaven), before he and his brothers fell on their swords.

The cracks, which one has to imagine were being made even during the lifetime of the First Emperor, became impossible to gloss over a year after the First Emperor's death, in 209. In what used to be the kingdom of Chu there was a plowhand, Chen She, who had been drafted into the Qin army and placed in charge of a slave gang. Then, because of a bad rainstorm, they were made extremely late for their next assignment. Under the ever harsher laws introduced by Zhao Gao's regime, Chen She and the workers under him would all die for tardiness, so they decided that if their choice was definitely being slaughtered on charges of desertion and perhaps being killed for treason then the latter was the vastly superior option. Even he may have been shocked at how well he did once he found himself in charge of a victorious rebel force and named the king of a resurgent Chu state. After a reign of six months, he had gotten into an argument with one of his own soldiers who later assassinated him. However, Chen She was only the first. Many of the former Warring States were now propping up kings who announced they were completely free from any obligations to the emperor.

While Qin's new adversaries plotted with and against each other, the tarnished imperial court was drowning itself in blood. The next on Zhao Gao's long hit list was Li Si. News that one of Li Si's sons had become a rebel leader provided the perfect pretext. Li Si was condemned to suffer the worst fate his own system of Legalism permitted, the Five Punishments: tattooing, mutilation, maiming, castration, and then, finally, being publicly cut in half. The last was also to be the fate of his wife and children. In his cell, as one last act of defiance, he wrote down a "confession" where, in one of the great sarcastic manifestos in any language and era, he agreed he was indeed guilty of elevating the kingdom of Qin into an empire that covered the entire civilized world, of ensuring prosperity and order for the state, and of always honoring his masters.

Li Si was erased as effectively and as brutally as he had erased the knowledge of countless generations. While led to his death, Li Si turned to one of his terrified and crying sons and said in memory of better times, "I wish you and I could once more take our yellow dog and go out the eastern gate of Shangcai to chase the wily rabbits. But there's little hope of that, is there!"[19] While his ministers and siblings were being butchered, the Second Emperor traveled ceaselessly from one country residence to another, his exact whereabouts a secret to even the members of his own government except Zhao Gao. It was an easy enough matter for Zhao Gao to keep the young Second Emperor off balance. In one anecdote preserved by Sima Qian, Zhao Gao went so far as to present the emperor with the gift of a horse, except that all the emperor saw before him was a deer. Zhao Gao and the other courtiers insisted it was a horse and whispered (within earshot of the emperor, of course) their fear that their lord might be going mad. His doctors, who were all in Zhao Gao's employ, advised him that he could recover but only if he stayed away from the stressful atmosphere of the court.

However, even the isolated emperor could not be sheltered from the news of growing rebellions and more and more new kingdoms swearing off imperial rule. He had the audacity to criticize Zhao Gao for failing catastrophically as first minister, which only fueled Zhao Gao's paranoia. It was now time to cut the puppet's strings. While the Second Emperor was at one of his country estates, Zhao Gao arranged to have soldiers loyal to him and led by his son-in-law feign an attack on the residence as a group of bandits. As the Second Emperor cowered in his chambers with one remaining faithful servant, a eunuch, he asked his sole remaining friend why he was not warned and received the stern answer that everyone who tried to warn him about the tightening noose he had executed and, for the survivors, silence was the only way they could save their own skin. Zhao Gao's son-in-law burst into the chamber and declared that the Second Emperor had lost the Mandate of Heaven and the only chance to save his dynasty was to commit suicide. The Second Emperor pitifully begged to be able to live out his days as a humble nobleman living out in the country or even as some commoner. He was refused.

Would there be a Third Emperor? Zhao Gao decided against it. The best bet for survival, for the Qin and more importantly for himself, was on the Qin renouncing their imperial pretensions and trying to resurrect the *status quo* of the Warring States. With Zhao Gao's blessing, Ziying, who may have been a son of the doomed Fusu, came to the throne not as the Third Emperor but as merely the new king of Qin. Ziying was no fool or already knew a great deal about what Zhao Gao had done and stabbed Zhao Gao to death with his own hands. It was much too late for such boldness. A ferocious general, Xiang Yu, who had titled himself Hegemon-King of Western Chu and was perhaps a relation of Chu's old royals, helped lead an invasion of Qin and lusted for revenge against the one-time conquerors of his beloved homeland. Ziying was executed, what was left of the royal family of Qin was rounded up and murdered, the entire population of Xianyang was cut down, and the city including its libraries were burned, wiping out in a stroke what was left untouched even by the Burning of the Books.

Even then, it was not the end of the imperial dream. Instead the splintering kingdoms were again united by 202 under one ruler, Liu

Bang. Liu Bang had been an alcoholic peasant who had also been tasked with handling a gang of convicts under the Qin government and, like Chen She, turned rebel out of fear that they would be executed for some petty offense. Taking the reign-name Gaozu, he would be the first emperor of the new Han dynasty, which would go on to rule for four centuries, a much more impressive track record than the Ten-Thousand-Year Empire the First Emperor had envisioned. One of the first acts of the new Han dynasty was loosening the burden of strict laws, punishments, and taxation that the Qin had imposed. So, although the body of the empire was restored, its guiding philosophy was mostly lost.

This leaves an interesting what-if. Could a Legalist empire have survived for long? Fusu is only given the most shallow of descriptions in the *Records of the Great Historian,* but even if he had little or no genuine compassion for the "black headed people" who groaned under his father's brutal reign he at least may have appreciated the importance of solid public relations. If Zhao Gao had failed in his coup, would Fusu have preserved the Qin? Given how quickly and disastrously the house that Qin Shi Huangdi built fell apart when faced with its first real crisis, the answer is likely not. The story of the many people who ripped the empire apart is filled with those characters who, from the peasant who had been forced into becoming a laborer to the nobleman who lost his prospects when the old kingdoms were dissolved, had their lives upended by the First Emperor's divine ambitions. Fear of an unforgiving and all-seeing penal system probably did succeed in keeping the people in check for a while anyway, but it also gave even the lowest of the low a reason to see the whole system toppled.

4.

THE CARTHAGINIAN EMPIRE
Bullied to Extinction

Few societies in history have respected someone who had attempted to annihilate them as much as the Romans respected
the general Hannibal. Even though the Romans swore that
Hannibal's home country Carthage was nothing but a breeding
ground for decadence and treachery, Hannibal himself became a symbol of honor and military brilliance. Introducing the topic of the war
Hannibal waged against Rome, the best-selling first-century Roman
historian, Livy, wrote, "I am about to relate the most memorable of
all wars that were ever waged: the war which the Carthaginians,
under the conduct of Hannibal, maintained with the Roman people.
For never did any states and nations more efficient in their resources
engage in contest; nor had they themselves at any other period so
great a degree of power and energy."[1] The Greek historian Polybius
went even further in heaping on the praise: "It is a remarkable and
very cogent proof of Hannibal's having been by nature a real leader
and far superior to anyone else in statesmanship, that though he spent
seventeen years in the field, passed through so many barbarous countries, and employed to aid him in desperate and extraordinary enter-
prises numbers of men of different nations and languages, no one ever
dreamt of conspiring against him, nor was he ever deserted by those
who had once joined him or submitted to him."[2]

Despite their congenial admiration of a worthy opponent, the Romans were merciless toward the society that Hannibal risked his life and those of hundreds of men to defend, Carthage. Thanks to the Romans, the Carthaginians have effectively been scrubbed from history, and even their language, Punic, is only known from some inscriptions here and a few lines from a Roman play there. However, there was a time when they very well could have obliterated the Roman Empire, rather than the other way around.

Carthage started out as a mere colony established by the Phoenician people in modern-day Tunisia. Spread out across North Africa in small city-states, the Phoenicians were a Semitic people, closely related to the Canaanites and the Hebrews. (Both ancient stories and modern theories disagree about where the Phoenicians actually came from originally. "Suspects" include somewhere along the Red Sea or the Persian Gulf, the Horn of Africa, Lebanon, or Palestine.) It was a Phoenician king, Ithobaal of Tyre, who was the father of the proverbially notorious Jezebel, the wife of King Ahab of Israel. The Old Testament connections are more subtle elsewhere. Hannibal's own name referred to a god shared between the Canaanites and Phoenicians who went by the name-title Baal, or "lord," and might possibly have meant "Baal is gracious." At their height the Phoenician cities thrived on the trade of the southern Mediterranean, so much so that it was the Phoenicians who taught the Greeks how to run a commercial society, from having loans with interest to the development of an alphabet designed to help keep records and inventories.

In the end, the Phoenicians were maybe a tad too successful and attracted the greed of the Assyrians, the Persians, and finally Alexander the Great, who allegedly deposed the king of the great Phoenician city of Sidon and replaced him with a gardener (although at the risk of ruining a great tale "gardener" might have just been some honorary court title, like Steward or Keeper of the Horses). Once the richest of all Phoenician cities, Tyre, had been ground under the Persians' and then Alexander's boot, and its colony Carthage was happy to fill the gaps in its old trade networks. Growing fat and healthy on the circulating wealth of the Mediterranean, Carthage soon grew into an empire whose agents were often merchants and colonists, not soldiers and magistrates.[3] At its peak, Carthage's trade spanned from what is now southern Spain to Sicily and Sardinia to modern-day Lebanon and made its top citizens richer than most kings of their day.

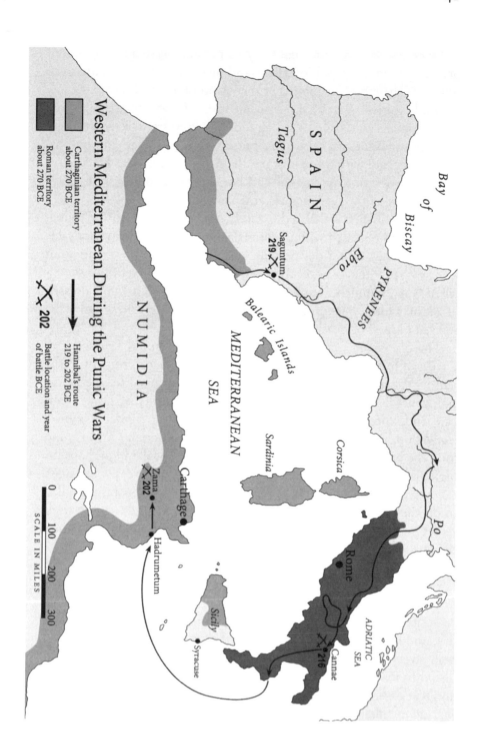

Of course, it is not unusual for even commercial empires to find it practical to spill a little blood now and then. Like the Athenians once did, the Carthaginians looked at the island of Sicily and saw the key to total control over Mediterranean trade. However, although the Carthaginians established a strong foothold in western Sicily, the powerful city of Syracuse refused to put up with Carthage's ambitions, just as they had with those upstarts the Athenians. By 405 BCE, Syracuse's democratic government had been torn down and in its place rose Dionysius the *tyrannos* (a term that gives us the word "tyrant" but is probably best translated in modern terms as "dictator"). Young, brilliant, and obsessed with imperial daydreams of his own, Dionysius drew Carthage into a devastating guerrilla war, which at one point went so badly that a general who was a long-time veteran of the Sicilian wars, Himilco, roamed around the streets of Carthage dressed in plain white robes and begged for divine forgiveness while he starved himself to death.

The occasional setback aside, the rivers of capital flowing into Carthage from places like western Sicily made its government a true plutocracy, and the reins were often jealously gripped by the politician-generals who ran Carthage in the fourth century BCE like Himilco and, after him, Hanno "the Great." Even under Hanno's leadership, the war in Sicily continued to be unpopular and Hanno took the brunt of the blame. Fearing for his political and perhaps his biological life, Hanno schemed to assassinate members of Carthage's executive body, the Council of Elders. Although the conspiracy failed to do the one important thing all conspiracies must do—keep itself secret—the council was afraid to create a public scandal by taking down such a prominent citizen. Overestimating his position as a result, Hanno next attempted to rally Carthage's slaves and the neighboring Libyan and Numidian peoples in a plot to make him dictator or even king. The Roman historian Justin described the grim outcome: ". . . he was captured, and after being scourged, having his eyes put out, and his arms and legs broken, as if atonement was to be exacted from every limb, he was put to death in the sight of the people, and his body, mangled with stripes, was nailed to a cross. All his children and relations, too, though guiltless, were delivered to the executioner, that no member of so nefarious a family might survive either to imitate his villainy, or to revenge his death."[4] Given all these theatrics from its failed military leaders, it is not too much of a surprise that

Carthage alone of all ancient Mediterranean societies punished its generals for incompetence with not only disgrace but with death by crucifixion.

The threat of overmighty citizens was a painful thorn in Carthage's side that just could not be removed. Carthaginian territory in what is now southern Portugal and Spain was entrusted to the Barcid family, who could boast the famous Hannibal as a member. A major spot in the Mediterranean's silver trade, the Iberian province, which had a "New Carthage" as one of its capitals, actually became wealthier than the homeland itself. The Barcids savored their position and found it both practical and satisfying to overawe both the natives and their mercenary troops by playing up their pomp and power. One Barcid, Hasdrubal, even had a local king as a son-in-law.[5] If history had turned in just a slightly different direction, maybe Carthage would have instead been smashed by an insurgent Barcid kingdom of the Iberian Peninsula. Instead, the real threat in hindsight was not Syracuse or the Barcids but a one-time backwater city somewhere in the middle of the Italian Peninsula.

In the beginning, Rome and Carthage were allies. In fact, their first trade agreement, signed in 509 BCE, was embraced as such a wonderful acknowledgment of Rome's mere existence by a great nation the terms of the treaty were preserved in a temple on bronze tablets.[6] Much later, in the late third century BCE, Carthage and Rome forged a military alliance against Pyrrhus, the king of the Balkan kingdom of Epirus. As Rome embarked on its own rise to power, first subduing all of Italy and then beginning to reach greedily over the sea into Greece, there was likely no way around a clash with their former friends. This squabble would only be the first of what Roman historians would call the "Punic wars," which pitted Rome against the only other major power left on the Mediterranean. At the onset of the First Punic War, Rome barely had a navy to speak of and Carthage commanded the sea. Unfortunately for Carthage, Rome already had the most disciplined war machine the Mediterranean had ever seen while the Carthaginians had the serious handicap of being heavily dependent on foreign mercenaries.

The cause of their first clash was, yet again, the siren call of Sicily. In 265 a band of Italian mercenaries, the Mamertines (meaning "followers of Mamers," an Italian war god), settled in Sicily and slaughtered the men of the city of Messana, taking their homes and their wives for themselves. Threatened by Syracuse, the Mamertines hedged their bets by petitioning both Carthage and Rome for protection. If not for Rome sticking its nose into Sicily, it might have been just another episode in the decades-long tug of war between Syracuse and Carthage over the island. Romans who wrote about the Punic War later gleefully claimed instead that Carthage's intervention in Sicily was actually just one step in Carthage's master plan to take over all of Sicily and from there Italy, a scheme heroically thwarted by their ancestors. Maybe that was what Rome's Senate at the time actually believed, or they were just eager for any excuse to set their sights on Sicily. In any case, even though Messana was already occupied by Carthaginian soldiers, Rome shipped an army to Sicily, pushing even the long-time rivals of Carthage and Syracuse into an alliance against the Roman interlopers.

As much as Rome's own historians loved to see their empire's ascendancy as destiny, the end of the First Punic War was not a foregone conclusion. Disasters and setbacks derailed the Roman war effort, and at one point, Rome lost almost its entire fleet. On the other hand, Carthage became fatally distracted by another threat, the Numidians in present-day Algeria. However much of a chance Carthage had at the start, in the end it was forced to give up Sicily completely.

The end of hostilities would prove only to be a brief reprieve. Hannibal, who had inherited control over southern Iberia, got into a violent confrontation with an ally of Rome, the city of Saguntum, in what is now the Spanish province of Valencia. It was this, the second of the Punic Wars, that most fired the imagination of later Romans, and in fact historians and writers throughout Western history. Images of Hannibal, marching across the Alps with his massive army and two hundred war elephants and nearly reaching the walls of Rome itself, echo from ancient Roman manuscripts to Hollywood film sets. Maybe it is more than an admiration for military skills. It could be that it is impossible to ignore that Hannibal himself marked one of history's major turning points, where one civilization could have triumphed instead of being forced to disappear from the history books, and in such a victory would have fashioned a world incalculably different from our own.

But that world was stillborn. For all his military brilliance that made admirers out of even his bitterest enemies, Hannibal irrevocably lost by 201. Sensing how close to total destruction they came, the

Roman Senate demanded unforgiving terms for peace. Carthage would cede all its territories in the Iberian Peninsula, would have to pay a massive indemnity, had to surrender its war elephants and all of its ships except ten, and could no longer start any wars without Rome's permission. Hannibal himself, after a successful but tense career as a populist politician and a desperate attempt to recapture his military glory, was forced to flee east, condemned to wandering from country to country as a celebrity exile. Eventually he happened to be staying at the royal court of the king of Bithynia in Asia Minor just when a Roman general happened to be visiting on diplomatic business. Eager to please Rome, the king ordered Hannibal's arrest, forcing the one-time hero of Carthage to gulp down a vial of poison he always kept on him.

Carthage's own demise would be even more cruelly prolonged. It was the death of a superpower in twilight at the mercy of another still in ascendancy. Yet Carthage after the Second Punic War, no longer needing to keep hordes of mercenaries fed and happy, was basking in a pleasant economic boom and Carthage's leaders quietly swallowed their new status as the tributaries of Rome. Livy records one episode between the Roman Senate and Carthage's emissaries during Rome's war with Macedonia:

> The Carthaginians reported that they had taken down to the coast one million modii [roughly eight quarts each] of wheat and half a million of barley, to be transported wherever the Senate should order. They knew, they said, that this gift, which they regarded as a duty, was not adequate to the services which the Roman people had rendered, nor was it what they would have wished to give, but on other occasions, when both nations were in a prosperous condition, they had fulfilled the duty of loyal and grateful allies.[7]

Once Carthage oversaw the entire Mediterranean Sea and its riches like a leviathan. Now it had to grovel simply for its right to exist. Worse, Rome was not alone in exploiting the situation. Numidia was positioning itself as Rome's most trustworthy friend in North Africa and a natural enemy to the treacherous Carthaginians, whom the Numidians slyly implied would grab any opportunity to recapture their lost glory. Masinissa, king of Numidia, decided to put this bias to the ultimate test by seizing Syrtis Minor, a region rich in coastal farmland on the Gulf of Gabès that had traditionally been Carthaginian land. Wealthy as it still was, Carthage still could not afford to lose the farmland in its backyard and there was talk of war between the two countries, likely just as Masinissa intended.

Masinissa may have already known he had a steadfast ally at Rome, Marcus Porcius Cato, a senator who was a hardened veteran of the Second Punic War in his eighties. A member of an official delegation to Carthage sent in 152, Cato was disgusted to find that, rather than still reeling from its defeat decades ago, Carthage had a young and well-fed population, a supply of weapons, and a surplus of wood that could be transformed almost overnight into a new war fleet. Multiple ancient sources attest that Cato became so obsessed as soon as he returned to Rome with the existential threat of a resurgent Carthage that he ended every speech, no matter the subject, before the Senate with the same rhetorical drumbeat, *Carthago delenda est*— "Carthage must be destroyed." Even a piece of fruit became a key prop in Cato's democratic theatrics:

> Burning with a mortal hatred of Carthage and anxious in regard to the safety of his descendants, at every meeting of the senate he used to vociferate 'Down with Carthage!' and so on a certain occasion he brought into the house an early ripe fig from that province, and displaying it to the Fathers [Senators] he said, 'I put it to you, when do you think this fruit was plucked from the tree?' Everybody agreed that it was quite fresh; so he said, 'Oh well, it was picked the day before yesterday at Carthage— so near is the enemy to our walls!'[8]

Not everyone agreed with Cato, and one senator, Publius Scipio Nascia, countered Cato's memorable phrase with the perhaps not as catchy "Carthage should be spared." In fact, Nascia argued that it was *because* Carthage was known as Rome's eternal rival that it must remain. According to Diodorus's account, Nascia pleaded before the Senate that "as long as Carthage survived, the fear that she generated forced the Romans to live together in harmony and to rule their subjects equitably and with credit to themselves."[9] Also the Roman Senate prided itself in its reputation for only engaging in just wars, however shaky that reputation actually was. Still, that anxiety about keeping up honorable appearances was enough that, for Cato to get his wish, there would have to be some kind of a pretext.[10]

Thankfully, the Carthaginians gave such an excuse when a dispute between the Numidians and the Carthaginians over more territory the Numidians tried to quietly annex turned violent. Carthage had once again been found guilty of attacking a Roman ally; it did not matter that this time they had been provoked by an act of aggression. In 150, the third and last of the Punic Wars was launched, although it was less of a war and more of a punishing raid. The leaders of Carthage desperately tried to make amends, which Cato urged the Senate to ignore: "Who are the people who have often broken their treaties? The Carthaginians. Who are the people who have waged war with the utmost cruelty? The Carthaginians. Who are the people who have disfigured Italy? The Carthaginians. Who are the people who ask to be forgiven? The Carthaginians."[11] To Cato, and no doubt to more than a few prominent Romans who had fresh memories of the Second Punic War, the only solution to the alleged threat Carthage posed was total extermination.

Starved of supplies and no doubt fully aware of Rome's intentions, Carthage fell under the dictatorship of a charismatic general named Hasdrubal, who casually executed any member of the Council of Elders who tried to undermine him. Unfortunately for him, the same catastrophic circumstances that allowed him to achieve absolute power, the dream of many a disgruntled Carthaginian general throughout the city's history, refused to recede. By the spring of 146, the Romans under the command of Scipio Aemelianus had subdued all of Carthage's territory save the city itself. After just one week under siege, a cabal of members of the Council of Elders and much of the populace left the city to plead for mercy. Scipio gladly granted their request, although for the fifty thousand people who abandoned their city "mercy" would still entail a life of slavery. Inside the city walls only Hasdrubal, his family, and hundreds remained. They had holed up in the temple of Eshmun, the Phoenician god of healing, which was the most defensible building in the city, but even so they were eventually forced to take a last stand on the temple's roof.

Even Hasdrubal was broken. Abandoning his own family, he climbed down the temple walls and begged for Scipio's pardon. This last humiliation only steeled the resolve of the others, who set fire to the temple and shouted curses at Hasdrubal. The worst came from his own wife. "Wretch, traitor, most effeminate of men, this fire will entomb me and my children," she allegedly screamed from over the flames. "Will you, the leader of great Carthage, decorate a Roman triumph? Ah, what punishment will you not receive from him at whose feet you are now sitting." With that last prophecy, she killed her own children and pushed their corpses into the flames before following them.[12] In a perhaps anticlimactic postscript, however, she would be proven wrong. Seeing nothing to gain from Hasdrubal's death, Scipio had him exhibited in a triumphal march like all fallen opponents of Rome, but afterward he was allowed to live out the rest of his days peacefully in a villa in rural Italy.

Carthage itself could not be spared. The Romans burned the city down and had the land formally cursed, although the famous claim that the Romans salted the earth so that crops could not grow on it was only a modern invention. A close friend of Scipio Aemilianus who was present at the siege of Carthage, the historian Polybius, claims even Scipio was struck at the magnitude of what they had done. Scipio wept at the sight of Carthage burning and thought about all the cities and empires that had fallen in the past. To Polybius, Scipio quoted a verse from Homer: "The day shall come in which our sacred Troy / and Priam, and the people over whom / Spear-bearing Priam rules, shall perish all." When Polybius asked what he meant, he "did not hesitate to frankly name his own country, for whose fate he feared when he considered the mutability of human affairs."[13]

In fact, the ghost of Carthage would haunt Rome more than any of its other vanquished rivals. After all, the epic struggles with Carthage had left Rome as the only superpower in all of the Mediterranean. Later generations of Romans would blame the "Punic curse" for giving Rome literally more wealth and land than it knew what to do with and triggering a series of events that would mean mob violence and civil war for the Roman Republic and, eventually, the emergence of the emperors and the crippling of the Roman Senate. Even before the first emperor Augustus came to power, the Roman historian Sallust diagnosed Rome's problems as stemming from their own total victory, writing:

> For before the destruction of Carthage the people and senate
> of Rome together governed the republic peacefully and with
> moderation. There was no strife among the citizens either for
> glory or for power; fear of the enemy preserved the good morals
> of the state. But when the minds of the people were relieved of

View of the excavations of Carthage, Tunisia. (*Christian Manhart/UNESCO*)

that dread, wantonness and arrogance naturally arose, vices which are fostered by prosperity. Thus the peace for which they had longed in time of adversity, after they had gained it proved to be more cruel and bitter than adversity itself. For the nobles began to abuse their position and the people their liberty, and every man for himself robbed, pillaged, and plundered. Thus the community was split into two parties, and between these the state was torn to pieces.[14]

If that seems a great deal to blame on a destroyed society, it is at least true that the debate over how to allocate all the fertile land gained in North Africa, and how it should benefit the veterans of the Punic Wars who were (like many veterans of many wars throughout history) disproportionately poor, actually did ignite the first of the constitutional crises that would shake Rome to the core throughout the first century BCE. The end result would turn the proud republic into a monarchy in all but name.

However, this was not really the end for Carthage. Julius Caesar began and Emperor Augustus completed the rebuilding of Carthage as a Roman colony for war veterans under the untidy name of Colonia Iulia Concordia Carthago. In a nod to the old city's significance, this new Roman Carthage was made the capital of one of the empire's North African provinces. The area is still inhabited and called Carthage to this day, although it only exists now as a suburb of the city of Tunis. At the same time, the memory of Carthaginian civilization is preserved mostly through the tales told by the people that destroyed it, apart from archaeological discoveries. Despite Carthage's own survival of a sort, its story, from the perspective of its own champions like Hannibal, must remain a project of the imagination.

5.

THE HAN EMPIRE
Reign of the Eunuchs

A t the same time the Roman Empire was nearing its peak in 1 AD, China under the Han dynasty could already boast a highly sophisticated, centralized administration and a population of nearly 57 million.[1] Its capital, Chang'an, was home to a population of 246,200, making it easily the most populous city in the world at the time. Visitors to Chang'an could look at exotic animals and plants collected from across the empire and placed in public zoos and gardens or go shopping in the bustling marketplaces where officials were tasked with ensuring as much as possible that no customers were cheated. Radiating from this thriving urban climate was an intellectual culture that offered comprehensive historical writings that attempted to gleam the origins of the human race, erudite works of mathematics and literary criticism, and poetry that delved into both the natural world and humanity's inner emotional realms. To run such an empire, the Han emperors divided their territory which at its height stretched from what is now northern Vietnam to the northernmost regions of the Korean Peninsula into 1,587 prefectures, each of which was further split down into districts, which were all cut into wards. Each ward was governed by trained scholars selected through merit after a rigorous examination process.[2]

The cornerstone to all this was laid down by a peasant with a penchant for booze and a hatred for manual labor, Liu Bang. After being drafted as a patrol leader under the brutal Qin government and later leading a revolt, he managed to triumph over all the would-be kings who surfaced during the collapse of the Qin, even famously edging out the aristocratic general Xiang Yu, self-proclaimed Hegemon of Western Chu (in fact, to this day in China both sides of a chessboard are referred to as Chu and Han). Instead of completely tossing out the idea of imperial rule that the Qin emperor pioneered, the victorious Liu Bang gave himself the reign-name of Gaozu (meaning "high-forefather") and declared the ascension of a new dynasty, the Han. Gaozu and his successors relaxed or jettisoned many of the stern features of Legalism, although they kept the idea of group responsibility for crimes and punishment through tattooing, the amputation of noses or feet, and castration. Upon Legalism's former pedestal, they raised Confucianism, particularly emphasizing its comforting promise that if ritual, precedent, and the ancient virtues were carefully observed a harmonious relationship between the sovereign, his subjects, and the cosmos can be held in place.

At least, Gaozu's descendants did a far better job of keeping heaven's favor than the Qin did, although they too faced dangers. In 1 BCE, the Empress Dowager Wang Zhenjun selected her nephew, an accomplished Confucian scholar, Wang Mang, to rule as regent in the name of her very young son, the Emperor Pin. Like so many child monarchs beginning to reach adulthood, Pin resented the adults around him who were acting in his name and lashed out. Either Pin suddenly succumbed to the heart defect sources claim he had or Wang Mang handled the problem in the most direct and efficient way possible, by poisoning him.

Wang Mang scoured the Han's genealogical records for another malleable child heir to sit on the throne, but all the Emperor Pin's living male relations were well into adulthood. Refusing to surrender to the inconvenient necessities of hereditary monarchy, Wang Mang simply masterminded a propaganda campaign that promoted himself as the founder of a new imperial dynasty, the Xin (literally "new") dynasty. During the short existence of the Xin, Wang Mang would attack the empire's rich, overbearing landlords by abolishing all private ownership of land and outlawing the sale of land. Wang Mang dreamed of bringing Confucius's ideals into full reality, but instead he only conjured up a dreary period of revolts and civil war that lasted

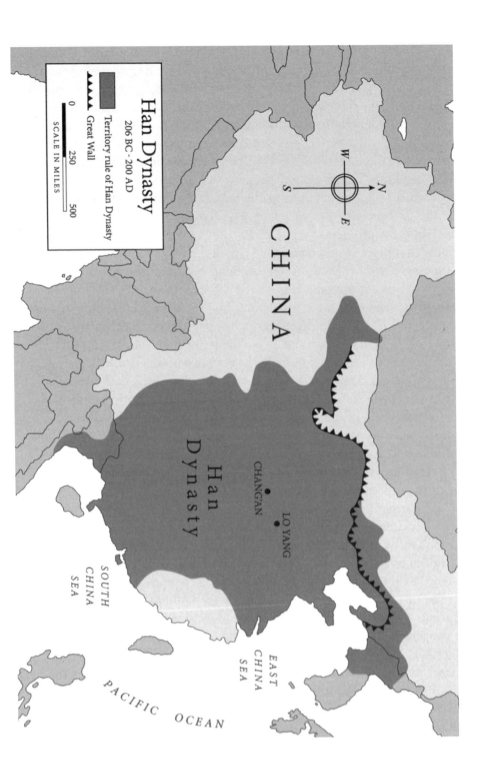

Han Dynasty
206 BC - 200 AD

Territory rule of Han Dynasty

Great Wall

SCALE IN MILES

0   250   500

CHINA

W   N
S   E

Han Dynasty

CHANG'AN

LO YANG

SOUTH CHINA SEA

EAST CHINA SEA

PACIFIC OCEAN

even after he was butchered in his own palace by a gang of young malcontents. The Han dynasty proved it could survive even after such a disastrous coup once another member of the Han, Guangwu, was able to seize the throne and restore order. Wang Mang's tenure as emperor would largely be remembered not as the fulfillment of Confucius's dreams of a perfectly ordered society but as a little blip in time that broke the history of the Han between the time of the "Former Han" and the "Eastern Han," the era of Guangwu and his successors, so named because they moved the imperial court to the city of Luoyang farther east.

Sadly, the problems that helped make Wang Mang's coup palpable in the first place would chase the Han all the way to Luoyang and become even worse. Wealthy landowning families, notorious among moralists even during the Han's heyday for extravagantly decking out even their slaves, began at some point to give little in taxes while soaking up much in profits from agricultural production. The frontiers were being held in place not by soldiers but by bribes showered on tribal chiefs residing just outside the empire's borders, which eventually proved to be as much of a burden on the state's coffers as any army. In the meantime, the imperial court became further detached from the world around it, as the Eastern Han emperors, who were mostly a series of powerless child emperors,[3] drowned in hordes of career-seeking retainers, ambitious empress dowagers and their grasping relatives, and the entrenched eunuchs, who would become a major feature of the Eastern Han court.

Like other courts that employed castrated men as servants and ministers, the original purpose of having eunuchs around was to make sure that the most important positions were held by men who had no children to enrich and that neither the women of the court and the men that served them were unwholesomely tempted. Most were recruited from commoner families and were willing—or at least their parents were willing—to sacrifice the most intimate part of themselves to ensure lucrative employment for life. Under the Eastern Han, the number of eunuchs at court skyrocketed, since as advisers and confidants to the emperor they were more reliable than the empresses and their self-serving relatives. At least, that was the hope. Eventually there were two thousand eunuchs at the imperial court of the Eastern Han.[4] With depressing inevitability, it was not long until the eunuchs became a government in and of themselves, and they too began to reserve important posts for their own relatives and crush any officials or even members of the imperial family who dared turn against them.

For example, there was the fate of Dou Wu, the father of an empress dowager, who made an attempt to dislodge the eunuchs, through the very direct tactic of slaughtering them all. The coup backfired when Dou Wu was found out and forced to commit suicide. Anyone in power who was remotely connected to him was relieved of their position and promptly replaced by a relative or friend of the eunuchs, tightening their stranglehold on the regime. The Emperor Ling, installed by his mother's family on the throne in 168 CE when he was only twelve years old, would, like many of the young Eastern Han predecessors, reign but not rule. The eunuchs guaranteed his obedience through a little bit of matchmaking, setting the young emperor up with a beautiful woman who would become the Empress Lingsi. The new emperor was content to just live in domestic bliss with his lady love. In the meantime, according to Rafe de Crespigny's introduction to his translation of the chronicles written by Sima Guang in the eleventh century, "the imperial civil service, and regular officials appointed to even the highest ranks were humiliated by the need to pay fines and bribes before they were permitted to enter upon their duties. With the favor of an inexperienced and irresponsible young ruler, and with the gratitude of the Empress and her family, the eunuchs could look forward to a long carer of steadily increasing power and wealth."[5]

Outside the isolated little world the eunuchs and the imperial family had created for themselves, matters were much more desperate and disorderly. There were failed harvests on top of the ever-stretching chasm between the great landowners and the rural poor. It was a time ripe for self-proclaimed prophets, violent rebels, and those who would be both. One such man was Zhang Jue who, drawing from the spiritual and philosophical tradition of Taoism, announced that he had in his sole possession a doctrine called the Way of Great Peace. Some people sold their property or abandoned their homes and families to follow him.[6] Backed by rich patrons who lived near the heart of the empire, Jue tried to overthrow the emperor. When the coup failed thanks to a traitor, Jue announced that he was the Lord of Heaven General and his followers, now in open rebellion, tore pieces of yellow cloth to wear as badges like soldiers in a war. The terrified populace would soon speak in dread about the Yellow Turbans.

Wherever the Yellow Turbans went villages were destroyed and government officials were butchered or sent scrambling for their lives. The Yellow Turbans were beaten after five years of bloodshed and outright warfare, with the cost of at least half a million peasants killed in reprisals by the overzealous army during just the first year.[7] However, the generals sent to quell the uprisings did not dismiss their forces even when they were victorious, but while still swearing loyalty to the emperor in Luoyang they took the opportunity to carve out their own power bases in the provinces. As this unfolded, any minister who suggested that reform must start with regaining confidence in imperial authority by breaking the backs of the eunuchs was eliminated. One such minister, Liu Tao, blamed the continued rise of rebels on the selfish and inept way the eunuchs managed the government. Sima Guang claims that the eunuchs countered the minister's report by appealing to the emperor with a potent combination of flattery and lies: "When the [Zhang Jue] business arose, imperial edicts displayed your majesty and grace, and since this time all the rebels have repented. Now the world is at peace, and yet Tao casts a slur upon your sage-like government and he takes it upon himself to speak heresy and evil. There have been no reports from the provinces or commanderies, so where does Tao get his information from?"[8] Tao would pay for his advice with his own death from torture.

The eunuchs themselves undertook no attempt to save their own golden goose even though there was no end in sight to military leaders shrugging off the central government or the rebels and bandits rampaging through the countryside. Instead they conducted business as usual, selling government posts to the highest bidder. Unfortunately for them, the emperor suddenly became as deathly sick as his empire. His only living sons were Bien, the fourteen-year-old son of his beloved empress, and the nine-year-old son of one of his concubines, who was named Xie. The emperor did not like his own son Bien but died in 189 before he could name a successor. Bien was crowned and given the reign-name Shao, but the real power over the Chinese Empire was up for grabs between all the various factions and powerbrokers at Luoyang. The summer of Shao's ascension, Bien's maternal uncle, He Jin, led a cabal of generals to take absolute power, going so far as driving Shao and Bien's grandmother, the empress dowager, and her nephew to suicide.

Han soldiers fighting Yellow Turban rebels. (*Wikimedia Commons*)

As always, the eunuchs had the final say. He Jin tried to enlist Lingsi in a plot to have all the eunuchs executed, but she rejected the idea. In Sima Guang's account, it was, in her words, because "the late Emperor has only just died and how can I maintain dignity and respect if I deal with strange men face to face?"[9] Desperate, He Jin next decided on a scheme to have generals stationed near the capital stage revolts with the demand that Lingsi consent to the extermination of all eunuchs at the court. One of the generals who answered the call was Dong Zhuo, who was a poor choice because of his almost psychopathic personality. Zhuo marched on the capital itself, ignoring He Jin's increasingly frantic orders to stand down. In the panic, rumors of what He Jin planned to do to the eunuchs leaked out and one of them assassinated him. It was too late for the eunuchs, however. Dong Zhuo's men were already at the palace gates.

"The affairs of the nation, aren't they my concern? If I want to do it, who shall contradict me?" Dong Zhuo once yelled at another general who dared disagree with him. "Are you saying Dong Zhuo's sword is not sharp?"[10] Indeed, Dong Zhuo could not be accused of being indecisive. Once he had secured the capital, most of the eunuchs were wiped out without trial. A couple of eunuchs in desperation had kidnapped the emperor and his brother. After they were hunted down and the eunuchs committed suicide by drowning themselves in a river, Dong Zhuo was disappointed by his confusing and incomprehensible interview with the emperor, who was understandably in shock or even had a nervous breakdown. So, without hesitation, Dong Zhuo had the emperor replaced by his brother Xie, who would take the reign-name Xian. The unlucky Shao was pressured into drinking poisoned wine, but at least he was allowed to say goodbye to his wife and concubines first.

The reign of the eunuchs had just concluded with blood, but the reign of the warlords was only beginning. Once Dong Zhuo himself was assassinated in 192, with much of his family and supporters including his ninety-year-old mother following him to the grave, Xian like his father and brother before him was only a living symbol while a series of warlords did the actual ruling. One, Cao Pi, finally became weary of the charade and announced that he would establish a brand new imperial dynasty. However, the damage to the legitimacy of the imperial office had already been done and China would split again, ushering in the hallowed era of the Three Kingdoms. For the last of the Han emperors, Xian, fate was more kind than it had been with his brother. He was allowed to live on as a nobleman and died peacefully in old age. It was a sad testimony to how much the Han name had diminished in value by his lifetime, but at least it was to his personal benefit.

6.

THE ROMAN EMPIRE

Murder in the Emperor's Court

"But the obedience of the Roman world was uniform, voluntary, and permanent," Edward Gibbon wrote in the first volume of his pivotal *The Fall of the Roman Empire*, published in 1776. "The vanquished nations, blended into one great people, resigned the hope, nay, even the wish, of resuming their independence, and scarcely considered their own existence as distinct from the existence of Rome."[1] In one sentence, Gibbon summarizes the success of the Romans, in that they not only promoted their political rule but a promise of a civilized and stable way of life. On top of Rome's efficient networks of paved roads, aqueducts that could service entire cities, and public bathhouses that included gymnasiums and libraries, Roman citizenship was meant to be seen not as oppression but as a gift.

Rome may have genuinely brought prosperity across Europe, Asia Minor, North Africa, and the Middle East, as Gibbon believed, but through much of the Roman Empire's history one of the most miserable people in the empire was the emperor himself. Yes, the emperor enjoyed virtually unlimited power (even in the early years when most emperors still pretended to follow Rome's old republican traditions and be just "first among equals") and as much luxury as he desired. But even if we waive away some of the more lurid stories from Roman historians, more than half of Rome's emperors did not pass away

peacefully in their beds. Augustus, the first emperor, was a phenom-
enally clever politician, but he did fail to leave a path for an orderly,
constitutional succession for the men who would follow him. Eventually it was proven that any man could become emperor at any time,
even someone like the Emperor Maximinus who started out as a peasant from the Danube who had enlisted with the Roman army, as long
as he had the love of the army. What is remarkable was not that the
office of emperor became so accessible through sheer brute force alone
but that it took until the third century for people to truly realize it.

This revelation drove what historians of Rome call the Crisis of
the Third Century, which began with Maximinus's own unexpected
rise to power and just as sudden assassination. From 235 to 284 about
nineteen of the twenty-three established emperors who ruled died
fighting in civil wars, were assassinated by rivals, were murdered by
their own soldiers, or were forced to commit suicide. In the midst of
the madness there were attempts by the Roman Senate to grab the
wheel through their own candidates, but most of the emperors that
tended to last were military officers from the provinces propped up
by their comrades with the meek consent of the Senate.

For the Roman Empire itself, real power no longer belonged to the
senatorial class or even to the historic imperial center of Italy, as the
city of Rome itself relinquished its ancient significance. The Emperor
Diocletian at the end of the third century did not even find it necessary
to visit Rome itself once until the celebrations for the twentieth year
of his reign, and in the end he, who was like so many other emperors
from the era originally a lower-class soldier from the provinces, didn't
care for the experience.

Even so, the Roman Empire not only endured but still thrived. The
largest bathhouse complex ever built, the Baths of Diocletian, was finished by 306 when in hindsight the Roman Empire in the west was
nearing its twilight. A feat of both Roman engineering and the empire's
riches in spite of long decades of civil war, the baths covered about
1,300 square feet. The fifth-century writer Olympiodorus claimed that
the Baths of Diocletian could house over 3,000 people.[2] The ruins still
stand in Rome on the Viminal Hill at the Viale Enrico de Nicola. In
fact, even during the chaotic fourth century, Rome's aqueducts still
supplied eleven public bath complexes, 926 small public baths, 1,212
water fountains, and 247 water tanks.[3] Similar services were not just
for Rome, however, but for all the cities of the empire.

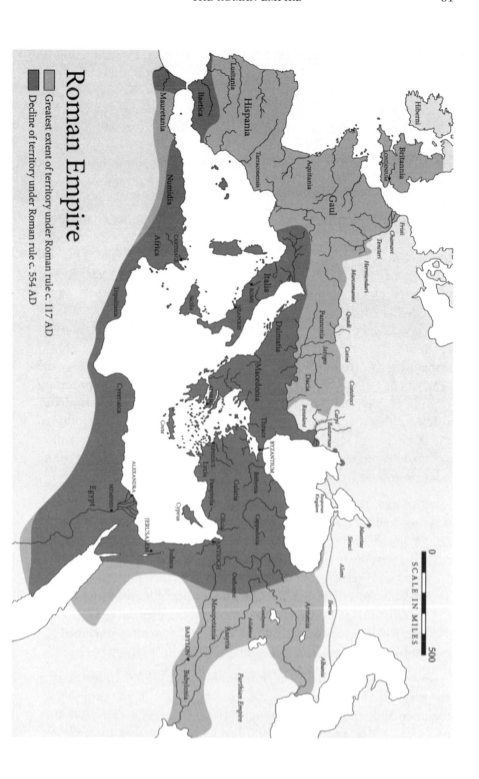

Roman Empire

Greatest extent of territory under Roman rule c. 117 AD

Decline of territory under Roman rule c. 554 AD

SCALE IN MILES

0 500

Why a political system that could provide such incredible public works would begin to collapse within a few generations has been subject to one of the great debates of Western history. Nonetheless, the festering problems are not too difficult to trace. The cities, which had always been the backbone of Roman civilization, were falling apart, their tax revenues channeled away toward the army by unsympathetic soldier-emperors who barely allowed them enough money to maintain their buildings and public works or repair them after they were damaged in the civil wars or barbarian raids. Pressed from above, city councils passed crushing taxes on those below, who were appeased only by the still running public games. One writer, Salvian, scolded the people of Treveri (today the city of Trier in the Rhineland) for still holding their civic games after the city had been recently attacked and plundered by German marauders three times. With bitterness he reflected, "The Roman people are dying and laughing."[4]

A good deal of the empire's wealth was being hoarded by landowners apathetic to the concerns of the empire as a whole, not even bothering like the Roman elites of better times long past to become senators or military leaders. Instead they were content with presiding over extensive estates that were practically outside the government's reach, with villages filled with rural workers accountable only to them, poets and scholars on their payroll, and even their own bailiffs and private prisons. Michael Grant paints a depressing portrait of the relationship between these grand landowners and the empire:

> Indeed, the leading men had the whip-hand in every way. It was even they who themselves levied the taxes payable by their tenants. This was part of their deal with the government, the deal which eventually placed most of the official posts at their disposal. And yet Valentinian III, in 450, still found it diplomatically advisable to express sympathy with the alleged hardships of the wealthy class of taxpayers. Even so, however, they did not move into patriotic obedience. On the contrary, they often remained hostile to the Emperor, and estranged from his advisers.[5]

In such a climate that was hospitable only to the rich, it is hardly surprising that many people across the empire decided to drop out altogether and join Christian monasteries, a process accelerated after 313 when Constantine I converted to Christianity and formally put an end to the persecution of Christians. The benefits of being a nun, to save women from the perils of abusive husbands (likely pushed on them by arranged marriages) and childbirth, were timeless. However, in this era long after Rome's peak life as a monk guaranteed freedom from the draconian legislation passed by Diocletian and maintained by his successors to try to stop the empire's bleeding, which actually mandated that many young men follow the occupation of their fathers. It is no surprise that for so many young women and men loyalty to a loving but distant God should trump loyalty to an overbearing and very near government.

Although even at the time of Constantine's conversion Christians were still a relatively small minority, enthusiasm for the new religion surfaced in aggressive and even violent ways. While Constantine I tried to maintain the Roman tradition of tolerance (however flawed and limited) for multiple beliefs as long as they bowed their heads before the emperor, Constantine's Christian successors soon began to nonchalantly abolish the most ancient and sacred rituals of pagan Rome. One of Constantine I's sons, Constantius II, had the statue of the goddess Victory removed from the Senate house. It was restored and its use defended by a pagan senator named Symmachus, but the bishop of Milan, Ambrose, objected and tried to win over the current emperor, Valentinian II. It is unknown exactly what happened next, except that no one followed Symmachus after his death in 402 or 403 in defending the presence of the statue.[6] It would be Ambrose's disciple, a Spanish soldier turned emperor, Theodosius I, who would decide matters by outlawing pagan rituals as harshly as the most anti-Christian emperor had ever tried to ban Christianity. Outside the corridors of power, Christian mobs took it upon themselves to eradicate all traces of pagan worship. For just one of countless examples, the Egyptian temple of Rameses II had at one point been extensively vandalized. The statues in its courtyard were smashed and the complex was covered by graffiti depicting crosses.[7]

The painful decline of what had once been the diversity yet unity in belief that helped bind the empire together was also felt among the Christians themselves. Appalled by the vicious infighting of the different interpreters of Christian theology, Constantine complained in a letter to Bishop Chrestus of Syracuse, "The very persons who ought to display brotherly harmony and concord are estranged from one another in a way that is disgraceful if not positively sickening."[8] A few emperors, like Rome's last pagan emperor Julian "the Apostate" and the Christian but open-minded Valentinian I, tried to extend tolerance and resuscitate Rome's old tradition of pluralism, but by 407 heresy was made a crime again. Augustine of Hippo, who would before too long prove to be the most influential theologian of his time, applauded the state-sponsored persecution of pagans and heretics, comparing it to forcing bitter medicine on a sick, reluctant patient.

The Romans were likewise failing to incorporate outsiders, as they had once tamed a multitude of peoples through both force and the tangible awards of Roman civilization. German tribes had been migrating into the Roman Empire, a threat the emperors since Constantine I tried to shift to Rome's advantage by recruiting Germans as mercenaries or even allowing entire tribes to settle permanently on Roman territory in exchange for them agreeing to fight for Rome. By the dawn of the fifth century, Roman armies were being staffed in no small part by Germans. Even Emperor Theodosius II was one-fourth German through his mother Eudoxia.[9] Despite this growing dependence, Roman intellectuals responded with an entrenched, haughty bigotry to their neighbors. "The Romans deliberately imposed on their new and unwelcome neighbors a kind of spiritual apartheid, viewing them as an unabsorbable lump of marked men, encapsulated by a wall of eloquent or silent dislike," says Michael Grant.[10]

These elements were all part of the Roman Empire's increasingly bleak situation when the future emperor Valentinian III was born in 419. The child was born not in Rome but in Ravenna, where the emperors had retreated to as the predicaments on the frontiers escalated. Ravenna was a small port city in northeastern Italy built in the midst of marshland and had a chronic lack of clean drinking water, but it offered an open port on the Adriatic while the swamps also made it almost inaccessible by land, forming a natural safe haven for the rulers of an empire under siege.

Valentinian III's mother Galla Placidia had impeccable imperial pedigree as the daughter of the celebrated (especially among hardline Christians) Theodosius I. It was the deathbed wish of Theodosius that the empire be divided between his sons Arcadius and Honorius, with Honorius presiding over the west in Ravenna and the east ruled by Arcadius in Constantinople. Galla Placidia herself had first been married to a Germanic king, the young and handsome King Athaulf of the Visigoths, who were settled in modern Narbonne, a match which was in and of itself a sign of just how much the Germans were able

A soldus coin featuring the portrait of Valentinian III, c. 430 AD.

to "invade" Roman society in ways other than war. If Galla Placidia genuinely loved her husband as legend claims, her happiness was short-lived, as Athaulf was shortly murdered in an old-fashioned German blood feud.

In his place, Galla Placidia married a popular general, who was named Constantius and who became Valentinian's father. She was clearly no dynastic pawn. At Galla Placidia's own insistence her son was named *noblissimus*, "most noble," which already singled out the infant as a possible heir to the imperial throne, and she arranged to have Constantius appointed co-emperor in 421.[11] Constantius III did not want such a promotion because it meant an end to his lifestyle of easygoing partying, but luckily he only had to live with it for less than a year since he died from an illness. Honorius himself would follow him, without any children of his own, just two years later. However, Galla Placidia's plans to continue her father's dynasty in the form of her son fell into a snag when a government official, Johannes, made a bid for the imperial throne. With the support of Galla Placidia's nephew in Constantinople, Theodosius II, and major segments of the army, Johannes was captured and beheaded by 425. Valentinian III's reign was assured, but it was a clear sign that even for heirs of popular families claims to the imperial throne rarely ran smoothly.

Although it was Galla Placidia who conducted the day-to-day business of governing, Valentinian III even as a child would have been idolized as God's viceroy on Earth. Long ago Augustus's genius had been in giving himself the power of a monarch while still wrapping himself in Rome's republican institutions and traditions, but it had always been a charade. Diocletian finally did away with it altogether with his reforms, mandating that the emperor always be surrounded by elaborate rituals and gestures of respect and awe. Even after Christianity became the state religion of the Roman Empire, the emperors encouraged their subjects to think that they represented not just the people and the Senate, as was the formula in the good old days, but the will of God as well. The Senate, which still regularly met in Rome, was for generations used to being compliant in all of this. Valentinian III himself would have witnessed this when he adopted the law code devised for Theodosius II in Constantinople, or at least he would have if it were not for the fact that he rarely left the safety of Ravenna. When the passage of the law code was announced to the Senate, the senators obligingly chanted 352 repeated praises of Valentinian III and Theodosius II.[12]

The boy turned emperor would not live up to such worship or even to the reputations of his ancestors Valentinian I and Theodosius I. He devoted himself to living a life of pleasure at his luxurious court in Ravenna. Once he reached his age of majority at eighteen, Galla Placidia was forced to share the reins of power with the general Flavius Aëtius until her death in 450. Valentinian himself did not seem to want the responsibility of power, only the benefits. In Valentinian's defense, being emperor was perhaps not the most desirable job in the empire. Even while he was a child, Germanic tribes had been migrating into and seizing territory across the western empire. By the time of Valentinian III's death, nearly all of Gaul, western Spain, and North Africa had been completely lost to fully independent Germanic kings.

The true threat, however, seemed to come even farther east, from the warlord Attila the Hun. At first, much to Valentinian III's relief, Attila only threatened the Balkan territories of the eastern empire, but then Attila turned his attention west, all because (or so the story goes) he had received a marriage proposal from Valentinian's sister Honoria and used that as an excuse to seize half the western empire as his would-be bride's dowry. Honoria, who was in many ways the bold intriguer her brother could not be, had rebelled against her lonely, pointless life at court by having a love affair. As soon as the affair was uncovered, her lover was executed and she was exiled to Constantinople. In the meantime, her brother arranged to marry her off to an affluent Roman senator. With the ultimate act of sisterly defiance, Honoria wrote to Attila, asking for his hand in marriage.

Luckily Attila was beaten back by a plague claiming the lives of his soldiers and the fact that the eastern empire was attacking his lands in the Balkans. More good news from the western Roman Empire's shrinking frontiers was that Aëtius did much to give the dying empire a new lease on life, rallying Germanic settlers to fight for Rome. As Aëtius fought on campaign or engaged in the gritty business of managing the empire, Valentinian stayed secluded in Ravenna, gambling all day with courtiers and nervously consulting astrologers about his fate and the future of the empire. According to a seventh-century chronicler, John of Antioch, Valentinian did have one other way to pass the time, womanizing:

> Valentinian, having fallen in love with the wife of Maximus, a senator, used to play at dice with him. When Maximus lost and was unable to pay, the emperor took his ring. Rising, he gave it to one of Maximus' friends so that the man showed it to Maximus' wife and, as though from her husband, ordered her to come to the palace to dine with him there. She came, thinking this the truth, and when it was announced to the emperor, he arose and without Maximus' knowledge seduced her. After the lovemaking the wife went to meet her husband as he came, wailing and reproaching him as her betrayer. When he learned the whole story, he nursed his anger at the emperor.[13]

John of Antioch claims that Maximus wanted revenge but believed the emperor was safe as long as the popular and talented Aëtius lived, so he contrived to turn Valentinian against him. Valentinian had reason enough on his own to fear the prospect of being eclipsed by Aëtius's rising star. Or perhaps Valentinian was acutely aware of an actual conspiracy that has been forgotten by history; certainly Aëtius would not have been the first successful general to set his sights on the imperial diadem. Whatever the motive, the emperor took drastic action. One day when Aëtius was routinely going over matters of state with Valentinian, the emperor suddenly screamed that he was a traitor and he and a palace eunuch both stabbed Aëtius to death before he could defend himself. In John of Antioch's account, Valentinian bragged about what he had done to a courtier, who could only grimly and wisely answer, "You have only cut off your right hand with your left."[14]

Valentinian did not realize or did not care how loved Aëtius was among the Germans in his army. The emperor, who had never in his life seen a battlefield, may have absolutely believed that he had acted courageously in the best tradition of the Romans, but his ignorance had brought about a political blunder that neither Julius Caesar nor Augustus would have committed even at their most paranoid and murderous. Just one year later, after Aëtius was struck down, two German soldiers, loyal to the memory of their commander, ambushed the emperor in a palace corridor and stabbed him to death in 455, apparently in the exact same manner he had killed Aëtius.

The Roman Empire's imperial dynasties tended to have short life spans, but Valentinian III's family endured the longest at nearly a century. As if their longevity was tied to the lifeblood of the empire they ruled, matters became even more dire for the entire empire after Valentinian's assassination. The empire's borders kept receding until they barely stretched outside Italy itself. Meanwhile the same Maximus who allegedly schemed to turn the emperor against Aëtius himself took advantage of the lack of clear successors and managed to make himself the new emperor. It would be a short and disastrous reign. While preparing to flee Rome from an invasion led by the king of the Visigoths, Maximus was himself assassinated by a group of slaves and his corpse dumped into the Tiber River. He had been emperor for less than a year.

Even with such a pathetic reign, Maximus would make a name of sorts for himself as the first of the last. He and the emperors that followed are remembered as the "shadow emperors," who were merely propped up—and disposed of at will—by a series of German generals. Finally, by 476, one such general, Theodoric, decided this was no longer necessary and sent the reigning adolescent emperor, who in one of history's great ironies bore the names of Rome's founder and first emperor, respectively, as Romulus Augustulus, packing to a country manor. In his place, Theodoric declared himself master, not as emperor of the western Roman Empire but as king of Italy. With that, the former territories of the western Roman Empire had become Germanic kingdoms, and so ended a long, bitter process whereby a group an empire had sneered upon as much as it relied upon took complete control.

7.

THE CAROLINGIAN EMPIRE

The Field of Lies

The eastern Roman Empire would outlive its western half for centuries. Still, the very Germanic kingdoms that mushroomed in the ruins of the western Roman Empire took over the administrative machinery and the political legacies that Rome left behind. One of these Germanic kings, remembered by history as Charles the Great, "Charlemagne," was granted the old Roman title of *imperator romanorum*, "emperor of the Romans," the first such emperor in the west since the collapse of the western Roman Empire. More than simply reviving a dead empire, Charlemagne left behind the ideal of all of Europe under one order. It is a fragile ideal still embodied in the *Karlspries* ("Charlemagne Prize"), which is awarded at Charlemagne's old capital Aachen to anyone who contributed toward European unity, an august list that has included Pope Francis I, US president Bill Clinton, Winston Churchill, and even the entire people of Luxembourg.

Charlemagne was crowned personally by Pope Leo III in Saint Peter's Basilica on Christmas Day of 800. Leo III felt the need for a powerful protector after he was nearly torn apart by a Roman mob, and the opportunity to handpick his own emperor was thrown wide-open when the position of emperor in the eastern Roman Empire was unthinkably usurped by a woman, Eirene, from her own son. Allegedly, his promotion came as an unpleasant shock to Charlemagne himself who thought he was simply attending a special mass presided over by the pope. According to Charlemagne's biographer and personal friend Einhard, "he declared that he would not have set foot in the Church the day that they were conferred, although it was a great feast-day, if he could have foreseen the design of the Pope."[1] If true, he did not turn his back on an imperial crown.

In spite of his supposed reluctance, it is possible Charlemagne felt that he was vindicating his family. Charlemagne's ancestors, the Carolingians, had started out as just the hereditary majordomos, the perennial right-hand men, to the Merovingians, the quasi-sacred royal family of the Frankish people that had come to rule over the old Roman province of Gaul. As the centuries went on and the Merovingians themselves fell on very hard times thanks to a series of helpless child kings and violent infighting, the Carolingians ascended. It was no Merovingian but an illegitimate son of a Carolingian, Charles Martel, who rallied Frankish forces in the Battle of Tours against the Islamic Umayyad Caliphate that had taken over most of modern-day Spain and Portugal.

Charles Martel's son and Charlemagne's father, the unassumingly named Pippin "the Short," was far too ambitious to keep his dynasty out of the spotlight. In fact, if Einhard's description of the everyday life of the last Merovingian king Childeric III is at least half-true, then one can hardly blame him for taking advantage of his employers:

> Beyond this empty title of King, and a precarious living wage which the Mayor of the Palace provided at his own discretion, the King possessed nothing at all of his own, except a single estate with an extremely small revenue, in which he had his dwelling and from which came the servants, few enough in number, who ministered to his wants and did him honor. Whenever he needed to travel, he went in a cart which was drawn in country style by yoked oxen, with a cowherd to drive them. In this fashion, he would go to the palace and to the general assembly of his people, which was held each year to settle the general affairs of the kingdom, and in this fashion he would return home again. It was the Mayor of the Palace who took responsibility for the administration of the kingdom and all matters which had to be done or planned at home or abroad.[2]

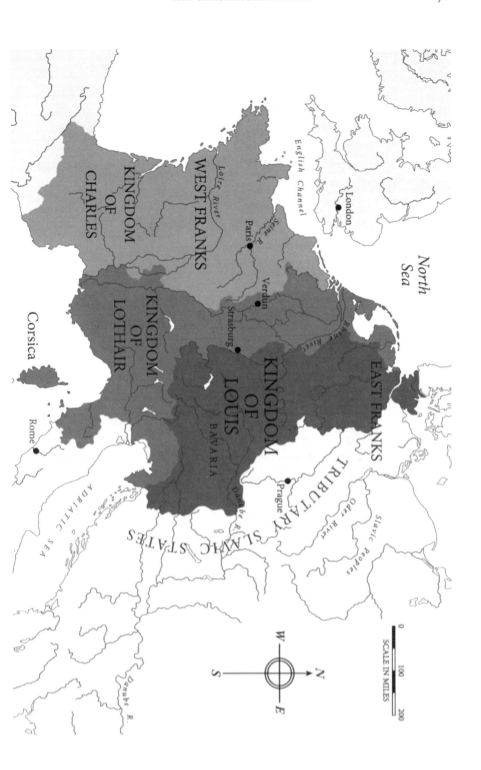

Pippin wrote to the reigning Pope Zachariah, inquiring if a king should only ever be the one who inherits the crown or if it was just that the one who actually steered the wheel of government had a right to the title. The Pope, who at the time just happened to need armed support against the Germanic Lombard kingdom in Italy, gladly gave Pippin his blessing for a coup. Childeric III and his teenage son Theudebert were promptly packed off to monasteries and out of the pages of recorded history. Pippin was now the king of the Franks in both name and fact.

It was Pippin's son, Charlemagne, who shaped the Frankish kingdom into an empire that could rival even that of the Romans in their glory days. At its peak, the Carolingian domain encompassed part of northeastern Spain, modern-day France (except Brittany), what is now the "Benelux" countries, much of northern and central Italy, and Germany. Charlemagne also looked the part of an emperor. He was broad-shouldered, physically strong, and over six feet tall, a contemporary claim about his appearance that was actually vindicated when Charlemagne's skeleton was examined by archaeologists in modern times.

The old historical stereotype is that Charlemagne's empire was really less of a cohesive unit and more of a feudal anarchy. That was not quite true. Each year a general assembly attended by the leading noblemen and clerics of the empire met to debate over political matters, ending with the *capitula*, "ordinances," being decided upon, issued, and imposed. The empire was divided into over three hundred counties, each one presided over by counts who were themselves assisted—and monitored—by other agents and representatives accountable only to the emperor.[3] Charlemagne trusted members of his family with positions of weighty symbolic authority, such as his son Louis who was crowned king of Aquitaine in what is now southern France. Of course, Louis, who was still just a child, was only a spokesperson for ministers handpicked by his father, but after Charlemagne's death future members of the Carolingian family would ask the question of why they had to obey the wishes of an emperor when they were kings themselves.

Charlemagne had hoped that this system could be preserved by his son and namesake, but young Charles died in 811. By the time of his own death in 814, Charlemagne only had one living son from a legitimate marriage, Louis. A devout and unpleasantly uptight man, one of Louis's first acts as emperor was to cast out his surviving sisters and other female relatives from the palace where they had always lived. This might have been a political act, crafted to avoid accusations of being under the influence of his female relations,[4] but Louis's anonymous biographer, known only as "the Astronomer," makes it fairly clear that he was at least also motivated by his distaste for the free sex lives and romances Charlemagne let them have. Even the Astronomer, who is usually sympathetic of Louis, writes, "they did not deserve of the emperor such treatment as they got."[5] Also, in a callous gesture of religious fanaticism, Louis had a collection of Frankish pagan poetry compiled under Charlemagne's direction burned.

His father may not have liked Louis as a son and heir or even as a human being, but the new reign did at first appear to have run better than Charlemagne could have hoped. The empire was in a relatively peaceful state and its frontiers were secure against both the Muslims of the west and the pagans and Byzantines to the east. Louis's nephew Bernard gracefully accepted his place as Louis's vassal as king of Italy, at least at first. Louis was able to enact his father's plan for the reform of the churches and monasteries, left unfinished by his death, and masterminded a successful attempt to streamline the imperial administration. After being uncomfortably reminded of his mortality by a narrow miss with a collapsing portico in the Aachen Palace, Louis named his eldest son Lothar his co-emperor and heir in 817, another son Pippin was crowned king of Aquitaine, and his youngest and namesake Louis, remembered by medieval chroniclers as "the German," was made king of Bavaria, ensuring the stability of the empire and the continuity of the dynasty for decades to come.

Unfortunately, there was one small flaw in the master plan: the Carolingian family itself. Bernard, irritated at some point in Louis's 817 declaration on the succession, rebelled. The twenty-year-old man had no real chance since he was almost immediately forced to surrender and dragged off to be tried at Aachen. Bernard was not sentenced to life at a monastery, but, taking notes from the Byzantines, Louis had him blinded, an operation that killed him several days later (unless we trust the Astronomer, who hints that Bernard committed suicide).[6] Another biographer of Louis, Thegan, says that when he heard Bernard died Louis, who had actually commuted Bernard's sentence from the death penalty, "wept with great grief for a long time and made confession in the presence of all his bishops and undertook penance by their decision for this reason: because he did not prohibit his counselors from doing that maiming. Therefore, he gave much to the poor in order to purge his soul."[7] While one hand was handing out alms, with the other Louis preemptively struck at his illegitimate half-brothers, Drogo, Theodoric, and Hugh, having them tonsured and banished to monasteries. Louis's piety apparently did not stop at treating the church like his own personal prison.[8]

After his wife Ermengarde died, Louis went looking for another wife and found the perfect replacement in Judith. Judith brought wealth and political connections as her dowry. Her mother was distinguished Saxon nobility while her father was a rich landowner. However, Louis may have been motivated by other, more personal considerations since Judith was not only quite beautiful but also had a lively personality and quick mind to offer. As it would turn out, she was also fertile, always a premium in an aristocratic medieval wife, and after bearing a daughter, Gisela, she later gave birth to a son, Charles, on June 13, 823. Louis's other sons, painfully aware of how Carolingian family values usually panned out, were hardly filled with fraternal joy at the news of the birth.

Lothar, who had been Louis's presumptive heir, had the most to lose. Before Judith even gave birth to Charles, Lothar, whom Louis had named the new king of Italy after Bernard's death, hurried to have himself declared emperor by Pope Paschal I while cultivating support among the nobility and the clergy. Judith and Louis fought back by showering territories and honors on the child Charles. Nerves were already being stretched to the limit when, from the comfort of his exile, Wala, a distant relative and friend of Lothar's, launched a propaganda campaign against Judith, alleging that she was a sorceress, the secret lover of her ally Bernard of Septimania, and that with Bernard she was scheming to see Louis dead so she could see Bernard crowned in his place.[9]

Naturally, none of this propaganda could be launched against the son of Charlemagne, but Judith and Bernard were much easier prey. While in the spring of 830, when Louis was preparing at Compiègne for an invasion of Brittany, he was confronted by Pippin, Lothar, the young Louis, and their supporters. Bernard managed to dodge the disobedient sons' clutches, but Judith was caught and forced into early retirement in a convent, Judith's brothers Conrad and Rudolph were tonsured and Bernard's brother Heribert was arrested and blinded, and Louis and Charles were both put under house arrest at the monastery of St. Denis. Lothar made sure to place little Charles under the care of monks, who were under strict orders to encourage the boy to heroically give up life as a prince and embrace the duties of a monk.

Such an abrupt change in regime could only put the imperial state into shock. "But the state of the empire grew worse from day to day, since all were driven by greed and sought only their own advantage,"[10] one writer who lived through Louis's reign lamented. Neither was the coalition between the three brothers running smoothly. Lothar helped himself to most of the power behind the throne, so Louis opened secret communications with the young Louis and Pippin, offering to not just pardon them but give them more land if they restored him to power. Louis's stratagem worked—human greed is always a reliable factor in any historical era—and Lothar was forced by his brothers to give their father his freedom and his crown and agree to a new partition of the empire. Yet Louis's three little Absaloms were not kept happy for long. By 833, Louis was at the mercy of his sons again, who this time had Pope Gregory VI and a sizable faction of the Frankish clergy in their corner.

With their soldiers and followers around them, Louis and his sons, accompanied by the pope, met on June 24, 833, at a field near Colmar in Alasce. The event and the place was labeled by chroniclers with the colorful but apt title "The Field of Lies." The Astronomer justified such a melodramatic christening: "For those who had sworn fealty to the emperor lied, and the name of the place where that occurred has remained ever since a witness of the faithlessness."[11] The conference lasted for days, but then one night most of Louis's followers abandoned him as though he were a leper, "leaving their tents, they went over to his sons. On the next day those who remained came to the emperor who admonished them, saying 'Go to my sons. I do not wish any of you to use your life or limbs on account of me.' And they, filled with tears, withdrew from him."[12] Judith was sent away to Italy and Charles was once again put under the tutelage of monks. As for Louis, at the cathedral of St. Médard in Soissons his greatest humiliation waited. "Under constraint, the emperor abased himself before all and avowed whatever was demanded: he confessed to sacrilege, homicide, spreading scandal, upsetting the peace, despoiling the goods of the church, breaking his vows to God and his fellow men, making arbitrary partitions and distributions of land. In a word, he confessed to every felony unworthy of a Christian king, and he 'spontaneously' renounced his imperial dignity."[13]

This time Lothar went too far. Not only was he so publicly humiliating a father who was already well known for his genuine piety, but he was acting as though the Frankish Empire was already his personal property. The brothers' squabbling, escalated by Lothar's imperial arrogance, quickly burst into a full-out civil war. In the chaos, Louis not only quietly slipped back into the role of emperor but was reunited with Judith and Charles. Chastised and beaten, Lothar was nonetheless allowed to keep Italy, but at the same time he was unofficially exiled to the peninsula for good. Nothing stood in the way of Louis having himself crowned as emperor again in 835. Three years later, he faced no opposition when he made Charles, who had become an adult by Frankish standards, the successor to Pippin's Aquitainian kingdom after Pippin's death, no matter what Pippin's two sons had to say about it.

The emperor Louis left the imperial crown to his new son Charles, just as Charles's brothers had feared. They, including the exiled Lothar, still would not stand for it. There was a fresh outbreak of civil war with Charles and Louis the German on one side and Lothar and Pippin II of Aquitaine (the disinherited son of Pippin I) on the other. The fighting climaxed with the Battle of Fontenoy, which in contemporaries' eyes was less a battle and more of a massacre. The poet Engelbert, although a confederate of Lothar's, writes with horror on the blood that was spilled on both sides:

> Let not that accursed day be counted in the calendar of the year,
> Rather let it be erased from all memory,
> May the sun's rays never fall there, may no dawn every come to
> [end its endless] twilight.[14]

Atrocity or no, the battle ended with Lothar being stripped of any advantage. Lothar tried to bribe Charles away from Louis the German, but instead on February 12, 842, they swore the Strasbourg Oaths, remarkable for linguists as well as medieval historians because

Opposite: The Carolingian family tree drawn during the twelfth century. 1. Charles Martel; 2. Charlemagne; 3. Louis the Pious; 4. Charles the Bald; 5. Lothar; 6. Louis the German. (*State Library of Berlin*)

while Louis the German spoke the oath in "Germanic" Charles rendered it in "Romantic."[15] Then, their alliance insured, the two brothers managed to invade the Aachen Palace itself, but not before Lothar made off with most of the palace's treasury. Still, even the tenacious Lothar was backed to the wall, and he soon left Pippin II to fend for himself while he approached his brothers for peace.

The finale of the negotiations between the unfraternal brothers was the Treaty of Verdun which, as the historian Janet Nelson suggests, was probably made just as a makeshift band-aid for the ruptures in the Frankish Empire[16] and had no grander purpose than giving all three brothers a fair share of the rich vassals, bishoprics, and monasteries in the Frankish domains.[17] Yet generations to come would see the Treaty of Verdun as a rare seismic event, its ramifications echoing loudly down throughout history. With the treaty, the Frankish Empire was cut into three segments: Charles's Western Kingdom, which was composed of modern-day France and the Spanish March (which, under the Counts of Barcelona, would one day become the kingdom of Aragon); Lothar's Middle Kingdom, roughly forming Belgium, the Netherlands, and Switzerland as well as Italy, Lorraine, Alsace, and parts of what is now western Germany; and finally the Eastern Kingdom, recognizable today as Germany and Austria. Perhaps the Treaty of Verdun can be said to be the time when France and Germany were "born," but it really was not the catalyst that awakened national consciousness in those countries, as it was once fashionable for both French and German historians to patriotically argue.[18]

One thing the Treaty of Verdun definitely did achieve was making the title of emperor more hollow than ever. The emperor still had special responsibilities to the pope and held power in Germany and northern Italy, but he had little say over what the other kingdoms of the Franks did.[19] A contemporary, Florus of Lyon, wrote a poem blasting the decision:

> It has lost both the name and the glory of empire,
> and the united kingdom has fallen to three lots.
> For there is no longer any one recognized as emperor:
> instead of a king, there is a kinglet; for a realm, but the fragments thereof.[20]

This happened just before the Frankish realms needed a steady hand most of all. A flood of migrating Slavic tribes were pressing on the eastern borders of the empire, while a brand new menace, the Vikings, were coming in from the north and looting without fear the prosperous abbeys and monasteries of the empire. Although the Carolingian Empire did painfully wither away in the harsh centuries to come, leaving in its place the kingdom of France and what would become the shaky conglomerate of German and northern Italian states remembered as the Holy Roman Empire, its shadow would haunt Europe's history, holding out the alluring promise of a unified Europe to all the would-be Charlemagnes of history.

8.

THE ABBASID CALIPHATE

The Razing of the Center of the World

"Iraq is indeed the center of the world," the scholar and traveler Ahmad ibn Abu Ya'qub ibn Ja'far al-Ya'qubi declared in his praises of Iraq and its flourishing capital of Baghdad. "Not only is the climate regular but the terrain is excellent, the water is sweet, the trees flourish, the fruit is of perfect quality, the harvests are magnificent, good things abound, and the water supply is almost at ground level." The perfection of the landscape, according to Ya'qubi, was rivaled only by that of its inhabitants. "The people also excel through their knowledge, their understanding, their good education, their perspicacity, their distinction, their commercial, industrial, and business sense, their ingenuousness in all controversy, their competence in all trades, and their ability in all industry."[1] As surely as Ya'qubi must have been looking at Baghdad through rose-colored glasses, he was nonetheless recognizing in the moment what future historians would claim—that Baghdad in this era was the tangible culmination of the Islamic world's golden age.

Belief that there is no god but God and that God's own words were transcribed by his final prophet Muhammad in the form of the Qu'ran, held the realm of which Baghdad became the capital together. This empire of faith was under the wise guidance of the caliph, the divinely ordained and unquestioned successor of the Prophet Muhammad. At least, that was the ideal. The split between Sunni Muslims, who acquiesced to Muhammad's companion and father-in-law Abu Bakr being chosen as the first caliph, and Shia Muslims, who believed that Muhammad's son-in-law, Ali, had all along been the rightful leader of the *umma,* the Muslim community, had nearly smothered the Islamic Caliphate in its infancy.

Nonetheless, the caliphate not merely survived but thrived. Under the Umayyad family, who by 644 claimed the office of caliph for themselves despite not being related in any way to the prophet, the reach of the caliphate expanded relentlessly until its natural boundaries were the Atlantic Ocean and the Caucasus Mountains. Even so, murmurs against the Umayyads never died down. "The Family of the Prophet remained the last great hope of all those, old Muslims and new converts alike, who felt that the Islamic state represented by the Ummayads . . . had betrayed the ideals of Islam," Hugh Kennedy describes the situation. "Or, more prosaically, had not brought them the prosperity and status they felt they were due. . ."[2] The last Ummayad caliph, Marwan al-Himar, ended his reign at the point of a sword, wielded by As-Saffah, a descendant of an uncle of the prophet and the first of the new dynasty that would claim the title of caliph, the Abbasids. The Umayyads were slain wherever they could be found— sixty in one bloody swoop—although one member of the family, Abd al-Rahman, managed to not only escape the wrath of the Abbasids but take over the caliphate's territories in modern Spain and Portugal. As for Marwan himself, his head was sent to the new caliph, "who gazed upon it, and it was removed, when a cat came and tore out the tongue and began to gnaw upon it; whereupon [As-Saffah] said, 'if the world had shown us none other of its wonders but the tongue of Marwan in the mouth of a cat, it would have been sufficient for us.'"[3]

By the time the Abbasids were firmly at the helm, the caliphate's lands in Portugal, Spain, and much of North Africa were torn away by their own independent Muslim rulers, and over time Persia would also slowly slide away from the caliphate's orbit. The *umma* would never again be held together under one government. Nonetheless, the Abbasids did in a sense fulfill the golden promise of a society guided by the prophet's heirs. The Islamic world was now deeply divided between different nations, but the caliphate was more than ever before awash with both material and cultural riches.

Perched on the crossroads between Asia, Africa, and Europe, the caliphate was undeniably wealthy, and these riches were filtered through a sophisticated banking and trade system that sustained a healthy urban middle class. Samples of the caliphate's gold coinage, the *dinar*, rivaled the international value of the Byzantine gold coin, the *solidus*, and was spent as far away as Scandinavia.[4] Still, like all societies that existed before the nineteenth century, the Abbasid Caliphate derived most of its wealth from the soil. Iraq itself was the healthy heart of this agricultural economy. Its farmland was so heavily yet carefully nourished by irrigation that one eighth-century bureaucrat calculated that Iraq produced four times more revenue than the caliphate's next richest province, Egypt, and five times as much as Palestine and Syria. This miraculously efficient network of canals would be damaged badly by the civil wars that besieged the Abbasids in the tenth century and would never be truly restored, even in modern times.[5]

At any rate, what remains a point of pride for modern Muslims isn't usually the Abbasid Caliphate's mastery of irrigation but its influence over matters of the mind. Islamic doctors and philosophers in the era pioneered what might be described as a form of psychology, prescribing treatments that can be recognized today as music therapy. A ninth-century Persian philosopher and doctor, Muhammad ibn Zakariya al-Razi (known as Rhazes in the Christian West), wrote about mental illness and in Baghdad became the director of one of the earliest known facilities dedicated entirely to dealing with problems of the mind. Although the mathematicians and scientists tapped into what they gleaned from the recorded knowledge of the ancient Greeks, some scholars like Thabit ibn Qurra, who devised ways to use numbers to express the ratios between geometric quantities, went further than the ancients. Perhaps the most ambitious intellectual project of the Islamic Golden Age was an attempt by scholars to measure the circumference of the Earth, which reveals a comprehensive use of the full scientific method, down to obtaining experimental evidence and testing if the results could be replicated.[6] Also a library's worth of historical evidence testifies to the existence of a rich and varied literary and musical culture in the Abbasid Caliphate. Poems, even ones with risque subject matter, were read or sung both during court gatherings or out at public receptions. Sadly, since a system of musical notation was unknown to the caliphate, all of this musical heritage has been lost to time.

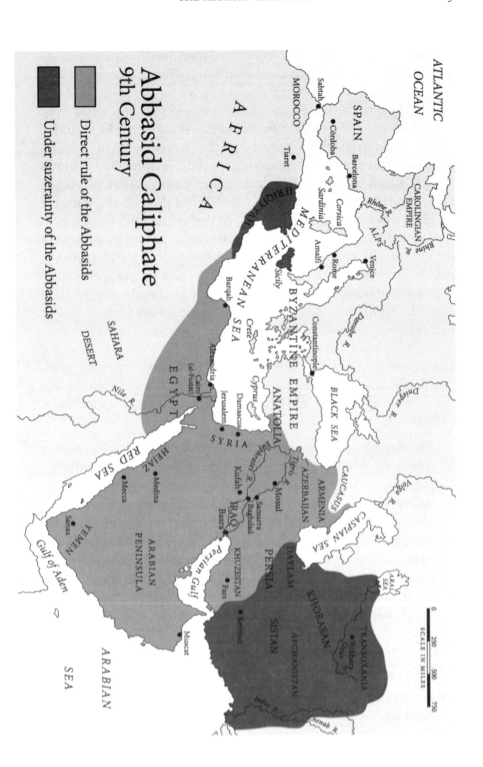

Abbasid Caliphate
9th Century

Direct rule of the Abbasids

Under suzerainty of the Abbasids

The Abbasids consciously worked to draw intellectuals and artists across their empire to Baghdad, a fortuitous Persian name meaning "Gift of God." It was probably built near or on the site of a pre-Islamic village of the same name, but nonetheless the city was a child of the Caliph Al-Mansur, the second of the Abbasid caliphs. Baghdad was designed to lie within a circle with the circumference of one kilometer and was placed in an area between the Tigris and the Euphrates Rivers, which had for millennia been the major arteries of Middle Eastern civilization. A system of canals laced through the southern suburbs, which were passable by arched bridges, and this canal system provided fresh water. There were strictly defined commercial areas in the city and its suburbs, especially in the suburb of Karkh (which is still the name held by a Baghdad district), where shopkeepers had to practice their trade at designated streets and neighborhoods. Walking around Karkh one could find the Street of the Fullers or the Canal of the Chickens, named for the nearby large chicken market.[7]

Baghdad has endured much over the long centuries, from Mongolian cavalries to American cruise missiles. In name the city still exists, but the incarnation the great scholars of the Islamic Golden Age would have known is lost forever. Still, Kennedy extends some hope to historians and romantics:

> In a way, we can reconstruct a virtual Baghdad: we can see in the mind's eye where the canals ran, we can follow roads from the ceremonial city, from the suqs [marketplaces] and the booksellers' market. We can go through the winding unpaved streets, past the fast-food stalls to the corners squatted and the roads petered out in the dusty desert margins. We can pass the blank walls of the mud-brick, single-story houses with the flat roofs so useful for sleeping on in the hot summer nights, and know, though of course we cannot see, that each house surrounded a courtyard, which, whether grand or mean, would be the real center of family life.[8]

The loss of this city, and indeed the world of which it was the center, can be blamed on a new power, which, not unlike the Arabs themselves, appeared seemingly out of nowhere: the Mongols.

However, as is often the case, the crisis was not really born with the Mongols and their relentless drive across almost the entire Eurasian land mass. Instead a historian can find fault with one decision made by Sultan Mutasim, who became caliph in 833, to establish a bodyguard staffed with ten thousand Turkish slaves, called *mamluks* in Arabic. The *mamluks* were still mostly unconverted to Islam and unable to speak fluent Arabic. Mutasim had entrusted his safety and that of his empire to men with no loyalty to anything but a regular paycheck. Nor did his people gladly accept his decision. Tensions between the *mamluks* and the people of Baghdad festered so dangerously that Mutasim found it wise to relocate his entire court to the smaller city of Samarra, about sixty miles north. In Mutasim's defense, he could not have possibly predicted that within just a few decades the *mamluks* would make and break their own caliphs. Between 861 and 869, the *mamluks* had murdered and replaced no less than six different caliphs, and the unusually short life spans of these Abbasid caliphs only ended when they finally found a caliph, Mutamid, who was willing to put a seal on the political arrangement between himself and the commander of the *mamluks* by being given the title of sultan. The consequences were quite bleak for the empire as a whole. The caliph was "a pampered prisoner in his own palace under the control of Turkish mercenaries," to whom even provincial governors felt they owed only the hollowest gestures of allegiance. Over the course of the tenth century, the Abbasids discovered they barely had any authority left in nearby Syria, much less in faraway Egypt. The *umma* would now splinter even further.[9]

By some miracle, the Abbasids clung to the caliphate, although it became more of a purely religious office and real political power fell into the clutches of a series of *mamluk* sultans. Likewise Baghdad jealously gripped its old importance. Although the master of Baghdad could no longer expect his commands to be carried out in Libya or Arabia, it was still a city of tremendous cultural and symbolic value, a capital for Islam in every sense save the political. But to the east of Baghdad and a little after the dawn of the thirteenth century, events were unfolding over the mountains that would change not only the city's future but that of all Islamic civilization. A once exiled and impoverished man named Genghis Khan had totally beaten the odds and turned the steppe people of Mongolia into a force looked upon with supernatural terror by the many societies from Japan to Hungary that they encountered. The rumored ability of the Mongolian horsemen to ride endlessly without need for food or rest, their smashing victories against even well-armed and well-disciplined armies, and their mas-

sacres of entire cities that defied them, a method for ensuring obedience notorious even in an era hardly known for humanitarianism, created a force that could cause great cities to grovel at just the
appearance of a Mongol emissary. Already by the time of Genghis
Khan's death in 1227, the Mongols had conquered northern China
and much of central Asia, modern Russia, and the Caucasus—and
even then the Mongols did not consider their work done. After all,
"Genghis Khan had charged his successors with the task of annexing
the whole world."[10]

When Pope Innocent IV fired a letter off to one of Genghis's successors, Guyuk Khan, damning him for the slaughter of Christians in
Hungary and Poland, the khan wrote back, "I do not understand
these words of yours. The Eternal Heaven [the sky-god Tengri] has
slain and annihilated these peoples, because they adhered neither to
[Genghis] Khan nor to the Khagan, both of whom have been sent to
make known God's command."[11] Therefore Baghdad was an inevitable target, especially after neighboring Persia had been added to
the Mongols' staggering list of conquests, since the caliph's "claim of
authority over all Muslims were considered an affront to Tengri and
his representative on earth, the khagan."[12]

Although the Mongols' triumphs and brutalities were whispered
about with awe in the Abbasid court at Baghdad, Mutasim was unim-
pressed when in the spring of 1257 he heard from a Mongol ambas-
sador graciously offering to let him keep the office of caliph if he
acknowledged the sovereignty of the reigning khagan, Hulagu Khan.
With the haughtiness that only a leader oblivious to his insignificance
can exhibit, the caliph countered, "do you not know that from the
East to the Maghreb, all the worshipers of Allah, whether kings or
beggars, are slaves to this court of mine, and that I can command
them to muster?"[13] Once those words were sent back to the khagan,
the destruction of Baghdad was already a *fait accompli*.

Despite his boast, no Muslim rulers came to the Abbasids' help,
and even Mutasim's closest ally, the sultan of Syria, abandoned the
Abbasids without hesitation. In January 1258, the caliph could see
on the horizon three Mongol armies closing in on Baghdad. During
the siege, the Mongols indulged in their usual tactic of terrifying the
populace by firing letters through arrows over the walls, promising
that noncombatants and important officials would be spared.[14] A gru-
eling month of terror and famine later, the city succumbed. Ninety

Hulagu Khan's forces besieging Baghdad in 1258, from a fifteenth-century painting in the Persian supplement 1113, fol. 180v-181. (*Bibliothèque nationale de France*)

thousand of its inhabitants were said to have been killed, with only the Christian minority completely free from harm because, it was said, of the intervention of one of the khagan's wives, Doquz Khatun, who was a Christian. "The massacre was so great that the blood of the slain flowed in a river like the Nile," the Persian chronicler Wassaf recalled. "Palaces whose canopies had because of their rich design made the seats of Paradise hide in shame and cover their shortcomings were destroyed."[15] Few mosques, libraries, and hospitals were spared from annihilation. The "House of Wisdom," Baghdad's largest library, which included both Arabic works and translations of Indian, ancient Greek, and Persian scientific and literary texts, was razed without quarter. It was remarked that the Tigris ran with both blood from those killed and ink from books the Mongol troops had casually dumped into it. Only four hundred volumes had been saved, secreted by librarians out of the city during the siege.[16]

Mutasim himself was imprisoned, humiliated, starved, and then dragged before the khagan himself. Hulagu Khan personally berated the caliph for his incompetence and for not sacrificing some of his gold for national defense or to the khagan in exchange for his and his people's security. The accounts of the caliph's degrading interview with the khagan gave rise to a colorful legend, written down by Marco Polo, that the khagan had locked the caliph in his own treasure room, challenging him to live off his riches and effectively leaving him to starve to death.[17] More likely, but no less horrifically, the caliph was on February 20, 1258, taken to a field outside the city, rolled up in a carpet, and trampled to death by galloping horses, a tidy way for the superstitious Mongols to avoid what they considered the blasphemous act of spilling royal blood.

Even then, the Abbasids survived as caliphs at the behest of the sultans of Egypt. However, their authority was more nominal than even before, and by 1517 the Caliph Al-Mtawakki III meekly surrendered his title of caliph to Egypt's new conqueror, the Ottoman Emperor Selim I. As for Baghdad, the city would recover somewhat, with its Mongol destroyers themselves restoring several mosques and repopulating the city. However, most histories of the Islamic Golden Age end with the sack of Baghdad with good reason. Even if Islamic culture was already in decline as a result of the political fracturing of Islam and the mounting irrelevance of the Abbasids' sacred authority, the brutal harrowing of Baghdad's libraries and the wrecking of what had been for centuries a celebrated intellectual and artistic center was as much a strike against the cultures of Islam as any. A poem by Takiuddin bin Yusr, recorded by the fifteenth-century Egyptian historian al-Suyuti, preserves some of the despair caused by the fall of Baghdad, which would echo for countless years afterward, perhaps even to this day:

> Harrowing are the tales of Baghdad for whoever weeps.
> Why remain when your friends have departed?
> Do not approach Baghdad, pilgrims,
> For in this guarded enclosure and abode there are no inhabitants.
> The crown of the Caliphate, the sojourn of spring, where its memorials
> Were honored—destruction has effaced all of it.
> In this abode there are marks of the decay that has come upon it,
> And traces of tears upon its ruins.[18]

THE BYZANTINE EMPIRE

The Blasphemous Crusade

Over the course of his reign as pope, John Paul II had taken several steps to recant certain less-than-pristine acts committed by the Catholic Church in the past. The last gesture to this effect was made in 2004, when the pope welcomed the Patriarch Bartholomew of Athens to the Vatican and said, in reference to an event that had happened exactly eight hundred years previously, that "we cannot forget what happened. . . . How can we not share, at a distance of eight centuries, the anger and the pain?" This source of rage that called even across the span of about forty generations was one of the most catastrophic, self-defeating, and utterly pointless acts of violence between two peoples sharing the same religion in all of history. What started out as a campaign to liberate Jerusalem (again) from Muslim control became the pillaging of one of Christendom's greatest cities, a deathblow against the one empire standing between Christian Europe and its Muslim neighbors and the snuffing out of the one direct remnant of the ancient Roman Empire.[1]

Since the eighteenth century the "Eastern Roman Empire" has usually been labeled as the Byzantine Empire, named for Byzantium, the ancient Greek colony situated on the Bosphorus Strait, traditionally considered the boundary between Asia and Europe. The old name lasted, even after it was rechristened Constantinople by Emperor Constantine I in 320. Once the empire permanently split between east and west, the Byzantine Empire would face an impressive rogues gallery of rivals, from Attila the Hun to the Slavic tribes that swarmed across the Balkans to the Islamic Caliphate. Over the centuries, the Byzantine Empire lost its footholds on Italy and Spain and all its territories in Palestine, Egypt, Syria, and North Africa. Even after it lost any hope of ever recovering Rome and even though the local Greek eventually replaced Latin as the administrative tongue of the entire empire, the "Byzantines" still thought of themselves as *romanoi*. They were not just the inheritors of the invincible and glorious Roman tradition of universal empire but the true and only standard bearers of Roman civilization now that Italy and all the other western lands had succumbed to barbarism.

Their feeling of being as permanent a part of the world as the moon was perfectly understandable. While the emperors reigned from behind the all but invincible fortifications of Constantinople, troubled by the occasional crisis or attempted invasion yet still unshakably secure, their enemies slipped off the stage. Even the caliphate, which had absorbed nearly three-fourths of the empire's former territory, eventually fell apart while Byzantium remained. Upstarts like that barbarian warlord Charlemagne might call themselves Emperor of the Romans, and the Byzantine emperors might have to tolerate being dismissively called "Emperor of the Greeks" by their fellow Christians in the west, but just as there's always a God in heaven and a bishop in Rome there would always be an emperor in Constantinople.

It was just as undeniable that the Christians of Byzantium had been drifting away from their fellow Christians in the west. At first, it was cultural, with the Byzantines embracing their Greek heritage and language while Latin remained the *lingua franca* of western Europe even long after it stopped being the language people actually spoke in their everyday lives. Then the "Greeks" and the "Latins" were falling out over theological matters. For a time, the Byzantine emperors had the pope in Rome at their beck and call, but once the Byzantines were forced to completely abandon Italy the pope, now both a spiritual authority and a territorial magnate with his own lands and army in central Italy, was asserting himself over kings—and even emperors. In 1054, the rupture of Christendom into the two camps today recognized as "Orthodox" and "Catholic" began when a cardinal excommunicated the patriarch of Constantinople, who retaliated in kind.

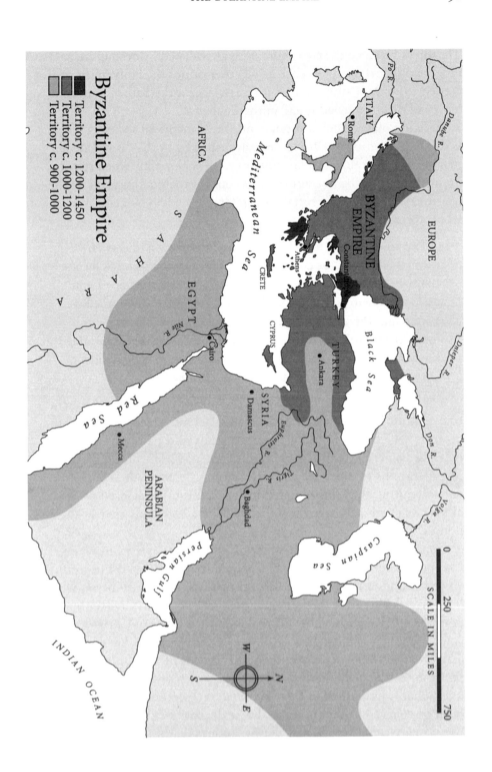

Byzantine Empire

- Territory c. 1200–1450
- Territory c. 1000–1200
- Territory c. 900–1000

The abyss between the two churches was widened by even more nagging theological disputes, such as whether or not the Holy Spirit proceeded from the Father and Jesus Christ or just the Father, and using leavened or unleavened bread in the Eucharist.

Religion played such a prominent role in medieval societies that it is difficult for modern Westerners, accustomed to the "isms" of secularism and pluralism, to imagine. Even in such a time when religion loomed so large, the Byzantines stood out for their enthusiasm. In the fourth century, the influential bishop Gregory of Nyssa remarked on Constantinople:

> The whole city is full of [theological arguments], the squares, the market places, the crossroads, the alleyways; old-clothes men, money changers, food sellers: they are all busy arguing. If you ask someone to give you change, he philosophizes about the Begotten and the Unbegotten; if you inquire about the price of a loaf, you are told by way of reply that the Father is greater and the Son inferior; if you ask "Is my bath ready?" the attendant answers that the Son was made out of nothing.[2]

The centuries apparently did not do much to change this element of Byzantine life. For instance, the iconoclast movement of the eighth century, which saw priceless religious icons and paintings smashed by radicals acting with the blessing of the government, had violent reverberations that echoed through the church as much as the state, demonstrating that the emperor in Constantinople aspired to have almost as much say over his subjects' beliefs and souls as over their bodies.

This was quite a different situation than what existed in western Europe. There was a patriarch in Constantinople who had a powerful voice in ecclesiastical and theological matters, but the emperor, who had an authority over the faith inherited straight from Constantine I, also had a place in the religious realm that the kings of Christian Europe and the so-called Holy Roman Emperor would have envied. There was certainly no reason, from the viewpoint of Constantinople, that the bishop of the holy but still far-off city of Rome should unquestionably have more of a voice than the emperor in what was practiced or believed in Byzantine lands. At the root of all the theological brawls between the pope and the Byzantines was a fight to see if the direct successors of the first emperor to embrace Christianity would have to kiss the ring of the pope, who had long claimed to be the shepherd of the entire Christian flock and the first and final word on doctrine.

More than a century later, in the spring of 1182, the grumbling between east and west became much more than a matter of words. By then, the Republics of Venice and Genoa had a stranglehold over Byzantine maritime trade, in spite of the best efforts of the emperors to play the republics off against each other. After the Emperor Manuel I died in 1180, his wife Maria of Antioch, a daughter of French nobility, took power as regent in the name of her son Alexios II and bluntly favored Italian merchants over their native competitors. Exploiting the resentments that were especially high in Constantinople itself, Alexios's cousin Andronikos overthrew Maria and had her strangled. The crowds that welcomed Andronikos into Constantinople celebrated, but the festivities stopped being innocent once the crowds turned their attention to the city's "Latin quarter":

> The city's populace regained their courage and incited one another to fight side by side, and strife broke out on land and sea. Surrounded and hemmed in by both throngs, the Latins were unable to resist. They attempted to save themselves as best they could, leaving behind their homes filled with riches and treasures of all kinds such as are sought by men bent on plunder; nor did they dare to remain where they were or to attack the Romans or to submit to, and endure, their onslaught. Some took their chances by scattering throughout the City, others sought asylum in the homes of the nobility, while yet others boarded the long ships manned by their fellow countrymen and escaped being cut down by the sword. Those apprehended were condemned to death, and all lost their properties and possessions. The triremes, loaded with refugees, put out from the City's harbors in the direction of the Hellespont and spent the rest of that day anchored at the seagirt islands which are neither far from the queen of cities nor far out in the open sea: I speak of Prinkipos and Prote and all the islands around them rising up from the deep. The next day, after burning down and destroying several monasteries on these islands, they departed, plying all oars and with sails unfurled. Pursued by no one and putting in wherever they wished, they inflicted as much injury as possible on the Romans in these parts.[3]

Rioters stormed into hospitals and slaughtered even the sick. Survivors were rounded up and sold as slaves to the Turks. Although eventually trade and diplomatic relations between the Byzantine Empire and the Latin nations were restored, the "incident" of 1182 left scars on westerners' psyches. The "Greeks" may be Christians—Christians of a sort, at any rate—but in the eyes of many Latins they had just shown they were just as untrustworthy as any heathen.

It was this distrust, if not outright loathing, that was in the back of the minds of a group of French noblemen as they began to realize their dreams to be the ones to finally and permanently "liberate" the Holy Land, plans that would almost certainly have to involve the Byzantine Empire in some fashion. Their ultimate objective to bring Jerusalem back into Christian hands had a special urgency. For a while a Christian Kingdom of Jerusalem had been established thanks to the First Crusade, but in time it was chiseled down to a blip on the Palestinian coastline, not even in charge of the city of Jerusalem itself. However, word had reached even France that the Islamic territory surrounding the Kingdom of "Jerusalem" had been in disarray since the demise of the famous Saladin. The crusaders decided to exploit these divisions and attempt to conquer Egypt, which could provide a more enduring foundation for the future of a crusader island in a hostile Muslim sea.

How the crusaders went from striving to seize Muslim territory to stabbing at the nerve center of the oldest Christian empire in existence can be blamed on two men. One was the doge of Venice, Enrico Dandolo. Elected doge in 1192, Dandolo was about ninety years old and blind by the time he was approached in 1201 by the crusaders, who were seeking to rent ships to Egypt. No less savvy for his age and ailments, he had the crusaders sign an agreement and, when the crusade leaders sheepishly admitted that they lacked the funds they had hoped for, Dandolo kindly suggested that the crusaders' debts to Venice for ships and supplies could be written off if they helped conquer the city of Zara (today Zadar in Croatia), which had thrown off Venetian rule years ago. "Was this Venetian empire-building or just an ingenious way to keep the crusade going?" one historian of the Fourth Crusade asks. "The answer is probably both, yet as the campaign unfolded, it was a combination that increasing numbers of crusaders found themselves unable to stomach."[4]

In the other corner, there was Alexios IV Angelos. He was the young but hopeless son of the emperor Isaakios II, a general who had overthrown the old Komnenoi dynasty but had proven spectacularly inept at dealing with the empire's ongoing feud with their neighbors, the Bulgarians. While Isaakios was out on a hunting trip, his brother—also named Alexios (confusingly for us), becoming Emperor Alexios III—had himself acclaimed emperor by the army in Constantinople. As soon as Isaakios returned to his capital, he was shuffled off to a prison and, like so many unwanted members of Byzantine imperial families, his eyes were stabbed out. Meanwhile his son had fled Constantinople by boat and spent his days desperately trying to scrape together enough funds and support to try to reclaim his father's throne, depending on his brother-in-law the Holy Roman Emperor, Philip of Swabia, for a roof over his head and at least two coins to rub together. It was at Zara, after the crusaders had helped the Venetians capture the city, that they were approached by Philip of Swabia's envoys on January 1, 1203, promising that if they gave the whole Byzantine Empire back to Alexios IV he would subsidize the crusade, give them an army to conquer Egypt, and most incredibly lead his people back into the loving arms of the pope.

Alexios IV was barely into his twenties and had no experience as anything but an exile—and one absolutely dependent on the good will of his brother-in-law, at that. Plus attacking Zara alone had already provoked the wrath of Pope Innocent IV, who blasted the crusaders for shedding "for demons your own and your brothers' blood" and excommunicated them all as punishment.[5] Regardless, the offer was enticing to the crusade leaders but not for the skeptical rank and file of the crusade. It was only after the leaders dropped to their knees, weeping, before their soldiers and made an oath not to stay in Constantinople for longer than a month that the crusade departed for Constantinople, about a thousand miles away from Egypt.

The stars were aligned for disaster but for which side? Alexios III proved no more capable for the job of running an empire than the man he stole it from. He surrounded himself with garish ceremonies and skilled flatterers, as if compensating for the reality that he had no stomach for bloodshed, either on the battlefield or under the executioner's blade, and no brain for governing.[6] The emperor did not even lift a finger to stop the crusaders. His implacable critic Niketas wrote that the emperor's "excessive slothfulness was equal to his stupidity" and he expended his mental energy not on plans for defense, but on "after-dinner repartee."[7] Only when the crusaders' fleet was nearing the waters around Greece did the emperor put the army on alert and secure Constantinople's fortifications.

Admittedly the emperor had plenty of justification to be cocky. The empire's armies were not the effective hammer against the empire's foes east and west they once were and the once unparalleled Byzantine navy had been left to rot for many years, with much of the fleet packed with ships and sailors for hire. Even so, the Byzantine military towered over the crusaders, something even they may have realized when they sailed within sight of Constantinople, a city far more packed with life and wealth than any they had ever seen before, even Paris and Venice. Obviously Alexios III had poured assurances into the crusaders' ears that the people of Constantinople were waiting just for one small omen before they would revolt and invite back their "rightful" emperor. Yet not a single message was smuggled out of the city welcoming the crusaders as liberators. When the crusaders hoped that showing off the young, wayward prince would rouse the people against his evil uncle, the people of Constantinople did not shower them with cheers but with laughter and stones. The crusaders felt they had irrevocably committed themselves to Alexios IV's cause, however hopeless it was. More to the point, it was unlikely that they had enough food and coin to reach Egypt or even Palestine without the backing promised by Alexios IV.

Perhaps still hoping that the Greeks would turn against their emperor if there was a show of force in his favor, the crusaders and the Doge of Venice made a mutual decision to go to war. In spite of the odds, they were able to infiltrate the Golden Horn, the city's main dock, and capture the Tower of Galata on the city's walls. "Much were those of the host comforted thereby, and much did they praise the Lord God," writes Geoffrey de Villehardouin, one of the crusaders present.[8] Even with these early victories, it would have probably taken a miracle to take over the actual city. The crusaders were short on both morale and basic supplies, and Constantinople's legendary walls had staved off much more massive invasions than they could ever hope to muster. However, there was one factor in their favor they could not have anticipated: Alexios III's incompetence and paranoia.

Convinced that the city was on the brink of turning against him because of how he managed (or mismanaged) the crusaders, Alexios

III abandoned his own capital. He looted the imperial treasury and left behind his daughter Eudokia and wife Euphrosyne, who always had a tense relationship with her husband that hit its nadir when she was subjected to a very public accusation of adultery. To be fair, Alexios III may have thought that the threat the crusaders posed would be temporary and that his wife could manage matters until he raised enough support in the provinces. Unfortunately, he only gave his many enemies exactly the excuse they craved.[9] The throne was now considered vacant and the imperial officials and courtiers pulled the elderly, blind, and sickly Isaakios II out of the dungeons and reinstated him as emperor.

In the coming days, Isaakios may have considered that he was better off with his former accommodations. Sitting on a throne in full regalia before the leaders of the crusade, Isaakios was stunned into silence when for the first time he learned about the reckless and, really, impossible promises his son had made. One eyewitness among the crusaders would claim that Isaakios said bluntly, "These are very hard conditions and I do not really see how we can put them into effect," although he also allegedly admitted that he owed his entire empire to the crusaders.[10] Having little recourse, especially since the safety of his son and now co-emperor was still in the crusaders' hands, Isaakios had his secretaries draw up a formal agreement legitimizing all of his son's original concessions. Also, Isaakios allowed the crusaders to stay in the city, where like tourists they marveled at the mammoth size and timeless history of the city. One visitor gawked at the silver lamps and the purple and jasper columns in the Hagia Sophia, which the sick could touch to be miraculously healed.[11] They were all especially impressed by the number of sacred relics held by Constantinople's many churches, including the crown of thorns placed on Jesus Christ's head, a marble slab that still reportedly showed the stains from the Virgin Mary's tears, and fragments of the cross Jesus was crucified on.

Although he drank and gambled from dusk to dawn with the crusade's leaders, there is little doubt that Alexios IV was as desperate as his father to see the crusaders on their way. After all, the crusaders, overawed by the magnificence and holiness of Constantinople as they may have been, were still determined to collect. Thanks to years of instability in the government and the fact that the renegade former emperor made off with a good slice of the treasury, Isaakios and Alexios were terminally cash-strapped, barely able to see to their own needs much less truly pay off their "friends." In desperation, the emperors ordered that some of the crucifixes and images of saints be pried off of church walls and melted down for silver and gold. Most of these sacred coins went right into the crusaders' hands. Some of it was spent on preparations for the holy task of freeing the Holy Land from infidels, but much of it also mysteriously wound up in Constantinople's taverns and brothels. Even more than a disgusting act of impiety by the very men who were supposed to defend the empire, it was a humiliating act of subjugation to a pack of foreign and heretical adventurers. No wonder, then, Alexios found himself in the impossible position of needing to keep the very cause of his unpopularity close to protect his crown—and his life.

The storm clouds were ready to burst. It finally happened in August when a mob descended upon the Latin quarter and set fire to several houses, forcing many residents to seek refuge in the crusaders' camp. The crusade's leaders tried to keep the peace, but just one day later several of the crusaders along with some local Venetians and Pisans sailed in fishing boats to a seaside mosque, which was one of several in the city but the only one to lie outside the city's walls. The motive is unclear; perhaps frustrated that they could not attack the Greeks of the city without risking their relationship with the emperors, the crusaders decided to take their frustrations out on the nearest and most vulnerable non-Christians. Whatever the truth, the Muslims fought against the armed crusaders with whatever objects they happened to have, and the mosque's Greek neighbors rushed to their defense. The Latins were actually driven back, but during the chaos they set fire to the mosque and several neighboring houses. Helped by winds, the fire spread from the suburbs into the city, devouring slums and great mansions and cathedrals alike, as well as completely devastating Constantinople's largest marketplace. The fire burned for three days, leaving 440 acres of the city in blackened ruin.[12] The people of Constantinople had no doubt who was to blame, and all the remaining families in the Latin quarter made the prudent decision to flee the city and stay in the crusaders' camp. Meanwhile Isaakios and Alexios kept stripping off the riches of the city's churches—not for the restoration of Constantinople but in order to enrich the very men responsible for the worst fire the city had ever experienced in its long history. Even with such willingness to risk the wrath of God and the church, the payments fell short of what Alexios in his eagerness had guaranteed. On the crusaders' side, they began to suspect that the perfidious Greeks were cheating them. After all, had not the Greeks betrayed and murdered their fellow Christians once before?

Finally, the crusaders sent their envoys to the imperial palace, demanding that Alexios pay the rest of the money due or else force might have to be applied. Before the emperor, his family, and the court, the crusader delegation made its case but not without exposing their bigotry before the emperor by passive-aggressively remarking, "[T]hey [the crusaders] have never acted treacherously—that is not the custom of their country."[13] Emperor Alexios thundered back that his obligations to the Latins were null and void after the chaos and devastation they brought to his capital. The crusaders returned to the camp and decided to hold their ground, unsure that they would even be able to reach the Kingdom of Jerusalem, much less salvage the original plan to invade Egypt, with the funds they had. Under the weight of suspicion, desperation, and bigotry, that December, fighting would finally break out between the Greeks and the Latins.

Any lingering hope that peace could be saved ended when a court official, who was much to the consternation of future historians also named Alexios (but can be known by his family name Dukas), rushed into the emperor Alexios's bedchamber in the middle of the night, frantically warning him that a mob joined by Alexios's mutinous bodyguard was at the palace doors. Instead of helping his master escape on a ship, Dukas tossed a cloak over Alexios and conducted the terrified emperor as he mumbled prayers to a prison. Isaakios II died almost immediately afterward. Perhaps he was quietly murdered, but it is plausible enough that the mentally and physically crushed man, who never truly recovered from the savage operation that robbed him of his eyesight or the eight years he spent imprisoned, had his demise sped along by the latest bad news. With no more obstacles, the usurper had himself crowned Emperor Alexios V in the Hagia Sophia. His ascension was paid for by the unspoken promise that he would show no mercy to the Latins. Nor did he show any compassion to his predecessor. The young man was strangled in his cell late on a February night. Such was his ultimate reward for all his struggles to return to his homeland and handing the capital of his empire over to its bleak fate.

While getting rid of the former emperor had brought an end to the stranglehold the crusaders had over the imperial office, the murder of Alexios IV also had an impact on the crusaders themselves, who were understandably unconvinced by reports spread by the new emperor that Alexios IV had died a sudden but natural death. In spite of the very explicit orders from the pope that the crusaders should avoid any more conflict with other Christians no matter what, the priests among the crusaders assured them that outright war with the Byzantines was not only justified but could be interpreted as a righteous act. After all, the former emperor had sworn an oath to reconcile the Byzantine church with Rome. The deposing and cruel execution of a legitimate monarch who might have united Christendom and brought the schismatic Greeks under the care of the one true Mother Church surely had to be grounds for a new holy war, even against those who professed to follow Jesus Christ.

Under normal circumstances the crusaders would not have stood half a chance, but they were already camped within the fortifications around the Golden Horn, which alone gave them an advantage when they attacked Constantinople in April 1204. At first, in fact, the crusaders' siege went in favor of the city's defenders. Then, however, the crusaders were able to capture one of the towers on the wall and from there throw open the city gates. After that moment, Constantinople, the greatest Christian city in the world, would receive only rage and greed from its cross-bearing conquerors. Niketas Chroniates leaves behind an eyewitness account:

> When the sacred vases and utensils of unsurpassable art and grace and rare material, and the fine silver, wrought with gold, which encircled the screen of the tribunal and the ambo, of admirable workmanship, and the door and many other ornaments, were to be borne away as booty, mules and saddled horses were led to the very sanctuary of the temple. Some of these which were unable to keep their footing on the splendid and slippery pavement, were stabbed when they fell, so that the sacred pavement was polluted with blood and filth.
>
> Nay more, a certain harlot, a sharer in their guilt, a minister of the furies, a servant of the demons, a worker of incantations and poisonings, insulting Christ, sat in the patriarch's seat, singing an obscene song and dancing frequently. Or, indeed, were these crimes committed and others left undone, on the ground that these were of lesser guilt, the others of greater. But with one

consent all the most heinous sins and crimes were committed by all with equal zeal. Could those, who showed so great madness against God Himself, have spared the honorable matrons and maidens or the virgins consecrated to God? Nothing was more difficult and laborious than to soften by prayers, to render benevolent, these wrathful barbarians, vomiting forth bile at every unpleasing word, so that nothing failed to inflame their fury. Whoever attempted it was derided as insane and a man of intemperate language. Often they drew their daggers against any one who opposed them at all or hindered their demands.

No one was without a share in the grief. In the alleys, in the streets, in the temples, complaints, weeping, lamentations, grief, the groaning of men, the shrieks of women, wounds, rape, captivity, the separation of those most closely united. Nobles wandered about ignominiously, those of venerable age in tears, the rich in poverty. Thus it was in the streets, on the corners, in the temple, in the dens, for no place remained unassailed or defended the suppliants. All places everywhere were filled full of all kinds of crime. Oh, immortal God, how great the afflictions of the men, how great the distress![14]

Niketas himself was staying at a friend's house, since his home was destroyed in the fire, when the sack of Constantinople unfolded. One of the people in the house was a Venetian-born wine merchant, who donned armor and a sword in order to pretend to be one of the crusaders who had just commandeered the house. Still, the merchant was not sure the ploy could keep the house from falling to the invaders forever, so he urged everyone to leave. The merchant pretended to be holding Niketas and the others prisoner. The company, which desperately drifted from refuge to refuge for nearly the next week, was a sad sight, with Niketas's heavily pregnant wife and many of them (including Niketas himself) carrying infants and children too young to walk. Occasionally they were accosted by Latins who searched them for valuables and showed an ugly interest in the young women in the party. In one incident, Niketas saw the young daughter of a judge grabbed and dragged away by a crusader and risked his own life to wave down a few passing crusaders, pleading with them to stop their compatriot and even bravely pulling them by their hands toward the scene of the crime. Unsurprisingly, the women found it advisable to wipe dirt on their faces and walk where crowds were thickest as they tried to make it to the Golden Horn in order to escape by ship, which to Niketas's joy, they did.

For three days, the customary time for the sack of a conquered city, the crusaders ripped through the capital that not long ago astonished and humbled them. Everything in the Hagia Sophia, from its sacred ornaments to the gem-encrusted altar, was stripped of anything of monetary worth. Mules were needed to go into the Hagia Sophia and the city's cathedrals and mansions to carry away all the loot. Even the clerics among the crusaders could not resist. Over the wails and pleas of Constantinople's monks, nuns, and priests, the crusade's clerics took their pick of Constantinople's sacred relics. Bishop Conrad of Halberstadt alone lifted relics of four of the apostles, the finger of Saint Nicholas, and the hair of the Virgin Mary. He was rivaled only by Bishop Nivelon of Soissons, who claimed the Virgin Mary's robe, the head of John the Baptist, the crown of thorns, and two pieces of the cross.[15] Priceless artistic and literary works of antiquity were also surely lost. Enrico Dandolo arranged to have the Roman bronze statues of four horses that once adorned Constantinople's own coliseum, the Hippodrome, shipped back to Venice, among other treasures including *another* head of John the Baptist. The hundreds of other bronze statues decorating the Hippodrome were unceremoniously melted down for coin.

The emperor Alexios V Dukas himself had joined the horde of refugees fleeing the city. This left the way open for the crusaders to elect one of their own as the new emperor: Count Baldwin of Flanders. To help prove that Baldwin was truly the rightful emperor, an elaborate and traditional ceremony was held (only with a good Catholic mass as part of the ritual, of course) followed by a sumptuous feast. Still, the rich beginning of Emperor Baldwin's reign was made a joke by the new regime's endemic poverty. Emperor Baldwin was nothing more than a beggar-emperor presiding over a skeletal capital that was badly depopulated and still scarred by the fire of 1203. A year later Dukas was captured in a battle against the Latins and executed, but members of the old Komnenoi dynasty came to power in the geographically isolated but wealthy port city of Trebizond in northeastern Anatolia and declared themselves the much-wronged true rulers of the empire. To the south, Alexios III's son-in-law Theodoros Laskaris fled to the ancient city of Nicaea and

A fifteenth-century miniature depicting the Crusaders attack on Constantinople in 1204 from the *Croniques abregies commençans . . .* par David Aubert. (*Bibliothèque nationale de France*)

surrounded himself with prominent refugees from Constantinople to form a dangerously legitimate government-in-exile. It was not only the various Greek claimants to the throne that Baldwin and his successors would have to contend with. Other crusaders took advantage of the Byzantine Empire's disintegration by carving up Greece and setting up their own fiefdoms such as the duchy of Athens or the principality of Achaea (in southern Greece), which soon enough acknowledged the "real" emperor in Constantinople with only words, if that. On top of all that, Baldwin quickly found that he had also inherited the Byzantine emperors' traditional enemies, namely the kingdom of Bulgaria to the west and the Seljuk Turks to the east.

Like their former protégé Emperor Alexios IV discovered, the prize the crusaders fought and spilled blood for was far more tarnished than it appeared. Baldwin and those that unluckily followed him were driven to desperation for precious metals. The roofs and adornments of buildings were torn clean of all metal of value. Priceless monuments, many dating back to the days of the great Emperor Justinian I or even to antiquity, were pulled down and dragged off to the furnaces to be melted down. One victim was an ancient bronze statue of the Greek goddess Hera, which was so massive that it allegedly took four yokes of oxen to drag just its head to its doom. The Hippodrome, once a cultural heart of the city and a prime tourist hotspot, was rendered barren. Across the city, only jarred pieces of metal jutting out from empty pedestals still gave witness to the treasures that the city once hoarded.

As if cursed for their crime, Baldwin and the rest of the "Latin emperors" had even more issues than poverty to cope with. Baldwin was captured in a battle against the czar of the Bulgarians, Johanitza, who had a personal grudge against the crusaders since they haughtily turned down his offer of an alliance. Baldwin was never seen again. There were conflicting reports as to the beggar-emperor's final karmic fate. One held that Johanitza flew into a rage and had Baldwin's arms and legs cut off at the knees and elbows. Then he left the emperor to die in a pit, where he managed to hang on to life for three hellish days. Another claimed that Baldwin's head was cut off and the skull used as the czar's drinking cup.

Under Baldwin's heirs, the situation somehow deteriorated more. While he had opposed nearly every step the Fourth Crusade took, Pope Innocent ultimately gave his blessing to the invasion of Constantinople, hoping that under Latin rule the Byzantine Empire could function as a reliable bulwark against Islam. His optimism was misplaced. Constantinople now competed with the ailing Kingdom of Jerusalem for donations and fighters from back west. Even then, the empire continued to be plagued by poverty. Baldwin II, who inherited the imperial crown in 1228, had to scavenge his own palace's roof for tin to sell. Also, he was not too proud to make trips across western and central Europe, haggling with monarchs and merchants over the price of the sacred relics left in the Byzantine Empire. He sold Jesus's crown of thorns to a Venetian for 13,134 gold pieces, although the artifact ended up being acquired by agents of King "Saint" Louis IX of France. Today the crown, once a centerpiece of the Byzantine Church's revered treasures, rests in the Cathedral of Sainte-Chapelle. The tragicomedy that was the entire existence of this Latin Empire of the east finally had its denouement when Michael Palaiologos, now the exiled emperor in Nicaea, retook Constantinople by stealth for the Greeks on July 25, 1261. Although the dynasty Michael founded would never drive the Latins out of the empire's ancient heartland of

Greece completely, they would give the empire a new lease on life, albeit a life that would be snuffed out in 1453 when the Ottoman Turks seized Constantinople, this time for good.

Why, then, present the Fourth Crusade as an episode of imperial collapse, when the Byzantine Empire would survive for two more centuries? Although the Byzantine Empire had its dramatic cycles of waning and recovery before, the blow made by the Fourth Crusade was truly crippling. Even full reintegration of its wayward parts was beyond the enfeebled empire's powers. The "Empire" of Trebizond, never in control of more than the territory surrounding the city of Trebizond and the southernmost tip of the Crimean Peninsula, would remain stubbornly independent, eventually outlasting the Byzantine Empire itself until it too succumbed to the Ottomans in 1461. Likewise, the Byzantines could never reclaim all of Greece, including Athens, Rhodes, and the Aegean Islands, from the Latins. Perhaps most consequential was that the distance between the Greeks and the Latins was no longer bridgeable, if such a thing was possible after the first big rupture. The Pope and the regimes of western Europe schizophrenically switched between scheming to put the imperial crown into the hands of a Latin royal or offering swords and men against the threat of the Turks—in exchange for the Byzantine emperor herding all of his people back into the Roman papal fold, forcing the Byzantine emperors to waste precious energy and time in a tedious and unwinnable game. When the walls of Constantinople finally fell to the cannon of the Ottoman sultan, the Latins were as much to blame as the actual conquerors themselves.

10.

THE KHMER EMPIRE

The Abandoned City

Not far north of Cambodia's Great Lake lies what had once been the largest pre-industrial city in the world, Angkor. The capital of the Khmer Empire that covered modern-day Cambodia and beyond, this city, which along with its suburbs may have been the home of up to a million people, was completely abandoned by the fifteenth century for reasons that are still debated. When the French explorer Henri Mouhot went to visit Angkor in 1860, or "discovered" it even though the Cambodians themselves had never misplaced the city, he was so astonished he refused to believe that the Cambodian people he had met had much to do with the place. There are "ruins of such grandeur, remains of structures which must have been raised at such an immense cost of labour, that, at the first view, one is filled with profound admiration, and cannot but ask what has become of this powerful race, so civilized, so enlightened, the authors of these gigantic works?" Mouhot asked. All in all, Mouhot concluded that it "presents a sad contrast to the state of barbarism in which the nation is now plunged."[1] No wonder a few Europeans had felt compelled to theorize that Angkor was actually built by King Solomon or Alexander the Great, so hard was it to accept for Europeans that such grandeur could be carried out by people who were not truly "civilized."

Angkor is comprised of two complexes. There is Angkor Thom, the actual city where the king of the Khmers presided over his empire as the self-proclaimed universal monarch. The eight-meter-high walls and the deep moat encompassed a city that is three square kilometers or over one square mile wide. Two rows of fifty-four giants stand eternal guard over the city's five gates, each holding a *naga*, a divine serpent, on both sides of the paths. At the very center of the city was the Bayon, a highly decorated temple where great stone faces watch the city from high towers. A medieval Chinese visitor Chou Ta-kuan left a description of the temple's five gates: "Above each gate in the wall there are five great stone Buddha heads, their faces turned towards the cardinal points; the fifth head, in the center, is decorated with gold."[2] Later Portuguese and Spanish visitors, proceeding Henri Mouhot by centuries, were awed by such structures and worried that people back home would not believe their tales of a city that seemed like the "fantastic city of Plato's Atlantis or of his Republic."[3]

Perhaps more famous among modern tourists is Angkor Thom's companion, Angkor Wat, often described as a "temple-city" and which remains the largest religious site in the world. Dedicated to the Hindu god Vishnu by its founder, King Suryavarman II, in the twelfth century, Angkor Wat is a sacred city of stone. As one approaches it, the city is revealed to be a labyrinth of porticoes, terraces, courtyards, galleries, and towers, raised up on different levels and connected by a web of stairways and columned corridors. Faced with the magnitude of the wealth of buildings, Henri Mouhot remarked on one temple he explored, "What strikes the observer with not less admiration than the grandeur, regularity, and beauty of these majestic buildings, is the immense size and prodigious number of the blocks of stone in which they are constructed. In this temple alone are as many as 1,532 columns."[4] In Angkor's heyday, the human resources must have been as impressive as the effort that went into construction. Just one Buddhist monastery in the area of Angkor, Banteay Kdei, employed 79,365 staff, out of whom there were 2,740 officiates, 2,202 assistants, and 615 dancers. The monastery's property included a set of golden dishes weighing more than 500 kilograms, 40,620 pearls, 512 silk beds, and 523 parasols.[5]

Feeding such a mass of human beings was a feat in and of itself. A massive hydraulic system diverted water throughout Angkor. Just outside the city, irrigation fueled agriculture sufficient for the city's hundreds of thousands of inhabitants. At one point, the canals around Angkor may have been needed to supply 50 million rice paddies covering 12.3 million acres of land.[6] Large reservoirs were built to save enough water to furnish the fields in times when the rainy seasons proved lacking.

Sadly, historical records of the Khmer Empire and Angkor itself are few and far between. However, the hard work of archaeologists and historians has at least provided some broad strokes of the empire's story and that of its people. The Khmer Empire is thought to have been inaugurated by King Jayavarman II, who sometime in the eighth or ninth century felt secure enough to declare himself *kamraten jagat ta raja,* "the god who is king." But it would be Jayavarman II's successors who would gradually make Angkor into the empire's grand capital and "an artificial mountain of the gods."[7]

When the Chem people invaded the Khmer Empire and killed King Dharanindravarman II in 1160, his son Jayavarman VII was able to repel the invaders and contributed even more to both Angkor and the empire itself. He was celebrated by posterity for establishing a sophisticated road network, which had hostels and shelters built along regular intervals, and founding 102 hospitals across the kingdom.[8] For Angkor, among other things, he founded a religious university of sorts staffed by a thousand teachers and a royal reservoir, the Jayatataka, which had an island at its center decorated with a Buddhist shrine, icons of Hindu gods, and grottoes.[9] In order to organize such endowments and public works, the government had to be very well-staffed, especially by premodern standards. One inscription records that, one day in 1011, four thousand officials had gathered to swear *en masse* an oath of loyalty to the king.[10]

The countless engravings that cover the walls of Angkor give a little indication of what happened outside building projects, wars, and invasions. Carved inscriptions across one palace show the king sitting on a terrace floor surrounded by courtiers while animals are paraded before them, including a rhino, a buffalo, and a hare. Two fencers prepare to spar off. An orchestra including a violin, harp, and cymbals plays. An acrobat balances a tower of children.[11] Travelers' accounts also echo the experiences of the people who knew Angkor when it was still a vibrant city. Appropriately for a hydraulically fueled society, Chou Ta-kuan in the thirteenth century wrote disapprovingly, ". . . the people are often ill, which is to a great extent due to their too frequent

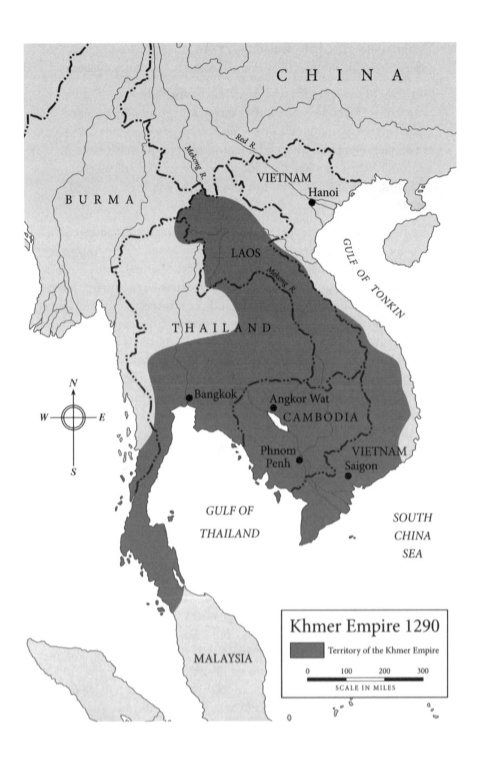

Khmer Empire 1290

Territory of the Khmer Empire

0   100   200   300

SCALE IN MILES

baths and incessant hair washing."[12] Another intimate aspect of Khmer life was also covered by Chou Ta-kuan, the village latrines:

> By two of three families they dig a ditch which they cover again with grass. When it is filled, they cover it over and dig another ditch. After having gone to this place, they go to the pond and wash themselves with the left hand, for the right hand is reserved for food. When they see the Chinese use paper, they mock them and close their doors. There are also women who urinate standing. It is ridiculous.[13]

Less certain is why Angkor would become practically deserted, although since the fifteenth century Angkor Wat remained an important pilgrimage site for Thai, Vietnamese, Chinese, and Japanese Buddhists. Despite its sacred standing, over the course of the fifteenth century Angkor's population plummeted and the royal court moved more or less permanently to the south, around the area where Cambodia's modern capital of Phnom Penh stands today. As the Khmer Empire itself withered, Angkor remained at least an outpost, but new construction ceased and it was no longer the heart of the kingdom. By then it was no longer an organic city but a museum fat with the relics and ghosts of a lost era.

Exactly why Angkor was abandoned is still the subject of hot debate, since none of the inscriptions left by the Khmers describe the reasons for their own decline.[14] One theory is that the Khmer kings, faced with the stark reality of the waning of their armies, had no choice but to retreat farther behind their borders after a Thai army struck the city twice in 1430 and 1431. Another argument is that Khmer society was totally undercut when Hinduism lost out to Buddhism in the marketplace of religions. However, there is one idea that looks toward factors outside warfare and religion and has disturbing ramifications for even people living today.

In an article published in 1974, Bernard Groslier made the more prosaic suggestion that the Khmers could not keep up with the task of keeping their canals clear of silt buildup.[15] Like Sisyphus, the workers of Angkor had a thankless and endless task in keeping the canals clear. This problem begat a crisis, especially since the extensive urban sprawl of Angkor, which has recently been verified through satellite views of the land, caused unstoppable deforestation and erosion. With the water supply failing and the local ecology disrupted, the soil died.

General view of Angkor Wat, from *Temple d'Angkor Vat. Premiere partie. L'architecture du monument*, published in 1929. (*New York Public Library*)

Likewise, the stagnant canals and reservoirs became a hospitable home for mosquitoes and the malaria they carried. Environmental decay chipped away at Angkor, already resting precariously on an ecological precipice, from many angles.

Looking at the growth rings of trees, research by climate scientists in 2010 from Columbia University has found that Angkor did experience harsh droughts from 1400 to the 1440s, the same years the city began to shed its population.[16] Rather than just a fluke, albeit an incredibly nasty one, the droughts may have been a symptom of the "Little Ice Age" that overtook the world, which in Cambodia meant that long arid seasons alternated with punishingly harsh monsoons that did more harm than good. Such a sour climate was like the proverbial bull in the china shop, easily becoming too much for an already overstrained system to bear. Perhaps it was even undernourished soldiers that gave the Thai forces the advantage in the first place.

"Angkor's end is a sobering lesson in the limits of human ingenuity," the *National Geographic* journalist John Stone concludes after his own look at the environmental causes of Angkor's collapse. "Its engineers managed to keep the civilization's signal achievement running for six centuries—until, in the end, a greater force overwhelmed them."[17] As of today, climate change has seeped from scientific journals into the halls of politics, while the question of ready supplies of fresh water has gone from being a subject for the "developing world" to an urgent matter for the western United States. Whatever the future holds as twenty-first century societies face fundamentally the same crises that overcame what was at one time the greatest city on Earth, Angkor remains a monument to the potential genius of human organization but also a testimony to the futility of hoping for nature's patient cooperation indefinitely.

11.

THE AZTEC EMPIRE

The Sun Will Never Rise Again

Today the Basilica of Our Lady of Guadalupe gazes solemnly over the Plaza de las Americas in Mexico City, drawing countless devout pilgrims to its centerpiece, an image of the Virgin Mary, as it has done since 1531. Although a newer building was constructed next to the old church in 1976 and claimed the Virgin Mary's holy icon for itself, the older basilica not only still stands but remains open to visitors. However, the entire site hides something of a secret. Where the entire complex stands today there was once a temple sacred to the goddess Tonantzin, the "Honored Grandmother" who guaranteed the fertility of the fields. This is far from the only case of Christianity placing a thin veneer over older religious practice, but it is perhaps more appropriate than most. More than a place for Catholics to prove their devotion to the mother of Jesus Christ, the Basilica of Our Lady of Guadalupe remains a patriotic symbol for the nation of Mexico, whose very name is derived from Tonantzin's beloved people, the Aztecs.

The place Aztecs hold in history is a rather morbid yet complex one. They have an undisputed position as the quintessential victims of European imperialism, their entire independence and civilization sacrificed toward the greed of the conquistadors and the pretensions of their king. Yet they are also, to use common academic-speak, the ultimate "other." Even the most casual accounts of the Aztecs summon images of priests cutting still-beating hearts out of victims, of prisoners from mock battles, the notorious "Flower Wars," being given one year as pampered gods-on-earth before being brutally sacrificed. For the Aztecs, human sacrifice was a selfless act on behalf of humanity, in imitation of the gods themselves who willingly butchered themselves to create the cosmos and to ensure that the sun will always rise and set. "Sacrifice was a way of life for the Aztecs," David Carrasco writes[1] as he argues that, rather than being a grotesque aberration, the Aztecs' penchant for human sacrifice is just one manifestation of the ways in which ritual violence continue to appear in societies even today.

Despite their gruesome reputation, the Aztec empire did not run on blood alone. Aztec society had the oldest compulsory school system in the world. There, both girls and boys, commoners and nobles alike, learned about religious practices and dances, history, rhetoric, and even art.[2] Sons of the nobility were trained to be warriors at the age of fifteen, finally departing for their first battle after they reached their twentieth birthday. In a ritual illuminating the glory of the path toward the battlefield, the young men's parents "gave them large, cotton capes, or carmine colored breech clouts, or capes painted with designs."[3] The system these warriors helped enforce was a well-oiled one, with cities and towns contributing to the Aztec city of Tenochtitlan and its allies' clothes and shields, which were meticulously counted and redistributed.

The ties holding it together were also those of faith. The ranks of priests, the *tlamacazqui,* came from all classes (although, of course, the cushiest gigs were often reserved for the nobility) and specialized in various tasks essential for Aztec culture. Some were teachers, some painted the records preserved in the codexes, while some dedicated themselves to memorizing to perfection the positions of the stars and the movements of the sun throughout each day of the year, essential knowledge for calculating the right days for religious festivals. A few had perhaps the more enjoyable work of interpreting dreams and visions or bestowing their own prophecies, aided in their work by peyote or psychedelic mushrooms and weeds. The Aztec priests were a downright terrifying sight to the Spanish invaders:

> They wore black cloaks like cassocks and long gowns reaching
> to their feet. Some had hoods like those worn by canons, and

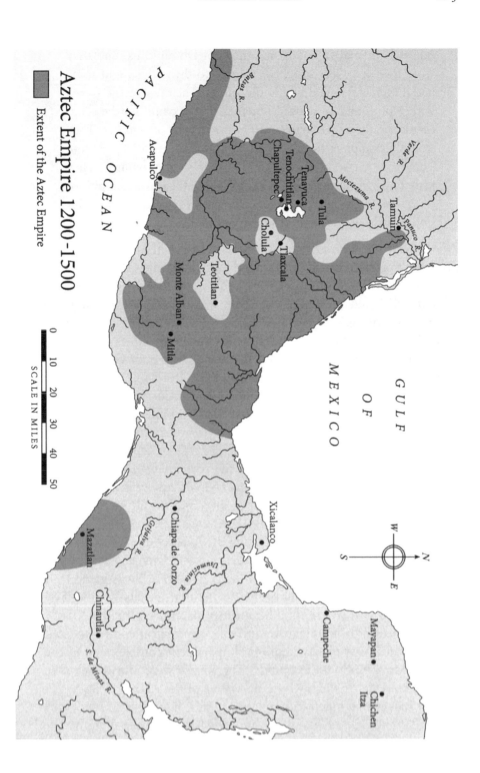

Aztec Empire 1200-1500

Extent of the Aztec Empire

SCALE IN MILES

0 10 20 30 40 50

PACIFIC OCEAN

Acapulco

Balsas R.

Tenayuca
Tenochtitlan
Chapultepec
Tula
Moctezuma R.
Cholula
Tlaxcala
Verde R.
Tamuin
Pánuco R.
Teotitlan
Monte Alban
Mitla

MEXICO

GULF OF

Mazatlan

Grijalva R.
Chiapa de Corzo
Usumacinta R.
Xicalanco
Chinautla
S. de Minas R.
Campeche
Mayapan
Chichen Itza

N
W   E
S

others had smaller hoods like those of Dominicans, and they wore their hair very long, right down to their waist, and some had it even reaching down to the ankles. Their hair was covered with blood, and so matted together that it could not be separated, and their ears were cut to pieces by way of penance. They stank like sulphur and they had another bad smell like carrion. They were the sons of chiefs and abstained from women. They fasted on certain days and what I saw them eat was the pith of seeds. The nails on their fingers were very long, and we heard it said that these priests were very pious and led good lives.[4]

Although the Spanish were shocked at the sight of self-mutilating priests who carried out the occasional human sacrifice, they could not help but compare the society they came across to theirs, once in a while finding that their home of Spain was rivaled or even came up short. "The city is so big and so remarkable that, although there is much I could say of it which I shall omit, the little I will say is, I think, almost unbelievable, for the city is much larger than Granada and very much stronger, with as good buildings and many more people than Granada had when it was taken," Hernan Cortés himself claims, in praise of just one city the conquistadors stumbled across. "There is in this city a market where each and every day upward of thirty thousand people come to buy and sell. . . . There is jewelry of gold and silver and precious stones and other ornaments of featherwork and all as well laid out as in any square or marketplace in the world."[5]

Even more impressive were the great capitals built by the Aztecs and their predecessors. One was Teotihuacan, which was perhaps once the center of an empire preceding the Aztecs but which had been abandoned by the time the Aztecs came across it. Even its name, Teotihuacan, literally "The City Where Gods Are Born," was given to it by the Aztecs themselves, out of their belief that the city was built by the gods and was where time began. An inspiration for the Aztecs' own ventures into architecture and city planning, the city boasted wide avenues, vast plazas, multilevel apartment complexes, and the massive Moon and Sun Pyramids. The Aztecs were in as much awe of the city as the Spanish would be in awe of the Aztecs' cities.[6]

The Aztecs had much to brag about their own capital, Tenochtitlan, still inhabited today under the name Mexico City. In fact, the settlement of the city's site was the stuff of patriotic legend. According to the Aztecs themselves, they emigrated into central Mexico from a land they called the "land of the cranes," Aztlán. The exact location of Aztlán was a mystery even to the Aztecs themselves, with the emperor Motecuhzoma I in the mid-fifteenth century dispatching an expedition of priests to find the holy land. Apparently they only returned with tales of a series of visions and a warning that the people of Tenochtitlan had grown too weak and self-indulgent. In any case, Aztlán's location remains a subject of pure speculation to modern-day historians and archaeologists. Nowadays most place the land farther north and west from modern-day Mexico City, possibly somewhere along Mexico's Pacific coast in the present-day Mexican states of Guanajuato, Jalisco, or Michoacán.[7]

Wherever it was, Aztlán was an island on a lagoon that was like a paradise, but sometime around 1000 AD the ancestors of the Aztecs fled *en masse* at the urging of the sun god Huitzilopochtli to escape a tyrannical ruler, possibly the ancient empire of the Toltecs.[8] After stopping at several points along the way, the Aztecs' ancestors finally settled for good at Lake Texcoco, where they discovered signs that had been foretold by Huitzilopochtli: frogs, fish, serpents, and weeds that were completely white and, more dramatically, an eagle perched on a cactus growing out of a rock, devouring a snake.[9] In spite of the marshiness of the terrain, the Aztecs started to build a city on the islands of Lake Texcoco in 1345.

Tenochtitlan began with a humble temple made out of dried mud dedicated to Huitzilopochtli, but by the time Cortés and his men gazed upon it the settlement had become so much more. Cortés estimated that the city sheltered sixty thousand houses and observed that safe drinking water was easily distributed throughout the city.[10] Like Venice, canals serving as passageways ran through the city, which were organized from the city center to its outskirts in a grid. Even the houses of the commoners were often colorfully decorated. Meanwhile the houses of the nobles in Tenochtitlan and other cities had amenities that rivaled the royal palaces of Europe, as Cortés claimed in a letter to the Emperor Charles V. "There are houses belonging to certain men of rank which are very cool and have many rooms, for we have seen as many as five courtyards in a single house, and the rooms around them very well laid out, each man having a private room," Cortés writes. "Instead there are also wells and water tanks and rooms for slaves and servants of which they have many. Each of these chieftains has in front of the entrance of his house a very large courtyard and some two or three or four of them raised very high with steps up to them and all very well built."[11]

At the time its eventual destroyers "discovered" it, the Aztec Empire was in what might have been its high noon under different circumstances. Once upon a time the Aztecs themselves were tributaries of other cities, and by the dawn of the fifteenth century they were under the boot of the Tepanec city-state of Atzcapotzalco, the most formidable city central Mexico had seen since the fall of the shadowy "gods" of Teotihuacan. Under the aggressive leadership of Itzcoatl, who had been chosen as *tlatoani* ("king" but literally "speaker") by the city's noble Council of Four despite having a slave woman as a mother, Tenochtitlan shook off the Tepanecs and forged a "Triple Alliance" with the nearby cities of Tlacopan and Tetzcoco. Under the force of their alliance Atzcapotzalco crumbled and its *tlatoani* Maxtla was handed over to his enemies by his own disgruntled people. Before a crowd of soldiers holding ornately painted shields with animal and flower motifs standing with their generals who marked their status by wearing jade, crystal, and obsidian from their lips, ears, and noses, Maxtla was held down on a block, his chest was stabbed, and his heart was torn out. His remains still received a funeral worthy of his former rank. It was the birth of what historians would come to christen the "Aztec Empire."[12]

Even though it was in truth not an "empire" in the usual sense but a partnership that Tenochtitlan would come to overshadow, Itzcoatl's nephew, Moctezuma I, who was elected to succeed him in 1440, was the first ruler to style himself the "great speaker," *huitlatoani*, meaning he "spoke" not only for the people of Tenochtitlan but all the towns and chieftains who paid the city tribute.[13] It was not a nominal self-promotion. By the time Moctezuma I died in 1469, Tenochtitlan's power could reach all the way to what is now the state of Veracruz and to the coasts of the Gulf of Mexico and the Atlantic and Pacific Oceans, far surpassing its own former masters.

And yet, in the words of one historian of the Aztecs, a mere half century after the great Moctezuma I's death a "whole nation [was] submitting to a handful of desperate Spanish soldiers."[14] Not long before Cortés arrived in Mexico, he was preceded by smallpox, which was already decimating the native populations of the Caribbean. Smallpox was still at the time deadly to Europeans, but to the unexposed Native Americans it was an unfathomable catastrophe. Over the course of the century and a half following the fateful year of 1519, Native American populations began to collapse, perhaps as much as 90 percent by the end, almost making the advent of the Black Death in Europe look like an outbreak of the flu in comparison.[15] The *Florentine Codex*, a history and cultural guide to the Aztecs written and edited by a Franciscan friar starting in 1545 with contributions from native converts, still shows the scars the plague made on survivors' memories: "But before the Spaniards had risen against us, first there to be prevalent a great sickness, a plague. [. . .] No longer could they walk; they only lay in their abodes, in their beds. [. . .] There was death from hunger; there was no one to take care of another; there was no one to attend to another."[16]

Still, Cortés could not have comprehended any of this. Also to him, no matter how advanced a society like the Aztecs' may be, they were still barbarians, by the will of God under the sovereignty of his lord, the Holy Roman Emperor and King of Spain Charles V. This was all because the pope for political convenience had arbitrarily divided what little was known of the "New World" between the kingdoms of Portugal and Spain. The Spanish were not shy about advertising this fact to their monarch's new subjects. Spain's conquistadors were required by law, whenever they came across an unfamiliar people in the Americas, to read a statement, the *Requerimiento*, solemnly informing the natives—in plain Latin, of course—that they were now at last being called upon to recognize the authority of the pope and the monarch he had chosen to rule over them. Any resistance would be treated as an act of rebellion. If the whole thing sounds like a joke to modern ears, they are not alone. Bartolomé de las Casas, the colonial soldier turned monk who dedicated his pen to the defense of Native Americans from abuse, supposedly remarked that he did not know "whether to laugh or cry" when he first heard about the practice.[17]

Although an earlier Spanish expedition in 1517 had been slaughtered by Mayans in the Yucatan, an undaunted Cortés set sail west from Cuba two years later. Riding along with Cortés— besides smallpox germs—was a roughly hundred-person crew of professional soldiers, young noblemen shouldered out of their inheritance by older brothers, and desperate colonists. There is no doubt that Cortés and many of the others genuinely wanted to spread the word of the one true God to the unenlightened barbarians, but it is also obvious that they came with the not particularly Christ-like thought that salvation could be brought to the natives without bloodshed here and there. "Truth to tell, it is war and warriors that really persuade the Indians to give up their idols, their bestial rites, and their abominable bloody sacrifices and the eating of men," reads the testimony of Cortés's own secretary, Francisco López de Gómara. "And it is thus that of their own free will and consent they more quickly receive, listen to, and believe our preachers, and accept the Gospel and baptism, which is what Christianity and faith consist of."[18] On top of a righteous mission, they had a sharp appetite for profit. It was an appetite whetted when, not long after their arrival, they met a delegation from Tenochtitlan bringing them large gold and silver disks and sacred clothing and masks made with precious stones, seashells, and feathers.

The delegation was sent instead of an armed force to eradicate the strangers, a decision that of course still perplexes scholars, students, and casual history readers alike. The *huitlatoani* who made this apparently odd and seemingly idiotic decision was Moctezuma II. A smart, scholarly man who enjoyed his education in the religious temple, especially in astronomy, the second Moctezuma was either a son or a cousin of the first[19] and was chosen as *huittlatoani* in 1502. Even though by the standards of his own society he was more inclined to be a priest, Moctezuma was nonetheless a talented administrator and conqueror, sometimes leading his armies in person hundreds of miles to expand the Aztecs' sphere of influence even further. By the moment of Cortés's arrival, Moctezuma II's domains reached from coast to coast and from modern Veracruz and Michoacan to southwestern Guatemala.

Why, then, didn't this intelligent and warlike monarch recognize the Spanish as the threat those of us enjoying the luxury of being on this side of history can see? And how did an educated man like Moctezuma react to the mysterious coming of strange men from across the sea who wore metal, rode on strange beasts no one had seen before, and seemed oblivious to even the most basic social rules that had been passed down many generations? After all, almost right after their arrival the strangers were already causing unrest among the Aztecs' vassals. A popular myth that pops up in documentaries and school textbooks, one that may have had its roots in accounts spun by native writers themselves when trying desperately to make

Cortés receiving gifts from Moctezuma's emissaries, from *Historia de las Indias de Nueva España e islas de la tierra firme* ("The History of the Indies of New Spain") by Diego Durán, 1579. Note Cortés's African servant. (*Biblioteca Nacional de España*)

sense of the unfathomable reality of the conquest,[20] was that Moctezuma II became convinced that Cortés was in reality the exiled god-king Quetzalcoatl, returning after many centuries from the east to reclaim his rightful dominion. Besides having implications that are at best condescending about Native Americans, there is simply no proof that anyone, much less a man adept at running an empire like Moctezuma, believed that the Spanish were divine and heralded into the scene by ancient prophecies.[21]

But Moctezuma may in truth have been unnerved by an uncanny historical similarity. After all, his own ancestors had come from an unknown land and eventually established an empire over the remnants of an older people. It might have been a cautious curiosity that prompted Moctezuma, especially as he heard reports of the strangers' powerful weaponry and bizarre tactics in battle, which had already led them to emerge victorious from skirmishes with natives and even win several allies from among the Aztecs' enemies and vassals alike. No doubt the fact that natives thought of themselves as belonging to local communities, not to any kind of "Aztec nation," and many, even among the Aztecs' "allies," resented their lordship worked in Cortés's favor as much as, or perhaps even more so than, their guns.[22] Moctezuma's choice to invite the strangers into Tenochtitlan, the physical core of his power, was hardly a suicidal one but an attempt to learn more about a new people while hopefully also containing any danger they posed.

The Spanish were escorted to the main palace, which astonished them with its variety of courtyards and gardens. "And they were all dressed alike except that Moctezuma wore sandals whereas the others went barefoot; and they held his arm on either side," Cortés recalled this meeting. "When we met I dismounted and stepped forward to embrace him, but the two lords who were with him stopped me with their hands so that I should not touch him; and they likewise all performed the ceremony of kissing the earth."[23] Once the preliminaries were over, Cortés tried to explain that he was an emissary from a great emperor ruling over a land across the ocean and the sole representative of the one true creator of the world, the pope. Moctezuma did at least agree to send tribute, or pretended to do so, but things became awkward when the Spanish insisted on seeing the great temple. Their amazement at the splendor of Tenochtitlan and the palace of Moctezuma was quickly replaced with horror at the blood that flowed in gallons around the temple.

Two weeks passed with the Spanish as the pampered guests of Moctezuma, but it was hardly a relaxing vacation. Cortés knew that they were at Moctezuma's complete mercy, an anxiety that was certainly not assuaged by the Aztecs' penchant for human sacrifice. When a report reached Cortés that natives had gotten into a skirmish with his men in Veracruz, he believed that the fight was evidence that Moctezuma was scheming to kill all the foreigners in his empire and took preemptive action. Requesting an audience with Moctezuma in his apartments, Cortés and his men arrived, only to immediately take the emperor hostage. Over the tense days to come Moctezuma acquiesced to formally declaring himself the vassal of Charles V and allowing the Spanish to worship under a crucifix and an icon of the Virgin Mary in the sacred Great Pyramid. Before an assembly of nobles, Moctezuma was even prompted to give a speech of total submission, which de Gómara himself could not help but sympathetically note opened an outpouring of horror and grief:

"You will please me by giving yourselves to this captain as vassals of the Emperor and King of Spain, our sovereign lord, to whom I have already submitted as his servant and friend. And I implore you to obey him henceforth, as you have obeyed me, and give and render him the tributes, taxes, and services that you have rendered me, for you cannot give me greater pleasure." Moctezuma could say no more, because of his tears and sobs, and all the people wept so bitterly that for a good while they could not even answer him. They sighed and groaned so heavily that they even moved the hearts of our men; but in the end they said they would do as he commanded.[24]

No wonder Moctezuma today has a reputation as a cowering, inept ruler, but he was likely calculating that such grandiose gestures of degradation would not go unremarked among his people. If so, he was right. Moctezuma himself advised the Spanish that they should leave the city since even the *huitlatoani* himself could no longer ensure their lives. How this gambit of Moctezuma's might have worked cannot really be known, since Cortés had another problem. By staying in Mexico Cortés had disobeyed the explicit orders of his immediate superior, the Spanish governor of Cuba, and aggravated the offense by going over the governor's head to write directly to Charles V. Cortés had to abruptly leave Tenochtitlan to stop a squadron sent from Cuba to arrest him, leaving his soldiers in the city under the command of Pedro de Alvarado.

Although there are many details of what was happening in those days that have not been preserved, there is no doubt that a sword hung over both sides, but no one anticipated when it would drop. Moctezuma and the priestly hierarchy still went ahead with plans to celebrate Toxcatl, a religious festival filled with ceremonial costumes, singing, and dancing that would climax with the sacrifice of a young man who spent the previous year being coddled by the entire city as he impersonated the god Tezcatlipoca. On the day of May 7 or 8, 1520, men gathered at the behest of tradition in the temple courtyard to dance and sing in ceremonial warrior garb, fully armed, under the wary eyes of the Spanish garrison. In an instant and with no provocation, the soldiers descended upon the celebrants with swords drawn and began to systematically kill them. A compiler of the *Florentine Codex* may have heard an eyewitness account of a massacre that claimed the lives of much of the Aztec Empire's upper class in a single frenzied day:

> They came everywhere to block each of the ways leading out [and] leading in. . . . Thereupon they surrounded the dancers. Thereupon they went among the drums. Then they struck the drummer's arms; they severed both his hands; then they struck his neck. Far off did his neck [and head] go to fall. Then they all pierced the people with iron lances and they struck them each with iron swords. [. . .] Of some they struck repeatedly the shanks; of some they struck the belly; then their entrails gushed forth. And when in vain one would run, he would only drag his intestines like something raw as he tried to escape. Nowhere could he go. And him who tried to go out they there struck; they stabbed him. But some climbed the wall; they were able to escape. Some entered the . . . [buildings]; there they escaped. And some . . . got in among those really dead, only feigning to be dead. They were able to escape. But if one took a breath, if they saw him, they stabbed him. And the blood of the brave warriors ran like water; it was as if it lay slippery. [. . .] And the Spaniards went everywhere as they searched in the . . . [buildings]. Everywhere they went making thrusts as they searched, in case someone had taken refuge. [. . .] And when [the massacre] became known, there upon there was shouting: "O brave warriors, O Mexicans, hasten here! Let there be arraying—the devices, the shields, the arrows! Come! Hasten here! Already they have died, they have perished, they have been annihilated, O Mexicans, O brave warriors!"[25]

While the details of the horrors inflicted survive, those of the motive do not. Alvarado himself may have been the victim of a dupe. The main native allies of the Spanish, the Tlaxcalteca, a Mexican tribe that had resisted Aztec conquest, may have deliberately fed Alvarado false information about how Toxcatl was going to be used as a cover for a revolt against the Spanish.[26] Or maybe Alvarado justifiably felt entrapped by circumstances and acted out of simple fear and bigotry. However it happened, the Spanish conquest of Mexico had begun in earnest.

Moctezuma may have been trying to play a long game all this time even while he became a virtual prisoner, only allowed out for the occasional hunting trip, but news of the massacre which had claimed so many important lives and had taken place on one of the most sacred days of the year was too much for what remained of the Aztec elite. Cortés had returned to Tenochtitlan to find that the Aztec people had seized the initiative, besieging the Spanish with darts and stones. Overwhelmed, Cortés pleaded with Moctezuma to calm his people. Wearing his turquoise crown, Moctezuma emerged on top of a palace parapet, begging the mob to surrender. Voices rose in fury accusing him of being a coward, followed by stones, one of which managed to strike him in the head and fatally injure him. His captors hurried him to his bed, where Moctezuma would linger in silence and pain for three days before succumbing to his wound. Apparently the Spanish attempted to convert him to Christianity on his deathbed, but, in one last act of defiance against European domination, he refused, dying a believer in the gods of his ancestors. In the twentieth century Arthur Miller in his play *The Golden Years* has the fading Moctezuma bitterly quip to a remorseful Cortés, still hoping to atone by saving the monarch's soul, "Your god is bloodier than mine."

Moctezuma's brother Cuitláhuac was picked to become the new *huitlatoani*. He did manage to drive the Spanish out of Tenochtitlan, but rather than leading a smashing Aztec resurgence he died after a reign of eighty days, the victim of Cortés's invisible but most precious ally, smallpox. After his death, Tenochtitlan would soon fall to the Spanish. While in the early years of Spain's colonization of Mexico occasionally a native noble would be propped up as a new *huitlatoani* they would always be nothing more than a tool of the conquerors. Cortés's unexpected and impossible triumph, subduing in less than a year the most complex and formidable American society Europeans had yet encountered, set a dark tone for not only further European excursions into the Americas but for the next four hundred years of world history. That lust for land, power, and riches could be sanctified through the quest to spread the word of God and European civilization was a lesson that would not go neglected.

"New Spain," as the land of the Aztecs and their allies and rivals was humiliatingly named, wrested back its political independence in 1821 with the declaration of a Mexican Empire, which itself gave way to a republic only a couple of years later. Nonetheless, democratic ideals did little to erode Mexico's strict hierarchy of race and the absolute hegemony of Mexicans claiming pureblood Spanish ancestry.

Even so, the very name "Mexico" and the use of the eagle holding the serpent on a cactus as the country's coat of arms were acknowledgments of a buried but not dead past, still as visible as the Aztec goddess wearing the mask of the Christian messiah's mother.

12.

THE MUGHAL EMPIRE

A Rebel King

According to an English historian, an Indian once compared
the British to "*dimaks*" or white ants, which from dark or
scarcely visible beginnings pursue their determined objects in-
sidiously and silently, destroying green forest trees and in their exca-
vated trunks building edifices. . . . Attacking everything, devouring
everything, they undermine and sap and desolate," a comparison
which even the English commentator had to admit had merit.[1] The
colonization of India by the British began with the machinations of
the East India Tea Company, which had been allowed to operate in
India as not only a trade monopoly but as its own government. Eventually it culminated in the so-called British Raj, becoming the centerpiece of the greatest empire the world has ever known as well as the
symbol of peaceful resistance—and victory—over European colonialism in the twentieth century. However, the collapse of the Mughal
Empire, the Islamic state that had claimed most of the subcontinent
before the British Raj, had started long before all this. Arguably the
fissures were already showing as the Mughals struggled against re-
gional forces like the Marathas of the Deccan in southern India and
with the unending challenge of ruling over a vast land with a multitude of ancient and firmly rooted faiths and cultures.

The Mughals had not been the first. India had seen conquerors try
to claim the prestigious mantle of universal monarch, known among

Buddhists as the *chakravartin*. The Mauryans, the Satavahanas, the Guptas, and the Rashtrakutas were among the dynasties who seized large slices of India, and their declines are usually obscure because of a lack of written testimonies (like with so many ancient and medieval empires) except for the fact that they usually gave way to another ascending power. For just as long as India had seen the rise and fall of native and foreign empires, it had been a true mixing pot of religions and philosophies. In ancient India, one could subscribe to the teachings of Hindus, Buddhists, Jainists, or atheists, or some combination thereof, all offering not only different conceptions of the nature of the universe and human existence but a variety of ethical systems as well. No wonder the parable of the blind men and the elephant, where a group of blind men attempt to describe an elephant but can only talk about the parts they can touch without seeing the greater whole, is an Indian original and has been told and retold across the centuries by Jainists, Buddhists, and Sufi Muslims.

Islam reached South Asia by 712, with Arab armies conquering the Indus in the name of the Caliphate and independent sultanates overtaking modern-day Afghanistan and Pakistan and northern India, leaving Hindu kingdoms only in the southernmost regions of the subcontinent. While most Muslim rulers were willing to extend tolerance to those the Qu'ran named the "People of the Book"— Jews, Christians, and (depending on who was asked and what their mood was) Zoroastrians—Hindus were sometimes thought of as pagans, deprived of even the echo of divine revelation. There were Muslim rulers and generals who felt no shame over destroying Hindu temples and holy sites, such as Ulugh Khan who in 1323 had an expansive Svayambhusiva temple on the Deccan completely obliterated, although Richard M. Eaton has argued this was more a ritual act to discredit a Hindu king than what we would call a deliberate act of religious persecution.[2]

In fact, some degree of tolerance was often extended, although there were also spectacularly brutal exceptions, like the sultan of Delhi, Firuz Shah Tuglhuhq, who imposed the *jizya*, a property tax levied on non-Muslims, or the conqueror Timur (popularly known as Tamerlane in the West) who forced into conversion the hundreds of Hindus he did not slaughter. Nonetheless, in the northern and central parts of the country the Hindu masses for the most part went through their normal lives under Islamic aristocracies, with many Hindus

0   100   200
SCALE IN MILES

Kabul
KABUL
Peshawar   Shelum R.   Srinaga   Indus R.
Candahar   KASHMIR
LAHORE
Indus R.   Lahore
Ravi R.

HIMALAYAS

Dehli
THAR
DESERT   Ganges R.
OUDH
Agra   Lucknow   Gogra R.   BIHAR
AGRA   BENGAL
Benares   Ganges R.
ALLAHABAD

MUGHAL EMPIRE

Ahmedabad   Narmada R.   Calcutta
Tapti R.
Surat

Godavari R.

Bombay   Ahmadnagar   Bay
                                        of
Kistna R.   Hyderabad   Bengal

ARABIAN

SEA   Goa

N
W   E

S

Pondicherry

CEYLON

The Mughal Empire
c. 1700

Territory of Mughal Empire

ARABIAN SEA

INDIAN OCEAN

Bay of Bengal

working as secretaries and officials, while the Islamic elites indulged in the Hindus' own centuries-old traditions of music, literature, and architecture. Even after centuries of Muslim rule, by the era of British colonial rule about 70 percent of the population remained Hindu with 10 percent belonging to the various faiths and schools that made up India's complex mosaic, including Buddhism and Jainism, still making Muslims a 20 percent minority.[3]

The various sultanates of India themselves would succumb to Zahir-ud-Din Muhammad Babur, a royal of Mongolian descent who had the blood of Genghis Khan and Timur the Great in his veins. His father had been the ruler of a small kingdom in modern-day Uzbekistan, a tiny crumb of the once great Mongolian Empire, but from these unlucky beginnings Babur carved a new empire out of Afghanistan and northern India. His successors would go further, culminating in an empire that nearly controlled all of modern India and Pakistan except for the southern tip of the Indian subcontinent.

Although it never made it all the way south, the Mughal Empire was the closest thing to an independent pan-Indian state that would exist until the founding of the Republic of India in 1947. To run the largest empire India had yet seen the Mughal emperors designed and ran an efficient system that linked the empire's many regions. Roads held together the empire's major cities complete with rest stops providing separate accommodations for Hindus and Muslims and carefully maintained gardens to enjoy a nice afternoon's rest in. This network was also the backbone of an effective postal system. Beyond transportation and communication, the Mughal Empire offered across its territories religious endowments for both Muslims and Hindus, hospitals and hospices, and scholarships for teachers and students. As a matter of course, the government provided public parks and free kitchens for the public.[4]

Yet perhaps the most ambitious undertaking by the Mughal emperors was not some public works plan but an attempt to bridge the gaps between faiths, despite Islam's own claims to have the definitive guidebook to the whole elephant. The efforts of Guru Nanak, the founder of the Sikh religion, centered around his bold declaration that "God is neither Hindu or Muslim." The third Mughal emperor Akbar was lifted by the same wave of sentiment, even courting (although ultimately disappointing) a team of Portuguese Christian missionaries. Forging a seemingly impossible fusion of Islam, Hinduism, and

Portrait of Emperor Akbar Praying, in ink and gouache on paper, c. 1605, India. (*Metropolitan Museum of Art*)

Zoroastrianism (with perhaps a little Christianity thrown in), Akbar essentially laid down the cornerstone of his own religion, *Din-i-Ilahi* ("Religion of God"), preaching not unlike Guru Narak that God was One and known to many faiths and philosophies but adding the small detail that Akbar himself was God's viceroy on Earth. All Akbar's followers, among whom many of his courtiers proudly counted themselves, abstained from meat, venerated fire and the sun, and worshiped on Sundays.[5]

Akbar hoped to bring together a spiritually, philosophically, and culturally divided people under one creed that conveniently also venerated himself and his dynasty. Unfortunately, his successors were not inclined to uphold Akbar's own pet religion. Akbar's only son and successor, Jahangir, did join in Hindu ceremonies and, like his father, entertained himself by hosting debates with Christian missionaries and Hindu and Muslim scholars. Yet even though the tolerant dogma of the Sikhs was not unlike that of Akbar it was under Jahangir's orders that Guru Arjan, after he refused to pay a fine for breaking a law forbidding the proselytizing of Muslims and for keeping Islamic and

Hindu teachings together in his collection of spiritual readings, was tortured to death, becoming Sikhism's first martyr. Also he targeted a group of Hindus for marrying Muslim women and pressuring them to convert.[6]

Even though Jahangir had kicked off the beginnings of a new religion's oppression, he was not nearly as committed to Islamic orthodoxy as his descendant Aurangzeb, who ascended to the throne in 1658. A strictly orthodox Sunni Muslim, Aurangzeb was fastidious, consulting with only Islamic authorities on spiritual matters and indulging in neither opium nor wine. A Portuguese observer noted that "for a long time he pretended to be a faquir (*faqir*), a holy mendicant, by which he renounced the world, gave up all claim to the crown, and was content to pass his life in prayers and mortifications."[7] Aurangzeb was determined to prove his dedication to Islam by striking against any and all non-Islamic practices. A vast Hindu temple at Mathura was razed and replaced with a mosque, its bejeweled idols buried under the steps of another mosque. Also he revived the *jizya* despite opposition from even Muslim bureaucrats. Just as they feared, the tax inspired a mass protest in the capital of Delhi by Hindu merchants and bankers, to which Aurangzeb only responded by unleashing elephants and horses on the helpless crowd.[8]

There were more devastating strikes against Akbar's dream of a spiritually unified empire. Across the empire officials were commanded to demolish Sikh houses of worship, *gurdwaras*. The ninth Sikh guru, Tegh Bahadur, and five disciples were arrested for the crime of converting Muslims and for blasphemy. Carried to Delhi in chains, the guru was offered a chance to live if he converted to Islam or else performed a miracle or two to demonstrate he truly was a messenger of God. Guru Bahadur declined to do either and was promptly beheaded. The next guru, Bahadur's son, Gobind Singh, declared himself the last living guru and reformed the Sikhs from a religious order into a group of spiritual warriors, the *khalsa*. Vowing to never cut their hair and to always carry a sword and an iron bracelet, the Sikhs of the new *khalsa* vowed to protect the poor and people of all faiths and creeds from tyranny and oppression. In the words of Guru Gobind Singh himself, "between the Hindus and Muslims you will act as a bridge."[9] By ordering the death of one man, the emperor had made a devout and principled enemy of his mission to impose one faith.

An even bigger thorn on the side of the empire lay to the south in the Deccan Plateau of central and southern India. There a young nobleman of the Hindu Marathi people named Shivaji was leading devastating expeditions, robbing and seizing territory from the slowly collapsing sultanate of Bijapur. In one encounter that quickly became the stuff of legend, a Bijapur general tried to strangle Shivaji in his tent after negotiations broke down spectacularly, but Shivaji disemboweled his attacker with a secreted iron claw in his clothes and managed to give the signal for his troops hidden around the enemy camp to attack. Unfortunately, the weaker the sultanate grew, the more irresistibly Shivaji was drawn toward the Mughal Empire, which itself had been gleefully gobbling up the Deccan. Part king and part guerrilla terrorist, on the night of April 5, 1663, Shivaji and his men broke into the palace of the governor of the Mughals' Deccan territories and assassinated him and his family. Just half a year later, Shivaji and his forces looted Surat, the wealthiest port in western India. Overnight Shivaji had made himself the Mughal Empire's most wanted man. Adding spice to his heroic outlaw image was an episode that followed after Aurangzeb agreed to make peace and accept fealty from Shivaji but apparently snubbed Shivaji with childish deliberateness. When Shivaji vehemently protested, he was caught and imprisoned but soon escaped Mughal territory disguised as a Hindu monk.

However, Sivaji was not a Hindu militant by modern standards. He had trusted generals and officials who were Muslims and formed alliances with Muslim neighbors, even Aurangzeb's rebellious son Muhammad Akbar. Nonetheless, by June 1674, Sivaji had declared himself a Hindu king, in direct defiance of Mughal authority. "Insurgency against Mughal rule had acquired a new rallying point," notes historian John F. Richards.[10] Elsewhere in the empire there were serious Hindu revolts, where mosques were destroyed and officials collecting the *jiziya* tax were beaten with their beards plucked out.[11] These bouts of resistance were often crushed, but they raged on for many years and added to the massive drain on the empire's sources, which were already sinking from the endless wars in the Deccan. Shivaji himself made the connection when he personally wrote a letter to the emperor himself, rebuking him for bringing back the *jiziya* tax and for forgetting that Hindu and Muslim worshiped the same godhead according to their own customs.[12]

In March 1680, Shivaji died from dysentery. The loss of the daring and brilliant founder of the kingdom proved a catastrophe, especially since Aurangzeb had become obsessed with annexing more of the Deccan. Shivaji's son and heir Shambhaji was defeated and hacked to death, his remains fed to dogs. The Deccan sultanates of Bijapur and Golconda were added to the Mughal domains and the prodigal son Muhammad Akbar had been forced to escape to Persia. It should have been Aurangzeb's crowning achievement, but instead the emperor found himself fighting a guerrilla war against what was left of the Maratha kingdom. At home, he had alienated even his Muslim officials through his stubbornness on religious issues and the depressing fact that he had stamped out two fellow Muslim states with dubious justifications. From 1681 to 1706, the emperor had sacrificed the luxuries of Delhi to live in a series of war camps until, finally, worn out mentally and physically, he retired to the town of Ahmadnagar, still near his agonizing Deccan frontier, where he died a year later.

With the passing of Aurangzeb came the deluge. A succession crisis battered the empire as Aurangzeb's three sons wrestled against each other for the throne. This may not have been enough to erode the foundations of the empire—after all, the Mughals had a long, colorful history of bitter warfare between brothers and even between father and son—but at the same time another Sikh revolt erupted and the Marathas continued to loot Mughal towns with impunity. By 1757, when Britain's East India Tea Company seized control of the rich city of Benghal all but officially, arguably the true beginning of British colonization of India, the Mughal Empire was already a decaying edifice.

It should be made clear that the rot was not only caused by Aurangzeb's religious bigotry. Historians have also illuminated the shoddy tax collection policies that brought about a decaying system that hemorrhaged revenue and gave too much power to self-serving local officials.[13] Still, it seems the collapse of Akbar's dream left a void at the heart of the Mughal Empire. The sores may have broken out regardless, but the campaign to dismantle the ancient legacy of Indian pluralism aggravated them exponentially.

THE OTTOMAN EMPIRE

Liberty's Call

If one travels to the Mani Peninsula in southern Greece, one of the lesser-known historic sites is the small city of Areopoli. Serendipitously named for the Greek god of war, today Areopoli takes credit for being the cradle of the Greek War of Independence. In a small square, across from a church with an old-fashioned terracotta Byzantine roof, there is a twentieth-century plaque depicting an Archangel Michael presenting a laurel wreath for an unseen champion. An inscription declares to passersby, "From this historic square was launched the great uprising under the leadership of Petrobey, 17 March 1821." Three towns other than Areopoli make similar claims, yet none are wrong. Despite the multiple claims, in Greece today the official anniversary remains March 25, 1821, conveniently coinciding with the Greek Orthodox Church's celebration of the Annunciation to the *theotokos*, when the Virgin Mary was told that she would give birth to the son of God.

As much as the Greek rebels against the Islamic rule of the Ottoman Empire would invoke their faith, the Greek push for independence was not born out of a crusade for a free Christian state in the Balkans and Asia Minor or nostalgia for the Byzantine Empire, even though dreams of Greek soldiers marching into old Constantinople would linger in the minds of Greek leaders for many decades to come.

Instead it was stoked by the eighteenth-century fad for all things classical Greece; by the seeping of the Enlightenment into Greece through
translated works and trade networks with the French; and finally by
the revolution that began to unfold in France by the pivotal year of
1789. When they broke away from Ottoman rule the Greeks were
not looking back to the days their ancestors claimed the legacy of universal empire but toward a future of separate and independent nations
built around different languages, cultures, and ethnicities. In a sense,
the Greek War of Independence signaled not only the fall of the Ottoman Empire but the fall of *all* empires.

To be sure, at the beginning the Greek Orthodox Church tried to
repress the stirrings of rebellion. In 1798, well after the full blow of
the French Revolution against political and social tradition had
echoed across Europe, Patriarch Anthimos of Jerusalem issued a
scathing decree, holding up the four centuries of Ottoman rule over
Greece as God's unquestionable will: "The Almighty Lord puts into
the heart of the Sultan of these Ottomans an inclination to keep free
the religious beliefs of our Orthodox faith and, as a work of
supererogation, to protect them, even to the point of occasionally
chastising Christians who deviate from their faith, in order that they
have always before their eyes the fear of God. . . . Brothers, do not be
led astray from the path of salvation; but as you have always with
bravery and steadfastness trampled underfoot the wiles of the devil,
so now also close your ears and give no hearing to these newly ap-
pearing hopes of liberty 'for now salvation is nearer to us'"[1] Unfortunately for such conservative sentiments, it was too little too late. As
early as the 1750s, the writings of Enlightenment celebrities such as
Voltaire, Montesquieu, and Rousseau were being translated into
Greek, bringing with them the idea of legal rights innate to all people
and not granted by a government, skepticism of religious dogma and
the authority of priests, and the radical concept that regimes only rule
by the consent of the governed. The passion of Enlightenment celebrities for ancient Greece seeped back to the old land of Socrates itself
too. One French play, *Harmodius and Aristogeiton*, was translated
into Greek, telling the story of two ancient Greek heroes who lost
their lives in the attempt to overthrow Hippias, a sixth-century BCE
tyrant of Athens.[2] Then there was the French Revolution itself, which
not only asserted the right of the French to have representation in
their government but in its most radical stage gleefully toppled the

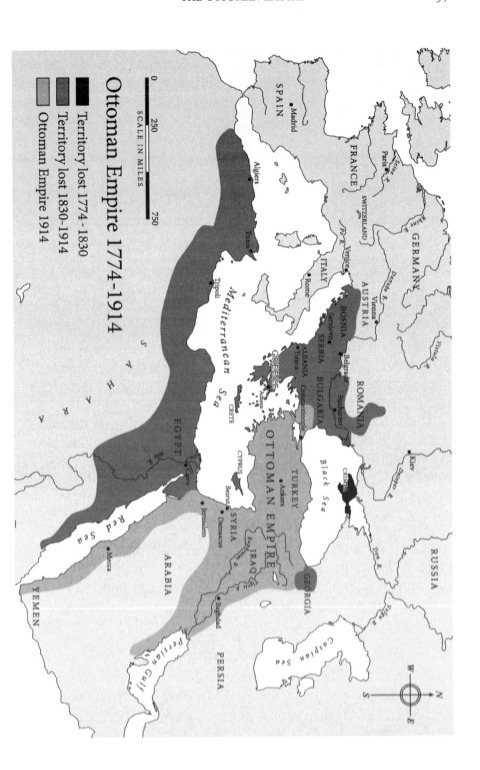

Ottoman Empire 1774-1914

Territory lost 1774-1830
Territory lost 1830-1914
Ottoman Empire 1914

SCALE IN MILES
0   250   750

age-old institutions of the monarchy and the church, a development that could not be comforting to either the sultan or the patriarch.

Even without the existential threat of enlightened rebels, the Ottomans had enough motive to want to cling to Greece. Besides lying near the capital of Istanbul, Greece had a symbolic value to the Ottoman sultans. It was the Ottoman conquest of Constantinople that represented the ultimate triumph of the Turks, staking out their claim to not only be the true leaders of Islam but the heirs to the Roman Empire. It was not just an empty brag. At its height, the Ottoman Empire's borders were broad enough they encompassed many of the most precious sites in the history of Western civilization, including Jerusalem, Mecca, Baghdad, Athens, Alexandria, and of course Constantinople. It was Süleyman the Magnificent (r .1520–1566) who renovated Mecca, refurbishing the city's water supply and building new minarets for the Great Mosque. Before him, Mehmed II (r. 1451–1481), the conqueror of Constantinople himself, visited the purported site of ancient Troy like a tourist, looking for the legendary tombs of the heroes Achilles and Ajax, and later had special copies of Homer's *Iliad* and an old Roman biography of Alexander the Great made for his library.[3]

True to their world-spanning ambitions, the Ottoman sultans both embraced their Islamic heritage and accepted the Christian and Jewish communities in their midst—for the most part. Christians and Jews were barred from the military, to the point they were not allowed to carry weapons, but under the Ottomans' *millet* system they were granted judicial independence. They had to pay a special tax in lieu of their military service, but their houses of worship and holy sites were officially protected from the whims of bigoted mobs and local officials. The early sultans themselves took their responsibilities as rulers over members of all three Abrahamaic faiths seriously. In 1463, Mehmed II formally promised to protect the rights of the Franciscan monasteries in Bosnia in what would become one of the world's oldest surviving documents on religious freedom. When the monarchs of Spain and Portugal expelled all Jews from their territories, Sultan Beyazid II (r. 1481–1512) issued an invitation for the exiles to settle in Ottoman lands, although they were not allowed to make Istanbul their new home. As such a ban in the midst of an otherwise warm invitation suggests, the relationship between the faith of the empire and the religions of the minorities occasionally ran aground on rocky shores. As the empire's religious heads became more dogmatic in the late sixteenth century, Jews and Christians were legally banned from wearing certain kinds of swank apparel. In 1660, when a fire decimated a rich port district of Istanbul, authorities blamed the local Jews for starting the fire and were unceremoniously exiled from the neighborhoods, a step the sultan did not reverse.[4]

Still, for Orthodox Christians in the Balkans, life under the Turks was vastly preferable to being under the rule of the militantly Catholic Hapsburg dynasty of Austria and Hungary. Certain groups of Jews would remain loyal to the empire until its very end. Nonetheless, once the seemingly invincible war machine of the Ottomans faltered while attacking Vienna in 1683, Christian unity became a potent rallying cry. Before the epoch-making siege of Vienna, the Ottoman Empire was already malnourished from an obsolete and inefficient taxation system and was further starved by massive inflation striking across all of Europe. Meanwhile the sultans, long accustomed to hiding away from the world amid the luxuries of Topkapı Palace, were at the mercy of their own elite Janissary corps, liable to be deposed at will if they displeased them in the slightest. After the siege, the empire found itself embroiled in a fifteen-year war against the Christian powers of eastern Europe, ending with the degrading Treaty of Karlowitz in 1699 where, for the first time, the Ottoman Empire had no choice but to relinquish large slices of territory to its Christian neighbors.

Sultan Selim III (r. 1789–1807) tried to learn from the Ottoman Empire's rivals to the west and created a modern army, one that even managed to stand up to Napoleon Bonaparte. For his trouble, he was deposed in a revolt, imprisoned, and eventually assassinated. When his nephew came to the throne as Mahmud II (r. 1808–1839), he had to cope with the somber lesson learned too late by his uncle that extensive Western-style reforms would inspire deadly resistance. Meanwhile he found that his inheritance was a wheezing empire burdened with a corrupt, archaic army and ambitious provincial governors who were, day by day, grasping for more independence.

A forceful, intelligent man, all too conscious of the empire's problems, Mahmud II possessed just the right mix of boldness and caution. He seized on the first opportunity to violently and utterly smash the Janissary corps and restructured the army, yet rarely took a single step without ensuring he had popular support behind him.[5] Unfortunately, Russia, whose czars had long nourished dreams of one day taking

Constantinople itself, was not slow in exploiting the Ottoman Empire's convulsions. During one war with the Turks, the Russians threw their considerable weight behind a series of Serbian uprisings that first erupted in 1805. The Turks were forced to surrender a great deal of autonomy to Serbia, up to the point where the sultan felt that in order to hang on to Serbia at all, he had to agree in 1817 to formally recognize a native, Milos Obrenovi, as the prince of Serbia. It was a concession that saved the empire's historic frontier against the Christian West, but it left a key question hanging: why shouldn't other Christian peoples living under the yoke of the sultan also at least have leaders of their own faith and race?

Even so, the revolt in Greece took Mahmud II and his ministers by surprise, especially given the patriarch in Constantinople's support of the sultan and the backing the Ottomans enjoyed from the Phanariots, wealthy Greek merchant families who were often entrusted with administrative posts around the Balkans.[6] Also the Ottomans had already decisively crushed a Greek revolt in 1770, the Orlov Revolt, so named for the involvement of the Russian diplomat Count Orlov, but it was quickly and effortlessly snuffed out when Russia declined to support the rebels. In the end, it seemed only to prove to the Ottomans that the only menaces they had to fear were from the outside.

However, the seed for revolution had already been planted in 1814, when a small band of Greeks in the Russian port city of Odessa, home to a large Greek expatriate community, swore together to uphold a new secret society, the *Filiki Eteria* ("Friendly Society"), consecrated to the goal of overthrowing the Ottomans and founding a new Byzantine Empire. Liberation of the homeland was dear to this society's identity. New members would swear by a "Great Oath" that "by the bitter tears which for so many centuries have been shed by thy unhappy children, by my own tears which I am pouring forth at this very moment; I swear by the future liberty of my countrymen, that I consecrate myself wholly to thee; that hence forward thou shall be the cause and object of my thoughts, thy name the guide of my actions, and thy happiness the recompense of my labours."[7]

In April 1820, the Filiki Eteria elected a prominent leader that had experience fighting as a general for Russia, Alexander Ypsilantis, a scion of a Phanariot family that could boast of having one of their own appointed prince of Moldavia by the Turkish government. Confident that he would be supported by Czar Alexander I of Russia, Ypsilantis dreamed of all Balkan Christians tearing off the Turkish yoke. At a monastery in the Romanian city of Iaşi, he issued a proclamation urging all Orthodox Christians in Ottoman territories to rise up. The patriarch of the Orthodox Church and the Orthodox Synod rigorously condemned Ypsilantis, going so far as to excommunicate him, but it was not enough. Czar Alexander I was still reluctant to sign off on an all-out war, but the would-be liberators found much more eager allies in the Mali region, long a hotbed of resistance to the Turks. By the winter of 1821, rebels for the Greek cause captured four key fortresses and had even scored a victory against the Ottoman navy. At the end of the year, an assembly met at Epídauros and pieced together a constitution for a new Greek nation. The document declared, "In the name of the Holy and Indivisible Trinity: the Greek nation, under the fearful domination of the Ottomans, unable to bear the heavy and unexampled yoke of tyranny and having with great sacrifices thrown it off, declares today, through its lawful representatives gathered in the National Assembly, before God and man, its political existence and independence." Further it established a senate and laid down that the future Greek state would adopt Greek Orthodox as the state religion and would guarantee civil rights such as security of property.[8] However, the Greeks themselves were hardly united, and different associations claiming to represent the "Greek nation" soon spread and fought among themselves.[9]

Divisions aside, the Greek revolt quickly drew international sympathy, as it helpfully coincided with both the ambitions of the powers of Europe to scrounge some advantages from the receding Ottoman Empire and the liberal mood of intellectuals and some politicians in the wake of the collapse of Napoleon's imperial ambitions and the reestablishment of Europe's old order. From his retreat in Pisa, Percy Shelley in 1821 declared his sympathy for the cause of Greek liberty through the poem *Hellas*, where Mahmud is disturbed by a dream where freedom returns to Greece. The artist Eugène Delacroix fanned the flames of popular sentiment when he displayed at the Salon of 1824 in Paris a painting depicting the slaughter, enslavement, and forced migration of tens of thousands of Greek civilians on the island of Chios on April 11, 1822.[10] Organizations for the express purpose of raising money for the Greek cause popped up across Europe, channeling individual contributions, small and large. As far away as Louisville, Kentucky, a barber humbly offered up a whole week's income.[11] For some, empathy for the Greeks inspired action. Many young men from Britain to Poland left for Greece to join the fighting or at least to act as not-so-neutral observers. Among them was the poet Lord Byron, whose artistic bad-boy celebrity became inexorable with the Greek cause among the British public. His friend Count Peter Gamba recounted Byron's words to him: "I have not, however, come here in search of adventures, but to assist in the regeneration of a nation, whose very debasement makes it more honourable to become their friend."[12] Lord Byron would die at Messolonghi on April 19, 1824, from a fever, falling ill just as he was about to participate in a military siege. His adopted nation would remember him by, among other things, naming a suburb of Athens "Vyronas."

Reports of atrocities committed by victorious Greek soldiers threatened to undo the neat narrative of an oppressed, noble people fighting against bloodthirsty heathens. When the city of Tripolitsa fell to the Greeks on October 5, 1821, the city's twenty thousand Turkish inhabitants were slaughtered, along with much of the city's Jewish population, which was just a precursor to later massacres against the Turks that would erupt in Athens and the Aegean Islands. No doubt news of such atrocities at least dampened passion for the Greek cause, but others justified it as retribution for centuries of tyranny by the inhuman Turks. This was the view of the otherwise liberal and humanitarian Mary Shelley, who in a letter acknowledged that the Greek side also unleashed cruelties but quickly added that such atrocities were merely the price paid by a tyrant's people.[13]

From the Ottoman view, losing so much territory that was practically within arm's reach of Istanbul was unthinkable. Mahmud also must have been painfully aware, to the point of paranoia, of how a major Orthodox Christian uprising would be an open invitation for a Russian invasion, and quite likely the dismantling of the entire empire. Even though the patriarch Gregorios V had condemned Alexander Ypsilantis, Mahmud became convinced Gregorios was part of an Orthodox conspiracy being orchestrated at the behest of Russian officials. On Easter Sunday 1821, Turkish soldiers dragged Gregorios to the gate of the Phanar quarter, a majority Greek district in Istanbul from which the Phanariot families took their name, and hanged him from the staple above the entrance, leaving the priest to slowly choke to death. For three days his body was left hanging by decree, forcing his successor to have to push it aside whenever he entered the eccle-

Le Massacre de Chios by Eugène Delacroix, 1824. (*Louvre Museum*)

siastical palace. Three other bishops and two priests were also hanged. Gregorios's corpse was finally handed over to a group of Jews, who dragged it through the streets and cast it, weighted with stones, into the waters of the Golden Horn. Mobs inflamed with government-sanctioned hatred rioted, storming into Orthodox churches and ripping apart the throne of the patriarch. When his body was found with some of its vestments intact, it was taken as a miraculous sign and he was buried like a saint. Ironically, in the end Gregorios became a potent martyr for the very cause he had condemned.[14]

Mahmud's other desperate gambit was appealing to Mehmet Ali Pasha, who governed Egypt and Sudan in the sultan's name but had carved out his own kingdom, which he molded using French-style economic and political reforms. The savvy Pasha demanded jurisdiction over the entire island of Crete as the price of his intervention, a degrading insult the sultan had little choice but to swallow. Mehmet's son Ibrahim landed at the head of ten thousand men, trained in modern Western warfare and armed with the latest artillery technology, on the shores of the southern Peloponnese. The finale of such a clash was not hard to protect. Although the fires of rebellion kept burning, by 1826 Mahmud could finally go to bed assured that the uprising would soon only be an unpleasant but easily forgotten little historical fact like the revolt of 1770.[15]

A good part of why Mahmud could sleep without that much stress was that so far the powers of Europe kept their support for the Greek revolt strictly moral. Even Russia was reluctant to lend a hand to fellow Orthodox Christians revolting against their heathen yet lawful sovereign. After all, the Polish in Russian lands had similar ancient claims on their own independent homeland, and the czar's Muslim subjects in the Crimea and central Asia could just as easily find inspiration for freedom from a Greek victory as any Christian subjects of the sultan. In Britain, however, Philhellene (pro-Greek) feeling was starting to prevail in diplomatic and political circles. Meanwhile the new Czar Nicholas I, who had been crowned in 1825, was in spite of his own reactionary inclinations more open to the argument that expanding the Russian Empire southward was worth even the cost of encouraging revolution. Still, he approved of negotiations mediated by France and Britain that would have resolved the rebellion by making Greece an autonomous nation-state that kept the sultan as its crowned head, much like Serbia. However, Mahmud rebuffed these diplomatic efforts and decided to stake everything on the power of Ibrahim's forces and the continued reluctant neutrality of the West.

He lost the wager, and badly. In July 1827, Britain, France, and Russia signed a treaty agreeing to use military force to push the Ottoman Empire into an armistice. At the Bay of Navarino on October 20, 1827, a combined fleet of Russian, British, and French ships wiped out two-thirds of the Egyptian-Turkish navy in only three hours.[16] Mahmud struck back by closing the Dardanelles strait between Asia and Europe to all foreign ships, but this only gave a pretext for all-out war Czar Nicholas could not resist. Backed into a corner by the Russian bear, Mahmud agreed to negotiate before a war with Russia could make his position even worse and signed the Treaty of Adrianople on September 14, 1829. Luckily for Mahmud, Britain and France had no desire to see Russian soldiers march unimpeded across the Balkans either, so the only territory the Ottoman Empire lost to Russia was what remained of the empire's holdings in Georgia. Yet the time to let Greece stay within the empire as a semi-independent state had long past.

The new and fully independent Greece, whose borders were fixed by further negotiations concluded in May 1832, was smaller than the Greece of today, holding only territory up to the modern city of Arta. It was also a painful birth for a new nation, burdened with war-torn cities, displaced refugees, and widespread poverty. Even though according to legend a Greek delegation arrived in England to try in vain to find the long-lost descendants of the Palaiologoi, the Byzantine Empire's last dynasty, the powers of Europe decided to import a foreign king for Greece: Otto, a Bavarian prince. A Philhellene himself, one of Otto's first acts was moving the capital of the kingdom to Athens, then just a town of a few thousand people, and commissioning an archaeological survey. In a way, it was a demonstration that Greece owed the support for its independence not just to the forces of nationalism unleashed by events around the dawn of the nineteenth century but also to their homeland's reputation as the cradle of Western civilization.

As for the Ottoman Empire itself, Mahmud had been ruthless but not at all misguided in trying to cling to Greece. Its loss caused a break in the foundations of his empire that could never be repaired. Just one year after the Treaty of Adrianople was signed, France invaded the Ottomans' territory in Algeria, allegedly on the pretext that the bey of Algeria struck a French diplomat with a fly whisk. In Egypt, Mehmet Pasha demanded compensation from the sultan for the devastation of his navy in Greece, and the entire province of Syria would suit him just nicely. Mahmud refused, and Mehmet Pasha's impulsive son Ibrahim marched on the Levant and Syria. Once more France and Britain stepped in, finding the Ottoman Empire's continued existence, however feeble, better than the alternative of an engorged Russia. No doubt choking back his rage, Mahmud still had to recognize Mehmet Pasha's rule over Egypt and Sudan, in exchange for nothing more than Mehmet acknowledging the sultan's sovereignty and the governorship of Adana, Damascus, and Aleppo.

In the decades to come, matters would only go from worse to worse. By the late nineteenth century, the Ottoman Empire had lost all of its former provinces in eastern Europe to independence movements or had to sign them away to its neighbors, except for Macedonia and the Marmara region immediately west of Istanbul. If the last sultans of the empire could take any satisfaction at all from events, it was from the *schadenfreude* that the forces awakened by Greek independence haunted their adversaries as well, in the guises of the independence movements launched by the Polish, the Irish, and the Slavic peoples of Austria-Hungary.

THE RUSSIAN EMPIRE

Bloody Sunday

O n the afternoon of November 1, 1894, a nervous, reserved, and remarkably unimaginative and unambitious young man was proclaimed the emperor and autocrat of all the Russias. Nikolai Alexandrovich Romanov, now titled Nicholas II, had become the absolute ruler of an empire that had a population of 126 million by 1897 and covered 22,800,000 kilometers of territory in 1866. In stark contrast to some of his colorful, eccentric, and unashamedly imperious predecessors, Nicholas II was more suited to be a quiet, stereotypically Victorian middle-class family man than a Russian czar. "The last tsar possessed personal qualities that many have admired, such as modesty, self-discipline, faith, patriotism, a deep sense of duty, and devotion to his family," the historians Nicholas V. Riasanovsky and Mark D. Steinberg write on the man who would be the last of the czars. "But these virtues mattered little in a situation that demanded strength, adaptability, and vision."[1] Nicholas was not blind to his own flaws, and it was said that early on in his reign he craved abdication.[2] He was not wrong to want out of his job. His reign would oversee a series of catastrophes that would shake one of the largest empires in history to its core, ultimately doom Nicholas and his beloved family, and help inaugurate the troubled, nearly apocalyptic history of the twentieth century. Perhaps the worst of these disasters, if not the one that sealed the fate of both Nicholas and Russia, was when Nicholas turned a public relations opportunity any politician would sell their soul for into a horrific blunder.

Nicholas II's inheritance was an empire with a manifest destiny wrapped in religion and nationality. The Russians proudly counted themselves as the inheritors of the kingdom of Kievan Rus', which was influential enough that it arranged a marriage alliance in the eleventh century with far-away France and, it was said, the Russian princess Anna knew how to sign her name on the marriage contract while her illiterate husband, King Henri I of France, could only scratch out a cross. Who was the civilized country and who was the backward kingdom then? Dynastic squabbles and Mongolian invasions shattered Kievan Rus' in the thirteenth century, but a principality centered on the city of Moscow threw off the Mongolian yoke and over time absorbed their Slavic neighbors. After Ivan the Terrible (r. 1547–1584) came to the throne, he invaded the Tatar and Muslim majority territories of Kazan and Astrakahn, turning what was an Orthodox Slavic kingdom into a multiethnic and multidenominational empire. Ivan himself put the seal on this transformation by declaring that Moscow was the Third Rome, now that Constantinople was in Islamic hands, and that he was the new Caesar, or "czar."

Isolated from Europe by the Mongolian conquests and practicing an interpretation of Christianity foreign to the Christians of the West, Russia was, for all the great wealth and territory the czars came to command, seen even by some Russians themselves as a land locked away in the past. Czar Peter the Great (r. 1682–1725) was actually not the first member of the Russian elite to have a fascination with western and central European culture and society, but he became the first czar to rip down Russia's Byzantine past and among its shreds erect a nation modeled on Western modernity, no matter what the Russian people actually had to say about it. Going about the task with his characteristic manic gusto, Peter forced the sons of the nobility to take education trips abroad, established newspapers and academies, and even mandated that men, except clergy, could not wear beards and that women had to wear more revealing clothing in French and German fashions.

What Peter the Great bequeathed to his successors was an unsolvable conundrum. With one hand, they beckoned their subjects toward a shining modernity, where at least the elites will be properly educated

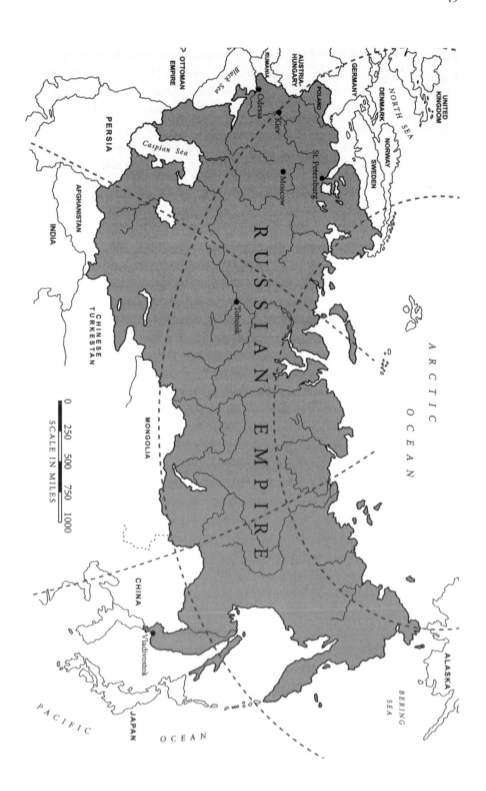

and society would keep pace with the latest technological, scientific, and social advancements. In the other hand, they held the old-fashioned scepter of absolute rule, denying the creation of any kind of true representative body and even keeping serfdom a fact of life for countless Russian peasants. So it was that Catherine II "the Great" (r. 1762–1796) could correspond with Enlightenment heroes Voltaire and Diderot and was praised for legislative feats like establishing the first compulsory schools for the children of landowners and the *bourgeoisie*. At the same time, Catherine casually handed over thousands of peasant serfs to her lovers once she tired of them as part of their retirement package.

By the nineteenth century, Russia found itself with an intelligentsia and a class of students nourished on the liberal and radical doctrines pouring in from western Europe after the French Revolution. The so-called "enlightened despotism" exemplified by Peter I and Catherine II was less appetizing in the shadow of the ruins of the Bastille. In even moderate circles across Europe, progress was seen more as something best manifested through the will of the masses, rather than the will of even a benevolent and well-educated monarch.

The Russian environment had become seismically fragile. In spite of the czars' ambition to fashion a modern and urban society, the Russian middle class remained small and anemic, gaining precious little sustenance from the crony capitalism that was rapidly evolving in a now-industrializing Russia. While more Russians were turning to the new factories for a meager wage, the population remained largely rural, agricultural, and uneducated, with a huge percentage of Russians bound to the land as serfs by the power of law. Although serfdom became subjected to more restrictions, like not being allowed in most of the new territories Russia had seized since Catherine II's day, in 1835 a little over half of the entire male population were still serfs, a number of over 11 million that overshoots the size of the population living in New York City today.[3] The liberal intelligentsia could not connect to this populace, who all might as well have lived in a foreign country of their own, nor could they expect much from a government that still preached as if the French Revolution never happened, that the czars were only accountable to God, not even to their own people. "Isolated from both government and people," Hugh Seton-Watson writes, the intelligentsia "pursued their thoughts to their logical conclusions, unaffected by experience of power."[4]

This uneasiness over reconciling autocracy with modernity was not unknown to the czars themselves. When he was still just the young heir to the throne, Czar Alexander I (r. 1801–1825) spent his days tormented by the alluring thought of forsaking the backwards and oppressive country his family ruled and embarking on a quiet life as a private gentleman in quiet, enlightened Switzerland. Instead he ended up rather accidentally becoming Europe's champion of conservatism and royalism against the armies of Napoleon. Disillusioned with how the French Revolution seemed to him to only spawn anarchy, massacres, and wars, after the Napoleonic Wars were finally over Alexander retreated from the prospect of serious political reform into a private realm of religion and mysticism.

His nephew and namesake, Alexander II (r. 1855–1881), was the next to submit himself to the cause of reform and made perhaps the most ambitious move since Peter the Great: the emancipation of Russia's serfs. Catherine II herself and her successors had each openly acknowledged that serfdom would eventually have to be done away with, if only because the economic and pragmatic reasons for doing so were just as compelling as the humanitarian motive insisted upon by a majority of intellectuals since the heyday of the Enlightenment, but all were dissuaded for one reason or another from this ultimate course. Ironically, it was Alexander II's ultraconservative father, Nicholas I, who had taken the furthest step by outlawing the sale of individual serfs. Announcing to the Assembly of the Nobility, "If we don't give the peasants freedom from above, they'll take it from below." Alexander II made the peasants' liberation the first major act of his reign, enacting it in January 1861.

However, it was no simple unlocking of a jail cell. Even though Alexander understood—in a way that few would-be reformers even today do—that freedom weighed down with poverty can only be worthless, in order to appease the landowners he had to limit the amount of land that would be allocated to the serfs and, worse, the former serfs would be expected to pay a reimbursement to their ex-owners. This stern reality clashed with peasant fantasies that this was the opening salvo in a campaign by the czar to sweep away all the corrupt landowners and officials who made the peasants' lives miserable for their own profit. Peasant unrest, put down by bullets, was the terrible but inevitable epilogue.[5] Twenty years later, an anarchist's bomb in Saint Petersburg would kill "the Liberator," just as he had in mind plans to establish a new elected representative assembly. It was a tragedy that only sanctified the prevailing reactionary opinion that in a tumultuous country like Russia reforms would only embolden those who wanted to tear the entire world down.

Just as the imperial rulers of Russia themselves took a hard right, the young, educated, and alienated became drawn to socialism and anarchism, especially those students and agitators who had been exiled from Russia. In spite of the impregnable wall between them and the still devout and often illiterate peasants, they glimpsed potential in the freshly liberated serf, who seemed to live out a primitive form of socialism though the practice of communal land ownership in their villages.[6] The peasantry, even the freed serfs who quickly found themselves legally exploited after emancipation by their former owners, were still overwhelmingly loyal to the czar, blaming their troubles on rapacious ministers and aristocrats who prevented the czar from knowing the true hardships of his people. When a radical named Stefanovich tried to win over peasants in the Chigirin district of the Kiev province, he felt he had to earn their loyalty by producing a forged imperial edict blessing any attempt by the people to rise up against the nobles, the bureaucrats, and the church. Over nine hundred peasants swore to fight and were organized like soldiers in a professional army. A single drunken indiscretion exposed the plot, and the whole plan was squashed when mass arrests were carried out in August 1877. However, the following May supporters broke Stefanovich and two of his co-conspirators out of their Kiev prison.[7]

Another contradiction that had become part of the empire's core was that it was a kingdom that proudly boasted its Orthodox Christian and Russian credentials even though large populations of the people living within its borders were neither. Since the eighteenth century Russia had embarked on conquests even Ivan the Terrible probably did not envision, spreading aggressively into central Asia and northern Europe and helping itself to a generous portion of Poland. At the dawn of the nineteenth century, less than half of the Russian Empire's people actually spoke Russian as their native tongue.[8] It did not help that later administrators heartily embraced European nationalism, incompatible as it was with the multinational essence of the empire, and forcefully tried to promote the Russian language and bring local self-determination to a heel. For just one example, Finland had been a peaceful and loyal part of the Russian Empire—at least until the fateful moment "Russification" was introduced by clueless officials in the first decade of the twentieth century.[9]

Such was the unwieldy, paradoxical empire Nicholas II had been born to rule. It also happened to be home to a young priest with an almost pathological obsession with working for the rural poor. Georgy Gapon came from a family of relatively affluent peasants living in modern-day Ukraine. A bright student, Gapon felt called to the priesthood, but becoming an avid reader of Leo Tolstoy and witnessing firsthand alcoholic, selfish priests steered him toward liberalism and social justice, especially principled pacifism, welfare for the poor, and even battling the corruption and greed of the church. This obsession fueled Gapon's own instability. His disappointment with the church manifested in illness and depression, culminating in an outburst where he threatened to kill a teacher and then himself. In the end, he received poor marks on behavior, which was just enough to cut short his aspirations. It was only through the intervention of a friend in the church hierarchy that Gapon became ordained and was granted a post as a priest in Poltava. There he became a popular priest overnight, cherished for his openness and informality.[10] An idea of Gapon's unique approach might be gleamed in a police record from later in Gapon's career when he became involved with the workers of St. Petersburg: ". . . for example, he would go along with workers on a boat ride. They would settle on some grassy island with food and wine; soon singing would begin, and finally they would dance. Father Gapon picking up the skirts of his robe, excelled with his usual vigor."[11]

Joining the St. Petersburg Theological Seminary, Gapon continued to be plagued by poor physical and mental health but was dedicated to helping with the plight of the city's industrial workers. This alone brought him to the attention of the city's governor and police force, always watchful for signs of inciters. Russia was notorious for its extensive and active police, always on the watch for radicals and to enforce laws against unlicensed public lectures and unapproved gatherings of more than a dozen people. However, the police were also proverbial for their corruption. The police chief of Ekaterinoslav, Rittmeister Krementski, was praised by higher-ups for managing to shut down three or four illegal presses each year. He received a stream of promotions and accolades until it was revealed he had set up all the presses himself.[12] The fact that Gapon chose to thoroughly cooperate with such a system has led to speculation that he was a spy and even a provocateur, but Gapon himself made no secret of his ties to the police, and such an arrangement was practically essential for anyone seeking to do outreach to the disadvantaged masses.

Gapon did have leftist and even socialist sympathies, but he was still a monarchist and in many other ways a traditionalist, keeping faith in the spirit of old Russia and not the revolutionary fantasies of the communists and anarchists. This was the philosophy that guided his decision to found a trade union devoted to St. Petersburg's mill and factory workers and improving not only their lot in life but their morals. "Essentially the basic idea is to build a nest among the factory and mill workers where Rus', a truly Russian spirit, would prevail," Gapon himself wrote. "From thence healthy and self-sacrificing fledglings could fly forth to defend their tsar and country and aid their fellow workers."[13] In fact, Russia seemed to need such an old-fashioned revitalization more than ever.

Even into the twentieth century, Czar Alexander II would prove to be only one of several high-profile victims of assassinations by radicals. Two of Nicholas's ministers of the interior, Dmitri Sipyagin and Vyacheslav von Plehve, were assassinated in succession. Nicholas II's own uncle, the arch-conservative Grand Duke Sergei Alexandrovich, would be murdered in February 1905 by a bomb thrown into his carriage. The already foreboding atmosphere was made positively toxic when Nicholas made the ill-advised decision to start a war with Japan over Manchuria. Instead of an easy and fast victory over a backwards island nation, Russia was instead fighting against a formidable country that had industrialized itself in reaction to just the type of Western aggression Russia was indulging in. As the war dragged on and the public's mood shifted from patriotic enthusiasm to dour bitterness, the liberal minister of the interior, Prince Pyotr Sviatopolk-Mirsky, pushed Nicholas in the direction of appeasement. On December 12, 1904, Czar Nicholas reluctantly signed a decree promising that the government would, among other popular but still timid reforms, consider giving more rights to peasants, to increase the powers of local governments, and to ease press censorship—but only promising that actual legislation would be drafted at some unspecified future date. That only added insult to a lackluster gift to the people.

Father Gapon had already decided that the time was ideal for making a grand gesture for real reform. His police contacts were afraid that Gapon was involved with the Union of Liberation, an organization of liberal middle-class intellectuals that advocated for a constitutional monarchy. They were also concerned about Gapon's plan to march with his followers to the czar's residence at the Winter Palace and present him personally with a petition that members of the Union of Liberation helped devise. Asking for such liberal, modern reforms as an elected legislative assembly, an eight-hour work day, universal suffrage, and the legal right to strike, the petition was nonetheless couched in the age-old idea that the czar would be sympathetic to the plight of his people if only he could be reached without his ministers around to interfere. The text of the petition read:

> We, the workers of St. Petersburg, our wives, our children, and our aged, helpless parents, come to Thee, O Sire, to seek justice and protection. We are impoverished; we are oppressed, over-burdened with excessive toil, contemptuously treated. We are not even recognized as human beings, but are treated like slaves who must suffer their bitter lot in silence and without complaint [. . .]
> O Sire, is this in accordance with God's laws, by the grace of which Thou reignest? Is it possible to live under such laws? Would it not be preferable for all of us, the toiling masses of Russia, to die? Let the capitalists and officials, the embezzlers and plunderers
> of the Russian people, live and enjoy their lives. [. . .] Do not turn Thy help from Thy people. Lead them out from the grave of lawlessness, poverty, and ignorance. Allow them to determine their own future; deliver them from the intolerable oppression of the officialdom. Raze the wall that separates Thee from Thy people and rule the country with them. . . .[14]

Also the whole event was to be given a sacred air. All the participants would be decked out in their Sunday best. They solemnly swore to die if it came to that, and that anyone who abandoned the march would be damned. When the petition was first read to the crowd, they crossed themselves.[15]

God may have been on the side of the protesters, but few others were. Rather than being moved by the love of his suffering people, Nicholas only remarked in his diary that there was supposed to be a demonstration led by "some socialist priest"[16] and decided to go ahead with plans to leave for elsewhere despite advice from his own family that he should at least stay in the city. Liberals aware of the march only thought (all too correctly) it would end in disaster. Gapon's own contacts in the police office believed that any sign of a crowd demanding concessions from their monarch, however symbolically and nonviolently, would set an undesirable precedent. Police officials even ordered Gapon's arrest, but he eluded them by dressing as a woman. On the eve of the demonstration, even Gapon was pale and clearly agitated.[17]

Nonetheless, the march was undertaken on January 22, 1905, as planned. Singing hymns and chanting "God Save The Czar!" while waving crucifixes and pictures of Nicholas II, a crowd of at least three thousand workers, the elderly, women, and children marched through the streets of St. Petersburg toward the Winter Palace. Ten thousand soldiers were stationed at the Winter Palace to monitor and contain the march, but orders were vague, leading to soldiers receiving conflicting commands from their superiors and the protesters being told at random that they could proceed or they had to disperse completely. Near the Narva Triumphal Arch, the cavalry started threatening to trample or attack protesters who kept marching despite commands to stop. At some unknown point, panicked soldiers turned their threats into shots. Casualty numbers varied wildly, especially between Russian officials and the regime's critics, but hundreds were killed and wounded. Leading one of the first segments that was shot at, Gapon was overheard screaming, "There is no God any longer. There is no Czar!" After being dragged to safety, Gapon wanted to rush back and share the fate of his followers, but he was barely persuaded to stop. On the spot his followers cut off Gapon's long hair and trimmed his beard. They stood around their leader, catching the falling locks of hair and murmuring, "Holy, holy."[18] "An occasion that the government could have exploited to its advantage became instead a rallying cry for the opposition," historian Abraham Ascher remarked in what can only be an understatement.[19] As for Gapon, he fled to Switzerland where he fell in with more radical Russian expatriates. Eventually he returned to his homeland, only to be hung by the neck, likely murdered by a man who was like himself an activist and a police informant, for reasons that remain a mystery.

Indeed, it did not take long for news of the massacre to spread, fueling riots and strikes across the capital. People shouting the likes of "Murderers! Bloodsuckers! Hangmen! You run away from the Japanese, but shoot at your own people!"[20] broke windows and threw

Urizky Square in front of the Winter Palace, St. Petersburg, is cordoned off by Tsarist cavalry, January 1905. (*St. Petersburg State Archive*)

stones at soldiers and officials. "Bloody Sunday," as it quickly became christened by the international press, was condemned far outside St. Petersburg. An American diplomat reported back to Washington, DC, that Nicholas II had completely lost his people's love.[21] Even in France, Russia's staunchest ally, denunciations of the czar as a blood-soaked demon echoed through the halls of the National Assembly.[22]

As for the monster himself, Nicholas II wrote in his diary, "It was a difficult day! In Petersburg there were disorders owing to the wishes of workers of the city; many were killed and wounded. Good heavens, how terrible and painful!" However, the rest of the entry only remarks on dining with his mother and a walk he took.[23] Whether or not the czar was capable of appreciating it, Bloody Sunday was a turning point that could not be reversed. The strikes and protests sparked by Bloody Sunday spread like a fire to other cities. After a series of half-hearted measures and unrelenting public pressure, by October 1905 Nicholas II allowed the establishment of an elected legislative body, the Duma, and this unprecedented move was soon followed by the drafting of Russia's first constitution.

No one realized at the time that the most dangerous wounds to the Russian monarchy inflicted by the shots fired on Bloody Sunday for the czar were actually more subtle and of a longer duration. The image of the czar as the benefactor of all, who was blinded to the hardships of his people by the truly evil and selfish, had been thoroughly dismembered. Instead, to many the czar was now no better than the landowners, the bureaucrats, and the capitalists who exploited their own people to sate their own greed. At the same time, a growing legion of industrial, urban, and underpaid and overworked laborers became more indoctrinated in politics and saw in liberalism or socialism their only hope for a better life. In the months after Bloody Sunday, workers founded at least fifty *soviets*, workers' councils, across urban Russia. Russia's future did not ultimately lie in the political events of 1905 but in the doctrines and activism being imbibed by the proletariat in the aftermath of one gruesome blunder.

15.

THE EMPIRE OF JAPAN
The Emperor's Broadcast

On December 1, 1941, a conference of Japan's officials was held in Room One East of the palace in the presence of the emperor. Prime Minister Hideki Tojo, a career military man who was handpicked as prime minister a couple of months before, fired off a convoluted lecture on American-Japanese relations, in order to impress the conclusion that Japan could never let itself succumb to American demands that Japan abandon their occupation of Chinese territory and break the Tripartite Pact that bound Japan to Italy and Germany. To do so would sacrifice the empire Japan needed for its prosperity, and indeed its very survival. The only option was war with the United States, Great Britain, and the Netherlands. The officers of the army and navy rose, with an admiral declaring that they were "burning with a desire to serve their Emperor and their country even at the cost of their lives." Emperor Hirohito (r. 1926–1989) sat silent and unmoving through all this, only nodding occasionally. Even though no one could truly assuage concerns brought up at the meeting over what could be done for civilians in case of air raids beyond providing basic shelter, the admiral Chūichi Hara said there was no point any longer in trying to appease the Americans. "The United States is acting in a conceited, stubborn, and disrespectful manner," he fumed. Capitulation would mean nothing less than giving up all the gains Japan had made since the Russo-Japanese War of 1904-1905, expensive victories that thousands of Japanese soldiers had traded their lives for. Thus the decision was made to strike the United States through Hawaii. And so, Japan was dragged into the Second World War, much to their future grief.[1]

Many times the path to empire starts in an urgent need for defense, and this was doubly true for Japan. Since 1639, Japan under the shogunate of the Tokugawa dynasty had fully enacted the policy of *sakoku*, which had strictly limited foreign trade to very narrowly specific zones. American warships put a stop to *sakoku*, forcing the Japanese into signing with the United States the Treaty of Peace and Amity, so named under the usual nineteenth century lack of irony, which allowed American trade at a couple of key Japanese port cities. Also Japan had many warnings from across the world and close to home of the European powers bullying other peoples in Africa and Asia into submission, if not outright exploitation. To put it simply, the leaders of Japan would decide that the best course of action was, if the colonial empires of Europe and the United States could not be beaten, Japan would join them.

This meant embarking on a painful process beginning in 1868 that history remembers as the Meiji Restoration. It was so named because it meant overturning the Tokugawa shogunate and erecting in its place a European-style imperial monarchy centered on the person of the Emperor Meiji; never mind the fact that for many centuries the emperor, or *tenn* ("heavenly sovereign"), held a ceremonial and religious significance and not a political one. The sullen and officious Emperor Meiji himself loathed the West and everything it offered, refusing to even allow his palace to be wired for electricity.[2] Nevertheless, the work of bringing Western-style capitalism and technology to Japan went apace. Japan completed a full railway system and imported 111 modern ships as part of a seven-year plan to stock the navy with up-to-date steamships and ironclads.[3] Japan's textile industry became industrialized and was soon able to compete globally with that of Britain. By the turn of the century, Japan was still in no small part an agricultural society, but its economy was becoming exponentially industrial.

The reformers were careful to sustain a precarious balance through imitating European and American economic and military models and preserving Japanese traditions. This was made possible through an

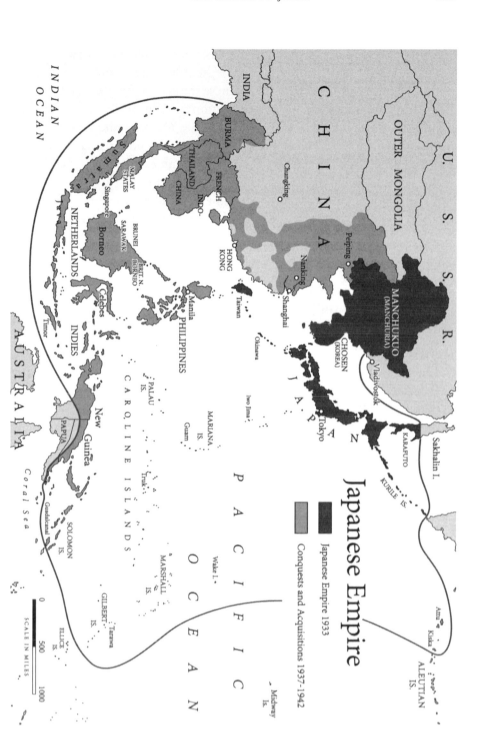

educational system designed to teach industrial and scientific advances alongside traditional values.[4] Such a venture could only invite painfully honest introspection, as Japanese statesmen traveled around the world and reported back their findings. The politician Kido Takayoshi, who joined a Japanese embassy to the United States, meekly noted in 1872, "Our present civilization is not true civilization, our present enlightenment is not true enlightenment."[5]

But becoming like the West did not just mean introducing science into the national educational curriculum or building some railways here and there. It meant ruthlessly building an empire that would span the seas, one that could furnish the nation's new industries with the needed raw materials. Japan only had to look over the sea toward its ancient neighbors, Korea and China. Korea was a particularly tempting prize. The peninsula had plenty of strategic and material potential, but it was also a possible danger, as the country had been for centuries a vassal of China and was at the time in danger of being taken over by Russia, which was also feeling the peer pressure to build its own ocean-spanning empire. Japan made the first move by pressuring the Koreans into making sizable trade concessions to them in 1876. China, which had already been bullied (no other word suffices) by the European powers for decades, could do little to counter this outrageous violation of their traditional sovereignty over Korea. Even so, Japan was not yet finished. Disgust at Japanese intrigue in Korea finally ruptured into open warfare, ending with China having no choice but to make humiliating territorial concessions in 1895 (although still not as much as Japan initially wanted) and to formally recognize Korea's "independence." Of course, this was shown to be little more than a sham when Japan abruptly annexed Korea and imprisoned its emperor Sunjong in 1910. With dark but perhaps unintentional humor a stated justification in the treaty of annexation was that annexation was necessary to *save* Korea from imperialism: "If we stand alone, we cannot exist."[6]

Korea was not enough to satisfy Japan's appetite. As the spoils of war, Japan also seized Taiwan from China, and it was only the disapproval of the European powers that stopped Japan from also claiming the valuable harbor of Port Arthur. However, Japan would have its revenge and prove itself no potential victim to the West in the Russo-Japanese War of 1904-1905. At the start of the war, Kaiser Wilhelm II of Germany solemnly warned his cousin, Czar Nicholas II, of the tremendous consequences of losing the struggle with the Japanese: "It is clearly the future of Russia to cultivate the continent of Asia and defend Europe from the inroads of the Great Yellow Race."[7] Beneath the obvious racism, Wilhelm II actually had a point. With this unexpected victory over one of the so-called "Great Powers," Japan had barged into the conference room of the world's leaders, no matter what the racial supremacists of the West had to say about it. Exploiting the spectacular collapse of China's Qing dynasty in 1912 and the subsequent struggle between the republican Chinese Nationalist Party and local warlords, Japan invaded China once again, setting up a proxy government, Manchukuo, in Inner Manchuria. There they propped up a puppet ruler, Puyi, the long-deposed last emperor of China.

However, Japan had learned more from the imperialistic West than just the need to ensure their security and access to raw materials through overseas conquest. Since the Meiji Restoration began, Japanese officials had sent various embassies around the world to study the technological, political, and social developments of other nations. The most successful of these was the Iwakura Mission, where diplomats, scholars, government officials, and students first sailed into San Francisco in 1871. From there, the Japanese visited Washington, DC, and then set sail again for Europe, where they stopped at Britain, France, Belgium, Germany, Austria-Hungary, the Netherlands, Denmark, Sweden, Italy, and Switzerland. On the way back to Japan, the embassy toured sites at Egypt, Yemen, modern-day Sri Lanka, Saigon, Shangai, and Hong Kong.

Alongside inspecting factories, mills, hospitals, and schools, the Japanese learned about the dirty business of imperial assimilation and ethnic cleansing. They had witnessed or learned second-hand about how Europeans and Americans tamed "the other," not only forcing their own ways and institutions on foreign peoples but convincing them to aspire to be Western like themselves. Japanese emissaries personally observed the treatment of black and Native American students in American schools and watched the British Empire in action in Sri Lanka (then known to English-speakers as Ceylon). From all that, as historian Mark E. Caprio argues, Japanese policy-makers were inspired.[8] In just one aspect of the mission to convince Koreans themselves that they were uncivilized, Japanese anthropologists were sent to Korean villages to take copious photos and write down everything worthwhile, all to provide quantifiable and scientifically respectable evidence of the stunted and inferior state of Korean society.[9]

Japan's assertion of itself as a civilized force in a world dominated by the nations of North America and Europe manifested in some rather more eclectic ways. Today visitors to the mountain village of Shingo in northern Japan can tour *Kirisuto no haka,* the "tomb of Jesus Christ" and for the low cost of a hundred yen they can visit the Legend of Christ museum. There they can learn about how Jesus came to Japan when he was twenty-one years old and learned about Japanese ethics. Jesus tried to spread what he learned back to his homeland, but this only earned the ire of Jewish and Roman authorities. Fortunately, he was saved from being crucified by his younger brother Isikuri, who took his place on the cross, and took the chance to return to Japan, where he settled down to life as a garlic farmer and family man. His descendants, the Sawaguchi family, still live in Shingo today. Naysayers and spoilsports suspect that the real body resting at the tomb of Jesus Christ is that of a sixteenth-century Christian missionary, who would no doubt be a little irked at what his time in Japan actually accomplished in the end, but what is certain is that these types of legends had more of a point than just helping local tourist industries. They helped position Japan as a center of the entire world rather than just a part of the quasi-civilized periphery many Westerners would instead consign it to. Thus, visitors to Japan could also add Moses's tomb at Mount Houdatsu to their itinerary. Accounts written up in the imperial era solemnly taught how Moses had received the Hebrew language, the Ten Commandments, and the first Star of David from the emperor of Japan.[10]

Although such tourist traps cannot help but seem a little odd to Westerners, if also more than vaguely blasphemous, they reflected a national mission the Japanese took very seriously. A December 1928 editorial in the *Yokohama Boeki Shimpo* newspaper, titled "Young Japan and Its Global Mission," read:

> Today's Japan should indeed not confine itself to its own small sphere. Neither should it remain in its position in the Orient or continue to occupy the place it holds in the world. This is an age in which Japan bears a global mission. It has become the center, the principal, and the commander and is advancing with the times to lead the entire world.[11]

A key part of this mission was engaging the great powers of the West like an equal but in a way that would hopefully keep Japan from getting dragged into the petty yet cataclysmic squabbles that always seemed about to break loose between the European nations. With such hopes in mind, the emperor signed off on the Tripartite Treaty between Japan, Germany, and Italy in 1940. The minister of foreign affairs, Yosuke Matsuoka, genuinely believed that the alliance would guarantee world peace. After all, a military alliance would keep a check on the United States, whose relations with Japan were deteriorating, and lay the groundwork for a grand global capitalist crusade against communism. Also Matsuoka hoped that cementing such a foreign policy coup would help ease the power struggles between the army and the navy being held at home. What could go wrong?

Ideally all officials in both the navy and the army were under the direct command of the emperor. A quiet, unassuming, and self-controlled young man, Emperor Hirohito experienced in 1928 an imperial coronation that presented him as both a monarch and a semi-divine figure of national unity. The long and sacred event ran from November 6 to December 2. In a series of rituals starting November 14, Hirohito, in garments of raw white silk and attended by handmaidens and a chef, entered a specially constructed compound of three wooden structures wherein he reenacted symbolically the descent from heaven as described by the holy texts of the Shinto religion. After purifying himself, he went farther in and performed secret rites. In one of the inner chambers, it was supposed that the emperor united with the sun goddess Amaterasu, entering a symbolic marriage to her. Hirohito made food offerings to her and other deities that completed the process of becoming an *arahitogami*, a "manifest deity." Leaving the site of his apotheosis, the emperor reviewed thirty-five thousand troops as they marched past him in Tokyo.[12]

While the emperor was among other things a living embodiment of the Japanese nation, Japan was not truly unified, and as happened in China modernity had helped attract a plethora of views of what direction society should go. There was an active communist party and also liberal groups pushing for more democracy in the Japanese government. By the 1930s, however, power in the state really belonged to neither the emperor nor the government ministers and the National Diet of Japan but to the army and navy, even though they were often at loggerheads with each other.[13] Generally, however, it was not war for its own sake that was the goal of military officials but simply keeping Japan from getting shut out of any burgeoning international order.

Of course, matters simply did not work out the way the military leaders hoped. Instead of intimidating the United States into at least a lukewarm friendship, the Tripartite Pact convinced the United States that Japan had deliberately declared itself its enemy. Even American public opinion had turned against Japan after 1930 as reports of Japanese treatment of Chinese civilians in occupied territories trickled in. After capturing the capital of the Republic of China, Nanking, on December 13, 1937, Japanese troops initiated six weeks of looting, rape, and slaughter, causing approximately two hundred thousand deaths, according to statistics tabulated by the International Military Tribunal for the Far East.[14] In retaliation for the Japanese invading French Indochina, the United States placed an embargo on oil and other industrial materials against Japan, a serious swipe against Japan's economy. So, at the end of 1941, Japan declared war on the United States, officially one hour after the bombing of the Pearl Harbor naval base, although officials meant the declaration to precede the attack by half an hour.

World War II would be the dark finale to the Japanese Empire's existence. Japanese atrocities carried out during the war in the Philippines, Korea, China, and Indochina haunt Japanese foreign relations and public memory to this day. Japan's post-war history has seen a series of official apologies (as well as non-apologies) and lawsuits over the so-called "comfort women," civilian women, mostly Chinese and Korean, who were forced into having sex with Japanese soldiers. This final act would end in August 1945 with two cities being consumed in a flash, claiming at least 129,000 lives. The sheer grotesqueness of the use of the atomic bomb, for not only Japan but for the world, is perhaps best proven just by its singularity: the bombing of Hiroshima and Nagasaki fortunately remain the only times nuclear weapons were used in warfare.

How much the atomic bombings forced Japan's surrender remains a taut, impassioned debate. What did happen for sure is that Emperor Hirohito was seriously disturbed by the news, and morale overall was further broken when the bombings were followed by a devastating air raid on Tokyo. Before a meeting of military officials, Hirohito announced:

Japanese citizens listening to Emperor Hirohito's radio broadcast announcing Japan's unconditional surrender on August 15, 1945. (*Kyodo/Japan Times*)

I have given serious thought to the situation prevailing at home and abroad and have concluded that continuing the war means destruction for the nation and a prolongation of bloodshed and cruelty in the world. I cannot bear to see my innocent people suffer any longer. Ending the war is the only way to restore world peace and to relieve the nation from the terrible distress with which it is burdened.[15]

There were officers in the army determined to see the war go even further, even if it meant carrying off a coup. It was decided that Hirohito should record an announcement that the Japanese government accepted the Allies' demands for unconditional surrender on a phonograph record, which would then be broadcast to the nation through a radio broadcast planned for August 15, 1945, the *Gyokuon-hōs* "Jewel Voice Broadcast."

After announcing that Japan was agreeing to the demands of the United States, the United Kingdom, China, and their allies, Hirohito began, "To strive for the common prosperity and happiness of all nations as well as the security and well-being of our subjects is the solemn obligation which has been handed down by our imperial ancestors and which we lay close to the heart." However, the war began "out of our sincere desire to insure Japan's self-preservation and the stabilization of East Asia, it being far from our thought either to infringe upon the sovereignty of other nations or to embark upon territorial aggrandizement" (one can only imagine the reaction of Yi Un, the one-time heir of Korea's last emperor who ended up serving as an officer in the Japanese military, to that particular claim).

The war, Hirohito admitted, had gone on too long and was harming Japan's interests, despite the best efforts of the entire population. "Moreover," Hirohito continued, "the enemy has begun to employ a new and most cruel bomb, the power of which to do damage is, indeed, incalculable, taking the toll of many innocent lives. Should we continue to fight, it would not only result in an ultimate collapse and obliteration of the Japanese nation, but also it would lead to the total extinction of human civilization." Because of this crisis, Hirohito asked, "how are we to save the millions of our subjects, or to atone ourselves before the hallowed spirits of our imperial ancestors? This is the reason why we have ordered the acceptance of the provisions of the joint declaration of the powers." Remarking on the soldiers who died in the fighting and their families, Hirohito added, "The welfare of the wounded and the war sufferers and of those who lost their homes and livelihood is the object of our profound solicitude. The hardships and sufferings to which our nation is to be subjected hereafter will be certainly great." Further addressing his subjects and their hardships, Hirohito concluded:

> Let the entire nation continue as one family from generation to generation, ever firm in its faith of the imperishableness of its divine land, and mindful of its heavy burden of responsibilities, and the long road before it. Unite your total strength to be devoted to the construction for the future. Cultivate the ways of rectitude, nobility of spirit, and work with resolution so that you may enhance the innate glory of the Imperial State and keep pace with the progress of the world.[16]

After the first reading of the speech, the emperor turned to a technician and asked, "Was it all right?" The technician reluctantly answered that a few words were not clear. Hirohito realized he had stuttered several times and offered to read the speech again. However, the second time his voice was pitched too high and he skipped a word.

"I'm willing to make another," he obligingly said, but the technicians thought it was "too great an ordeal" for the emperor. The second version became the one to be broadcast. To guard against the threat of a coup, the record was not kept at the radio station but in the offices of the Household Ministry.

The perhaps inevitable hardliner attempt at a coup had failed miserably, ending with the suicides of two ringleaders, and Japan submitted to military occupation by the United States. No longer the core of an empire that managed to stand firm against some of the largest colonial empires in human history for nearly a century, Japan's entire future was to be decided by its enemy. At first, that future looked ominous. Harry Truman, who became president of the United States after the death of Franklin Roosevelt on April 14, 1945, had signed off on the use of the atomic bombs and now demanded a complete purge of Japan's wartime government as well as a trial against the emperor. Still enraged by the Pearl Harbor attack, the American public would have gladly stood behind Truman. An unpublished Gallup poll taken in the summer of 1945 disclosed that 77 percent of the American public wanted to see the emperor brought before an international court. At the same time, the US Senate deliberated over a resolution calling for the emperor to be officially tried as a war criminal.[17] There was simply no question that many Americans, and perhaps President Truman himself, wanted the emperor of Japan to pay personally for the 1,503 people killed when Pearl Harbor was bombed.

However, General Douglas MacArthur, entrusted with the role of supreme commander of the allied forces in Japan, had a more serene and pragmatic view. Perhaps he had gained insight on Japanese politics during his time as commander of the Philippine Army, or he kept in mind the lessons taught by the example of Germany and World War I, where the seeds for a future war can be so easily planted with the degradation of a defeated nation. Either way, when Hirohito went to meet MacArthur at his makeshift offices in a Tokyo insurance company building, it was cordial, even though MacArthur, apparently in a deliberate gesture meant to deflate the emperor's sacred status, met Hirohito in a simple tan army outfit and only offered him a handshake. Hirohito himself was dressed in a plain coat, trousers, and a top hat. "I tried to make it as easy for him as I could, but I knew how deep and dreadful must be the agony of his humiliation," MacArthur would later recall. Instead of pleading not to be treated like a war criminal, Hirohito offered full responsibility for his people and their actions, impressing the general. MacArthur thanked Hirohito for his role in ending the war, but Hirohito remarked that it took the terrible bombing of Hiroshima and Nagasaki to finally give victory to the peace party. Asked why he consented to the start of the war in the first place, Hirohito finally cast aside his own humility and answered with some pride, "It wasn't clear to me that our course was unjustified. Even now I am not sure how historians will allocate responsibility for the war."[18]

MacArthur decided that the best approach was to lay the blame for the war on the heads of Japanese military leaders like Tojo, who became the ultimate scapegoat once he was hanged as a war criminal in December 1948. No matter what Hirohito's actual responsibility was over Japan's involvement in World War II, MacArthur early on decided that Hirohito had to be made an ally in order to ensure that Japan as a whole would become a steadfast ally as well. Standing up to President Truman himself, MacArthur declared, "His indictment will unquestionably cause a tremendous convulsion among the Japanese people, the repercussions of which cannot be overestimated. He is a symbol which unites all Japanese. Destroy him and the nation will disintegrate."[19] Truman personally loathed MacArthur and later in an interview called him a "dumb son of a bitch," but nonetheless he did let MacArthur's advice win the day.

History would justify the decisions of not only MacArthur but Hirohito's own urging of peace in his historic message to the nation, even if due to his use of the highly refined language of the imperial court not all listeners understood him. Japan would not share the same fate as Germany after World War I and MacArthur would be vindicated beyond even what he likely hoped for. The Land of the Rising Sun would make one of the most remarkable transitions in all of history, going from an imperial, colonizing power to the first nation in history to enshrine pacifism in its own constitution.

16.

THE BRITISH EMPIRE

Fiasco at Suez

"The episode was a catastrophic failure," the historian Eric Hobsbawm wrote on what history would mark down as the Suez Crisis, "all the more ridiculous for the combination of indecision, hesitation, and unconvincing disingenuousness by the British prime minister, Anthony Eden."[1] True, what happened in Egypt was only the latest in a series of shocks that struck the British Empire in the twentieth century. Yet it was the first time that the British, who had once commanded events from the Americas to Australia, had no choice but to surrender all initiative to a new power that would come to write the plot of world history down to the present day, the United States.

Since the dawn of the seventeenth century, Britain had gone from being a minor European power, often eclipsed by its rivals on the continent France and Spain, into two centuries later the "empire on which the sun never sets" that overshadowed the lives of one-fifth of the world's population in 1922.[2] Children growing up within the British Empire in the first half of the 1900s would have been all too familiar with the "red maps," showing in red British influence across all of Canada, Australia, India, and parts of the rest of Asia, the Middle East, Africa, Latin America, and Polynesia. An empire with the first industrial economy at its heart and holding the vastest amount of ter-

ritory in human history, the British Empire truly seemed unique, des-
tined to endure, although perhaps all empires appear that way in their
heyday. The British novelist Doris Lessing, born in 1919, reflected,
"You know, when I was a girl, the idea that the British Empire could
ever end was absolutely inconceivable. And it just disappeared, like
all the other empires."[3] In fact, many doubted that Britain would even
survive without it. A poll taken in 1948, asking the British public if
the nation could last without its empire, answered no. "We couldn't
live for five minutes without the Empire," one painter and decorator
believed.[4]

By the late nineteenth century, the signs were there, as the evidence
of decline usually is even if it is remarked upon by few. In Africa and
India and elsewhere, there were generations of middle- and upper-
class people who had been educated, often in Britain's own elite uni-
versities, on British ideals of democracy, liberty, and nationalism, and
they could not help but wonder why their home countries nonetheless
had almost no voice under British rule. One such gentleman was a
young Indian named Mohandas Gandhi. While a law student in London, Mohandas believed in Britain's benevolent promise that the peoples living under their flag would one day gain independence once
they were civilized and modernized, but he received his own personal
moment on the road to Damascus when he traveled to South Africa
to represent a labor organization, the Muslim Indian Traders, and experienced firsthand the racist system that had been engineered with
Britain's blessing when he was thrown off a train for refusing to give
up the first-class passenger compartment he had already paid for.

The hollowness of Britain's claims to be exporting political liberty
and economic prosperity for the good of its imperial subjects was felt
right next door to England. Except for the county of Ulster, Ireland
suffered slumping employment in the countryside but gained few industrial jobs to make up for it.[5] Between 1845 and 1852, the Irish
suffered a "Great Famine" of proportions that became the stuff of
real-life horror stories and alone drove over a million and a half to
abandon their homeland for alien shores, causing a steep drop in Ireland's population, which even today the island has yet to totally reverse. The Great Famine was not at all eased, to say the least, by
laissez-faire British economic policies pushed by officials like Sir
Charles Trevelyan who blamed the famine entirely on the "moral evil
of the selfish, perverse, and turbulent character of the people."[6] The

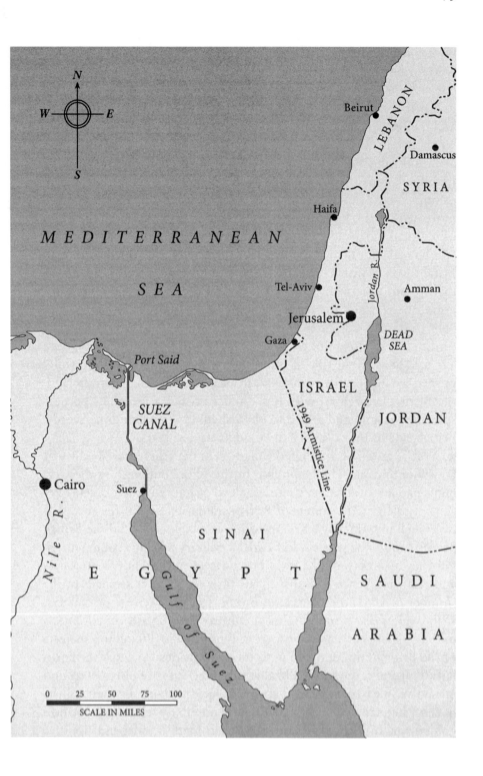

N
W—E
S

Beirut

LEBANON

Damascus

SYRIA

Haifa

MEDITERRANEAN

SEA

Tel-Aviv

Jordan R.

Amman

Jerusalem

Gaza

DEAD
SEA

Port Said

ISRAEL

SUEZ
CANAL

1949 Armistice Line

JORDAN

Cairo

Suez

SINAI

Nile R.

E   G   Y   P   T

Gulf

SAUDI

of

ARABIA

Suez

0   25   50   75   100

SCALE IN MILES

government in London had repealed official oppression of Catholics, who formed the majority in most of Ireland's counties, and gave some concessions toward Irish political autonomy. However, struggles between Irish supporters of the British government, Irish nationalists, and the British could not be eased by any act of parliament, especially when Britain insisted on the conscription of Irish men into their armies during World War I. In 1922, out of civil war emerged the Irish Free State, the predecessor to the Republic of Ireland. It was an example that Britain, for all the talk that it was a different, freer, and more democratic kind of empire, was not at all immune to the perils of national independence, even so close to the empire's heartland.

The real gauntlet for the empire would be World War II. Although Britain won, it was, at least for its empire, a pyrrhic victory. Even with the free aid Americans gave to the British under the Lend-Lease program, the war and the reconstruction ended with Britain in massive debt to the United States. Worse, India, which had been so essential for the British dream of empire that Britain's monarchs since Queen Victoria boasted the title of empress or emperor of India, successfully pushed for independence in 1947. Ironically, as they had with Ireland, the British left behind with India and Pakistan a legacy of borders splitting the land and sectarian bloodshed. In Piers Brendon's words, British rule of India "ended in blood as well as tears."[7]

Yet the mood of the United Kingdom in the years after World War II was optimistic. The nightmare of the Blitz bombings by the Germans had left over eighty thousand dead or injured, but it quickly became a celebrated example of British solidarity even at the mercy of overwhelming tragedy and impossible odds. Not only did the British people endure the worst Adolf Hitler's military machine could muster, but they also played a hand in bringing an end to Hitler's atrocities and restoring peace to Europe, this time for good it seemed. In the summer of 1951, the Festival of Britain was held across the country, with exhibitions promoting local cultures and British contributions to the arts, industry, and science. On June 2, 1953, 20 million subjects of the British Empire tuned in to their televisions to watch the coronation of a new monarch, Elizabeth II,[8] who was not only young and attractive but happened by a stroke of luck to share the name of the queen who presided over what was still popularly felt to be England's golden age and who too had lived when English independence was threatened by an implacable foe from the continent. Britain, it seemed, had been reborn out of the trials imposed on it, but the question remained, with India gone would it still have an empire?

At least Britain was not alone. The future seemed dim for all European colonial powers, even the ones who were the victors or neutral parties during World War II. A new wave of nationalist movements on the heels of the war washed over the world, with France losing Lebanon and Syria in 1945, Indonesia throwing off Dutch rule the same year, and Sri Lanka and Israel/Palestine breaking away from the British Empire in 1948. "What fatally damaged the old colonialists was the proof that white men and their states could be defeated, shamefully and dishonourably, and the old colonial powers were patently too weak, even after a victorious war, to restore their old positions," Eric Hobsbawm remarks.[9] Also it would become painfully clear to the old "Great Powers" that they had lost control of the board to two new major players, the Soviet Union and the United States, who in their war of ideas against each other looked toward the colonized lands that comprised what was now being called the "Third World."

This change in players and the very rules of the game did not dawn on Britain's leaders right away. Starting in 1944, Britain sided against the communist faction in a civil war in Greece, but it was really American support, not British guns, that was essential in driving communism out of Greece. Nor was it a promising sign that World War II basically ended with the United States and the Soviet Union dividing Europe between their own spheres of influence, splitting Europe right down the middle of Germany with the so-called Iron Curtain.

A crisis was brewing in the Middle East that would put the immortality of the British Empire to its most brutal test. Britain's hold over the Middle East had already been loosened when in 1948 they gave up Palestine, but their real stake in the region was the Suez Canal in Egypt, a passageway key to global trade, especially vital for oil shipments. By the 1940s, one-third of the world's oil shipments passed through the canal.[10] The Suez Canal had been an international zone since 1888, but British arms defended it, and Britain's "Canal Zone" by the middle of the twentieth century was at an impressive 750 square miles the largest military base in the world.[11] To keep the Suez Canal in their orbit, Britain kept up a strong if more often than not strained relationship with the Egyptian monarchy. Unfortunately, that monarchy happened to be on a downward spiral toward suicide. King

Farouk of Egypt made the impulsive decision to join other Arabic countries in attacking Israel, a choice that, rather than making Farouk the leader of the Arab world as he had dreamed, turned him and the entire underequipped and badly trained Egyptian army into a laughingstock. This was bad enough, but Farouk did himself (and the British, for that matter) no favors by being a manic playboy who owned around a hundred cars, indulged in casual kleptomania, and openly enjoyed a lavish night life with a series of mistresses on his arm. In July 1952, the king would be forced to abdicate and was exiled after a military coup, which was by no coincidence led by a wounded and embittered veteran of the Arab-Israeli War, Colonel Gamal Ab Nasser. Under Nasser's direction, Egypt was made into a republic and its government was purged of all rivals and dissidents.

Nasser was the son of a postal clerk and had personally witnessed the staggering inequality of wealth across Egypt during his time in the army, which made him a determined reformer. Once in power as president of Egypt by 1956, Nasser enacted sweeping agrarian reforms that eliminated the last traces of a feudal system that had been in place since the years when Egypt was still a province of the Ottoman Empire. It was not enough to help Egypt, however, but the entire Middle East, and to do so Nasser was determined to exorcise what was left of the British Empire from the region. Naturally from the beginning British politicians looked at Nasser with suspicion, if not outright hostility. The Baghdad Pact, a security agreement signed between Britain, Pakistan, Iraq, Iran, and Turkey in 1955, was ostensibly an anti-Soviet arrangement, but it was really mostly a way for Britain to try to resuscitate its waning influence in the region, a ploy called out by Nasser, who publicly denounced the pact as an imperialist sleight of hand.[12]

Nasser's archenemy in London was a privileged child of a gentry family in Durham and an Oxford graduate in oriental languages, Anthony Eden. Winston Churchill's former deputy and successor as prime minister, Eden shared his mentor's fixation on salvaging what was left of the empire and restoring its prestige. Eden and his government instinctively saw Nasser as a dictator in the same mold as Mussolini (with reason, given that under Nasser's influence the government of Egypt outlawed political parties), a view he emphatically tried to impress on his ally, President Dwight Eisenhower of the United States. In one meeting:

The Prime Minister and Eisenhower discussed Nasser, and this is clearly the unanswered question. The President said, "What kind of a fellow is Nasser?" [Foreign Secretary] Selwyn answered, he is ambitious, dreams of an Arab empire from Atlantic to Persian Gulf under his leadership. President: "Does that go well with the other Arabs?" The crucial question, he said, is whether Nasser is with the Soviets. If he proves to be, we shall have to back either Israel or the Arabs who don't like Egypt.[13]

Nasser had announced that Egypt would be neutral in the Cold War, but he still agreed to a weapons-for-cotton deal with the Soviet Union and opened diplomatic relations with Mao Zedong's new communist government in China. Both acts sanctified Eden's dread that Nasser not only wanted to head a pan-Arabic empire but would gleefully help open the entire Middle East to the Red Menace. "If we don't want to see the whole of the Middle East fall into Communist hands we must first back the friends of the West in Jordan and Iraq," Eden warned Eisenhower in a telegram dated January 16, 1956.[14] Eden's obsession drew him possibly to consider having the Secret Intelligence Service assassinate Nasser, but no plan seemed to make it far. "I just can't understand why the British did not bump off Nasser," Eisenhower wondered aloud to his secretary Bernard Shanley. "They have been doing it for years and then when faced with it they fumble."[15]

Instead Eden resorted to less straightforward tactics. In the spring of 1956, the Eisenhower administration, unhappy that Nasser extended the olive branch to Mao, gave in to Eden's request that it scuttle plans to give Egypt a loan needed to construct the valuable Aswan Dam on the Nile River. Nasser was quick to retaliate. To an ecstatic crowd in Alexandria, Nasser on July 26, 1956, announced that the army was already carrying out operations to secure the Suez Canal for Egypt. Nasser's promise that compensation would be paid to the canal's former owners did nothing to soothe Eden's outrage.

Eden's nightmare that he would have to watch helplessly as the British Empire receded from another corner of the world was coming true. In the weeks since Nasser determined that the Suez Canal by all rights belonged to Egypt, Eden, who had for years been plagued by medical problems, started depending on morphine to calm his nerves and took Benzedrine to cope with the highs. The cocktail of drugs running through his system inspired irrational declarations such as his outburst that he would rather see the entire British Empire fall down all at once than slowly fade away.[16] Just one day after Nasser's speech, Eden pleaded for support from Eisenhower:

> If we take a firm stand over this now, we shall have the support of the other maritime powers. If we do not, our influence and yours throughout the Middle East will, we are all convinced, be destroyed. [. . .] The Canal is an international asset and facility, which is vital to the free world. The maritime Powers cannot afford to allow Egypt to expropriate it and to exploit it by using the revenues for her own internal purposes irrespective of the interests of the Canal and the Canal users. Apart from the Egyptians' complete lack of technical qualifications, their past behavior gives no confidence that they can be trusted to manage it with any sense of international obligation. Nor are they capable of providing the capital which will soon be needed to widen and deepen it so that it may be capable of handling the increased volume of traffic which it must carry in the years to come.[17]

For all of Eden's fears that Nasser was a Stalin or a Hitler in the making, Eisenhower was reluctant to sign off on military retaliation. At the end of July, Eisenhower wrote back to Eden, "I have given you my own personal conviction, as well as that of my associates, as to the unwisdom even of contemplating the use of military force at this moment."[18] Nor was British public opinion or that of some government officials on Eden's side, with one high-ranking military official making his opinion plain: "Eden has gone bananas."[19]

Naturally Eden was undeterred and pushed forward with his case that Nasser nationalizing the Suez Canal was tantamount to a declaration of war. He had one ally in the French prime minister, Guy Mollet, whose government had a financial stake in the Suez Canal and who likewise flat-out compared Nasser to Adolf Hitler, branding Nasser's book *The Philosophy of the Revolution* a new *Mein Kampf*. Another natural partner was Israel, which had long been wary of Nasser's blunt hostility and his weapons deal with the Soviet Union. The entire cast for the farce was in place—except Britain's most cherished ally, the United States. In spite of Eden's treatment of Eisenhower as a personal friend, even tenderly assuring him that all of the people of Britain were relieved when Eisenhower made a full recovery

US president Dwight D. Eisenhower meeting with Egyptian president Gamal Abdel Nasser during Nasser's visit to United Nations in New York, 1960. (*Gamal Abdel Nasser Foundation*)

from a heart attack in 1955, Eisenhower was locked out of the loop. Instead British officials—some of the ones not openly revolting against Eden's directives, at any rate—went about the pretense that they had made no solid arrangements with the French and the Israelis, even as Israeli and French troops were setting foot on Egyptian soil on behalf of Britain.

It was all a joke that Eisenhower was in no mood to entertain, even from his supposed friend. Cranking up economic pressure and deploying American influence at the United Nations, Eisenhower forced Eden to agree to an abrupt cease-fire. Britain's so-called "police action" against Egypt lasted only a little over a week. The only one of Eden's allies to get anything out of the entire fiasco was Israel. Although the United States pressured Israel into relinquishing the Sinai Peninsula back to Egypt, Israel managed to force Nasser to agree to allow Israeli ships to pass through the Straits of Tiran. Egypt would keep control of the Suez Canal and, much to poor Eden's chagrin, Nasser would remain firmly in power as the president of Egypt until his death in 1970 from a heart attack—not, so we suppose, from British assassins.

Citing his debilitating health problems, Eden resigned as prime minister in January 1957. At about the same time, Eisenhower officially began to shape American foreign policy along the lines of the "Eisenhower Doctrine," which would seek to expand American influence into the Middle East before the Soviets could. The doctrine was based on the cold assumption that British power in the region was dead and had left the whole Middle East up for grabs. If nothing else, the Suez Crisis and the steely pragmatism of Cold War *realpolitik* had shown that the United States really thought of Britain not as a partner but as a client. The powerbrokers of the world like Eisenhower were now openly acknowledging that they lived in a world where the seemingly immortal British Empire was a spent force. At least King Hussein of Jordan, who himself had been a beneficiary of British imperial benevolence but now looked to woo Washington, DC, thought as much. Meditating on the Suez Crisis, the king remarked in a fitting epilogue, "What a tragedy: the day Britain finally fell off its pedestal, particularly around here."[20]

THE SOVIET UNION

Hands Across the Baltic

In Moscow, the premier of the Soviet Union, Nikita Khrushchev, attended in July 1959 a special and at one time unthinkable event, the American National Exhibition. As part of an attempt at mutual understanding between great rivals who practically held the world between them, the Soviet Union and the United States agreed to host exhibitions of art and technology in each other's countries to try to humanize the other. There Khruschev, who proudly described himself as very to-the-point, got into a polite yet spirited debate with the US vice president, Richard Nixon. The friendly squabble was notable enough the media and historians dubbed it the "Kitchen Debate" due to Nixon's insistence that modern conveniences of American life, such as kitchen appliances, proved beyond a reasonable doubt the virtues of capitalism. Unconvinced and wondering if technologically coddled Americans also needed a device to push the food down their throats, Khrushchev mused:

> The Americans have created their own image of the Soviet man and think he is as you want him to be. But he is not as you think. You think the Russian people will be dumbfounded to see these things, but the fact is that newly built Russian houses have all this equipment right now. Moreover, all you have to do to get a house is to be born in the Soviet Union. You are entitled to hous-

ing. I was born in the Soviet Union. So I have a right to a house. In America, if you don't have a dollar—you have the right to choose between sleeping in a house or on the pavement. Yet you say that we are slaves of communism.[1]

The Kitchen Debate might have helped make the point that the Soviet Union and the United States could possibly coexist. But it also exposed the fault lines that made any relationship between these two superpowers with diametrically opposed views on the best way to organize societies improbable. The instability also lay within the Soviet Union itself, as its very existence rested on a promise that the way of life it offered was better than anything the capitalist nations could offer.

This was all because the Soviet Union was a unique specimen of empire. Rather than being built around a city or nation, a royal dynasty, or a religious faith like all past empires, the Soviet Union was founded on an economic and social philosophy. That made it dangerous, potentially more frightening than any army. It was an empire that could suddenly convert entire governments and foreign citizens to its cause. Even though by about 1927 Soviet leaders had quietly shelved the dream of a global revolution,[2] the Western powers' nightmare of the nations of the world succumbing one by one to communism drove global politics after World War II. It did not really matter that communist China broke with the Soviet Union in a split as acrimonious as any divorce, or that even the Soviet Union's satellite regimes in eastern Europe began after the death of Josef Stalin to pursue their own national spins on communist practice. The Red Menace remained omnipresent.[3]

The birth of this bizarre empire of ideas and economics was itself a miracle, even in the eyes of its founders. It was conventional wisdom among Marxists that when the world revolution of the proletariat against the *bourgeoisie* began to unfold it would start in Britain, with the first industrialized economy and its cities filled with underpaid, undernourished factory laborers packed in substandard housing, or at least in Germany, which had also become heavily industrialized. The revolution certainly could not happen anytime soon in Russia, where instead of a large proletariat there was a mass of uneducated, religiously devout peasants and not even a strong *bourgeoisie* for the workers to rally against. When the czarist government collapsed and the communist Bolshevik party managed to seize the reins from the

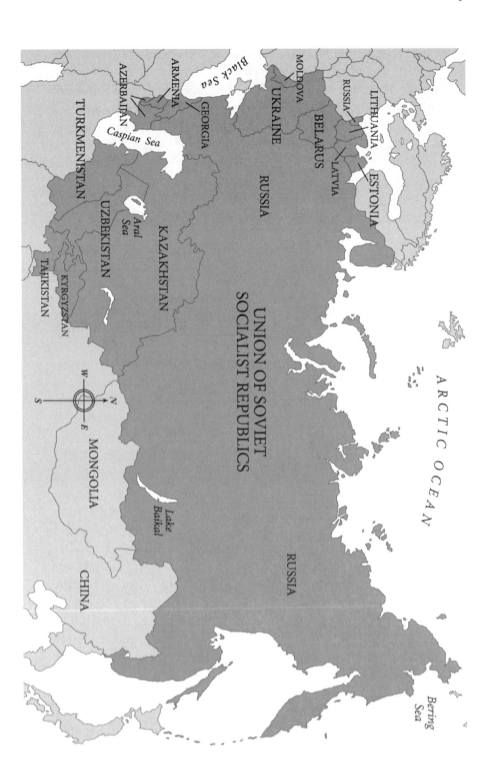

weak and fragmented Russian Republic in October 1917, even some communists outside Russia were startled.

The jolt of sudden power may have been too much even for one of the Bolshevik party's main architects and the new Soviet Union's first leader, Vladimir Lenin. Faced with the unenviable task of managing a Russia that had been sickened by long years of political uncertainty and civil war, Lenin had to make concessions, justified by the idea that the full revolution had to wait until Russians had their consciousness raised. Some private markets, especially of food, were allowed to function under Lenin's New Economic Policy, and factories were taken away from committees of workers, which was the communist ideal for industrial management, and handed over to single managers.[4] Still, despite these early compromises with the nasty reality of war, much had changed. Many landowners and business owners had fled Russia, the state took over the industrial and financial sectors, and the once kingly property of the Russian Orthodox Church was immediately nationalized.

Vladimir Lenin's eventual successor, Josef Stalin, had been a one-time seminary student who was converted to Marxism after he read the writings of Lenin. Dispatching his rivals and critics with clockwork efficiency, Stalin went further than Lenin, introducing collective farms and cracking down on the surviving private markets. Stalin's biggest push was to finally break Russia from its agricultural past once and for all with his audaciously ambitious Five-Year Plans, which culminated in the 1930s. The official line from the government was that rapid industrialization of the Soviet Union would bring everyday citizens a far better quality of life than their ancestors could have imagined. In 1936, the state's official slogan was, "Life has become better, life has become more joyous." This was not entirely untrue as more consumer goods from toothpastes to dresses became available, but the not so hidden costs were the staggering and indeed almost impossible quotas that weighed down on tens of thousands of managers and workers. Even Sergei Kirov, the official put in charge of industrialization, was so in the grip of the pressure that he came down with insomnia and heart problems.[5]

Yet, it worked, even in the wary eyes of the capitalist and fascist worlds. Outside the Soviet Union, governments that were fighting for solid ground at the height of the Great Depression could not help but notice that the Soviet Union was becoming an industrial powerhouse

overnight and moving forward in prosperity, not backward like virtually all the capitalist nations. From 1929 to 1940, Soviet industrial
production tripled, at the very least. Its output rose from 5 percent of
the world's manufactured products in 1929 to 18 percent in 1938.
Even the Nazis, who were literally defined by their loathing of communism, had their own "Four-Year Plan" debut in 1933.[6]

Nevertheless, few could deny that the stability and prosperity of
the Soviet Union was built on top of millions of bodies and displaced
lives. The contrast was right there for the public to see: "Newspapers
were filled not only with stories about enemies and purges but also
with advertisements for attractive new hats and shoes and reports of
dances and carnivals in parks."[7] Exactly how many died in Stalin's
purges is a contentious, obscured topic that will likely never be resolved to anybody's satisfaction, especially not for the descendants of
Stalin's millions of victims. In 1929, Stalin had taken aim against the
kulaks, landowning peasants, ordering "the liquidation of the *kulaks*
as a class."[8] Simply because their mere existence stood in the way of
Stalin's goal to make agriculture a collective matter, millions were sent
to die in the notorious work-camps, the *gulags*, or at least were
forcibly relocated. Then there were Stalin's countless political enemies.
It is telling that few of the old Bolshevik leaders lived to see the year
1938, with 80 percent of Stalin's own 1934 Central Committee executed or driven to suicide.[9]

After Stalin was felled by a stroke in 1953, his legacy was bitterly
denounced by Khruschev. Boldly Khruschev raged that Stalin should
only be remembered as a monstrous tyrant who demanded to be worshiped by his own "cult of personality" and had betrayed the principles of Marxism-Leninism in nearly every possible way. Even so,
Khruschev did not quite renounce the fact that the Soviet Union had
filled the borders of the old Russian Empire and beyond.

The Soviet Union as an imperial state had been born on December
29, 1922, when the newborn socialist republics in Russia and several
of the old imperial territories in the Caucasus and Ukraine agreed to
the creation of a union that would be governed by a central committee. Some of the agreement's architects clung to the hope that one day
the entire world would willingly join the revolution and the whole
concept of foreign borders and nationalities would become an em-
barrassing relic of the past. As the vision of a global revolution receded further and further into the horizon, the Soviet Union's tendrils

reached into Russia's old stomping grounds in central Asia and eastern Europe.

The most cynical land grab was perhaps what the Soviet Union had in store for the Baltic nations. A region that had long been subjected to violent, and indeed genocidal, invasions and colonization by Germanic peoples, the Baltic was through much of its later history at the mercy of the territorial ambitions of its neighbors like Poland, Sweden, and Russia. Even without a history of political independence, the Baltic peoples in the nineteenth century also enjoyed the fad for cultural nationalism sweeping across Europe, digging up and piecing together their own legacies of folklore and language. This paved the way for actual nation-states, with the new Baltic republics of Estonia, Latvia, and Lithuania flowering in the ruins of the old Russian Empire after World War I. But their fate would be decided by a handshake between Stalin's foreign minister, Vyacheslav Molotov, and his Nazi Germany counterpart, Joachim von Ribbentrop. According to a secret clause in the Molotov-Ribbentrop Pact between Germany and the Soviet Union, a number of inconveniently still independent territories in eastern Europe were to be cut up between the two powers, with all the Baltic states to be handed over in a doggy bag to the Soviet Union. Of course, technically the three countries would be their own nations under their own Soviet republics, but diplomats still delicately termed what was practically an imperialist coup by the Soviet Union as an expansion of the "sphere of influence."

Nonetheless, the Baltic remained relatively quiet, as the Soviet Union recovered from its epic struggle against its one-time ally, Nazi Germany, an apocalyptic war whose epic importance was crystalized in the dramatic Russian name for the struggle, the "Great Patriotic War." However, the decades after the Great Patriotic War that left the Soviet Union standing strong in eastern Europe were increasingly grim. In contrast to the halcyon days of the Great Depression when Soviet officials could boast of enjoying an economic health lost to their capitalist counterparts, countries like the United States, Japan, and West Germany were booming in the 1950s. Vindication seemed to finally come in the 1970s when much of the capitalist world was brought low by a crisis in oil prices, but the blow to the Soviet Union itself had only been delayed by a decade or so.[10] Even Stalin's Five-Year Plans had in the end backfired. Little of the Soviet Union's own industrial equipment had been updated since the 1930s rush, so by the 1970s the Soviets were stuck with "history's largest ever assemblage of obsolete equipment."[11]

Would-be reformers wrestled with not only a rusting industrial infrastructure but sinking Soviet morale. The promise of a better life for all workers willing to live under their system had given way to a bloated bureaucracy that existed only to feed a greedy military. A confidential report from 1965 by one official, Abel Aganbegyan, had noted how much money was spent on the military instead of on social services, consumer products, or even basic administration. It was a point he spearheaded with the absurd truth that the Central Statistical Administration did not have a single computer or was working on any plans to acquire one.[12]

None of this was lost on the public, especially the younger generation. Memories of the glory of the Great Patriotic War had faded for them, after all, and instead they could only see a party elite that enjoyed special benefits and access to entertainment and even scientific information completely denied to the general public. "What sort of a government is it [that] allows only selected people to live normal family lives?" wrote a "M.F." from the city of Kharkov to the newspaper *Facts & Arguments*, which had a Soviet readership in the millions. "Why is it that people in authority have everything, flats, *dachas* [vacation homes], and money, and others have nothing?. . . I am a simple woman. I used to believe in our government. Now I no longer believe."[13]

There was a potential savior in the wings: Mikhail Gorbachev, the child of a rural village that had suffered the brunt of both Stalin's purges and the famine of the early 1930s. Proclaiming that the Soviet Union was suffering a "spiritual crisis,"[14] a curious phrase for a country where the state "religion" was atheism, Gorbachev set about undertaking the most dramatic *volte face* since Khruschev took to the party pulpit to condemn the freshly buried Stalin. Since his appointment as the general secretary of the Communist Party, Gorbachev had tried to address the Soviet Union's myriad problems, from its economic decline to the plummeting standard of living and rising crime rate. In order to encourage a sense of involvement and investment with the government, Gorbachev introduced more democracy to local governments. Censorship was greatly relaxed with even novels, plays, and films critical of communism or of icons like Lenin being allowed and with amnesty being offered to political exiles and prisoners. By

1987, even the central planning of the economy was altered, with local officials being granted more discretion in setting prices and wages. The first real private businesses since the 1920s—usually small businesses like cafes but even a few private banks—began to surface. Gorbachev even tried to tackle the Russians' notorious love of alcohol by limiting the distribution of alcoholic beverages, although this only encouraged black market production and sale of alcohol, which itself brought on a massive sugar shortage.[15]

Arguably Gorbachev's most risky reform was hacking away at the culture of secrecy that had settled over the Soviet government, thanks to the influence of the KGB and the needs of Cold War intrigue. This included releasing more information about Stalin-era forced migrations in the Baltic states along with more details about the government's cynical maneuvering to pull the Baltic countries into the Soviet orbit. Rather than restoring confidence in the state, these disclosures only heated up anger that was already boiling in Lithuania, Estonia, and Latvia.

Relations between the Baltics and the Soviet government were already tense due to the heavy-handed exploitation of their natural resources. Estonians rallied against destructive phosphate mining while the Lithuanians objected to Moscow's plans to expand chemicals manufacturing and build a fourth nuclear reactor at the Ignalina nuclear power plant, especially so soon after the devastating meltdown of the Chernobyl nuclear plant in Ukraine.[16] The leaking information about the Soviet Union's dirty history with the Baltic nations only confirmed that the Baltic governments were far from equal partners in the grand communist experiment.

The first big movement for Baltic freedom was the Helsinki-86 group. They hosted a demonstration on June 14, 1987, at the Freedom Monument in the Latvian capital of Riga, which had been built to commemorate the Latvian War of Independence back in 1918. The demonstrators called attention to the dark anniversary of Stalin's mass deportations of Latvians in 1941. The marchers were harassed by KGB agents, but demonstrations continued. Protesters brought flowers with no consequences, an activity that would have entailed arrest just a few years ago. There were even more protests on the anniversaries of the Molotov-Ribbentrop Pact and Latvia's first declaration of independence. The police stepped in violently with the last, but the impression had already been made on the public.

The bonds that held the Soviet Union together were quite simply dissolving. In Estonia, the first large-scale noncommunist political coalition since the 1940s, the People's Front, had made its national debut in June 1988. That fall, Estonia asserted its right to reject Soviet laws whenever they conflicted with national interests. On January 18, 1989, Estonian, not Russian, became the official language of the republic, with the Latvian government also acknowledging mass protests demanding a revival of the Latvian language. The next domino to fall was a May 1989 resolution by the Lithuanian legislature, formally demanding more autonomy from Moscow.

The countries did see themselves as united in their struggle for more self-determination. One of the biggest and most remarkable protests in history, the Baltic Way, dramatically expressed this Baltic solidarity. When the fiftieth anniversary of the Molotov-Ribbentrop Pact rolled around on August 1989, about two million Latvians, Estonians, and Lithuanians reached out and created a human chain reaching across all three countries. "Together we made it," one Latvian writer proclaims on her government's website. "Looking back, it was not a time of sorrow—it was a time of decisiveness and unity. And when one looks at how things have turned out—with Latvia being a stable and trustworthy member of the European Union, NATO, having been reformed economically and politically—there is no doubt that it was worth it."[17] Two-fifths of the entire region's population participated, forming a 370-mile human chain that stretched from Lithuania's capital of Vilnius through Riga to the Estonian capital of Tallinn.[18]

This gesture undertaken by millions marked the beginning of the end. Even the Soviet official Alexander Yakovlev admitted as much when he described the talks he had with Baltic activists: "I had to admit to them that we had an empire, that there really was a centre which dictated to the republics. I had to agree with them. Anything else would have been blasphemy."[19] The spell was broken. By the end of 1989, Lithuania made the world-changing move of formally ending their Communist Party's monopoly over the government and even the Lithuanian Communist Party itself voted to break away from the Soviet Union. This was all just a prelude to moves by Lithuania's parliament to win full independence, which Gorbachev tried in vain to stop using an oil blockade.

Although Gorbachev was reluctant to use military force, the brunt of the Soviet military was called down, although perhaps not on the scale that might have been expected in another era. In Vilnius, Soviet troops made their way into a TV station where Lithuania's National Salvation Committee had announced that it had taken power. In the resulting chaos, thirteen Lithuanians and one KGB officer were killed. A woman, Loreta Asanavičiute, died when she tried to stop an armored personnel carrier by lying down in front of it. Violence also broke out in Riga, with several Latvians killed resisting Soviet takeovers of government buildings.[20] Nonetheless, even the threat of the gun was impotent. Over the course of 1990 and 1991, Estonia and Latvia would join Lithuania in reasserting their national independence, as new movements to break away from the Soviet Union rippled out from the Baltic. Remarkably, these separations were mostly non-violent except in Romania, where the regime of Nicolae Ceauşescu, as inhumane as it was incompetent, closed with more than a thousand deaths and the impromptu trial and execution of Nicolae and his wife Elena.

The Soviet Union itself was ironically brought to its end by the very country that created it. With support from a majority of the remaining Soviet republics, Gorbachev sought to negotiate a Treaty of Union that would preserve the Soviet Union in a looser form and create an elected federal president who would lead the military and handle foreign policy. Two days before the treaty was supposed to come into effect, all the leaders in the USSR from the KGB to the prime minister announced to the world that they had taken emergency powers to truly save the Soviet Union, putting the general secretary under a brief house arrest while he was on vacation in the Crimea. However, there was defiance from the newly elected president of the Russian Republic, Boris Yeltsin, whose entire office owed its existence to Gorbachev's democratization reforms. Surrounded by hundreds of supporters, Yeltsin braved the tanks camped in front of his headquarters. With determined casualness, Yeltsin went on to order the confiscation of all of the Soviet Union's offices and resources within Russian borders, a coolly bureaucratic end to what was meant to be the first paradise for workers on Earth. "The attempt to save the old structure of the Soviet Union had destroyed it more suddenly and irrevocably than anyone had expected," Eric Hobsbawm, himself a devoted Marxist, noted.[21]

Five years after Gorbachev announced his resignation from the leadership of the already defunct Soviet Union, he appeared with his

The Baltic Way in August 1989: Estonia, top, Latvia, middle, and Lithuania, bottom. (*Jaan Künnap/Uldis Pinka/Rimantas Lazdynas, Wikimedia Commons*)

ten-year-old granddaughter Anastasia in an ad for the American pizza chain Pizza Hut. It was shown in the United States but not in Russia, where Gorbachev remained a widely detested figure. It was probably for the best. If anything symbolized the total victory of Western capitalism over communism, it was the appearance of the Soviet Union's last leader, the successor of Lenin and Stalin, in a pitch for fast food pizza. Even so, perhaps gloating is unwarranted, since at the time of this writing the Soviet Union's greatest rival now also faces an out-of-control military budget, a population alienated from its leaders, an uncomfortable legacy of imperial hubris, and its very own "spiritual crisis."

CONCLUSION

If History Has Any Lessons

"Empires are restless organisms," Gore Vidal, the great modern chronicler of the American experiment, wrote. "They must constantly renew themselves; should an empire start leaking energy, it will die."[1]

Historians can and should avoid the trap of thinking that nations and the eras they navigate can be as cleanly categorized as geological minerals. Still, the world history of empire is filled with such repetitions and patterns. The profound stagnation that Gore Vidal describes is one of them. This is not just in terms of conquest and expansion, of course. It was Augustus in the early years of the first millennium CE who fixed the boundaries of the Roman Empire, which for the most part were not extended except famously through Trajan's conquests in the Middle East, Armenia, and modern-day Romania, and even then these new territories were generally not maintained for long. When Augustus did this, the best decades of the empire's lifespan were still over half a century away, the western half of the empire would continue to exist for another three centuries, and the eastern half far longer still.

One should never take too deterministic a view of history, but this stagnation does seem to reoccur in three ways. Perhaps the most obvious is how an empire becomes rich through exploitation of its new territories, resources, and subject peoples. At first, while the wealth is never distributed equitably, it does bring wide benefits to the imperial metropole, giving rise to new cultural movements, vastly improved infrastructure, and magnificent public works. However, over the course of generations, as the biggest beneficiaries of imperial largesse become entrenched, their personal interests diverge from and even conflict with the public good. Eventually they become an extremely insular elite, hoarding the sources of wealth, whether it be property, as in the case of all pre-industrial empires, or well-paying positions in influential industries such as media and academia and access to affluent social networks, something more familiar in the modern era. As the wealth pours more and more into the coffers of private interests who become apathetic or even hostile to their governments' need for tax revenue, the quality of infrastructure, public services, and social and cultural projects declines, in turn fueling people's escalating discontent and alienation from the government. Although its lifespan was cut short by the Romans, arguably one can see this beginning with the Carthaginian Empire, with the family of Hannibal gathering more wealth and influence than even the leading citizens at the imperial capital. The Carolingians, too, had failed in the end to strike that crucial balance between the well-being of the political center and the interests of the kings and nobles who ruled the empire's provinces.

Likewise, both Han China at its twilight and the late Roman Empire had their superrich landowners who could defy the emperor's tax collectors with impunity. "What middle ground there may have been earlier was squeezed by the concentration of income and wealth within a politically powerful elite," Walter Scheidel writes in *The Great Leveller: Violence and the History of Inequality from the Stone Age to the 21st Century*.[2] This was even true for the Soviet Union, where a small enclave within the government and the party enjoyed perks and a standard of living denied to the vast majority. Indeed, books and articles have been written claiming that the very same process is unfolding in the United States today, however much it may be shrouded by myths of capitalist meritocracy.[3] In other cases, it is the military that becomes the most affluent power in the government and dominates politics while robbing both public and private interests of economic resources, which was where Japan found itself by the time it was drawn into World War II and was not unlike the process that left the once-mighty Abbasids at the mercy of their own Turkish elite soldiers.

Another source of stagnation is another, much broader form of closing off: the shutting off of entire peoples from the benefits of empire. Some degree of openness to other peoples, cultures, and faiths has been an ingredient of imperial success since at least the Persians, whose respect for the religions and cultures of their conquered peoples went so far that Cyrus, despite being a Zoroastrian, became the unlikely savior of the Jewish people. Unlike the city-states of Greece, the Romans offered citizenship to other Italian peoples and later even to foreigners outside of Italy. Ultimately, by the early third century CE, the emperor Caracalla extended citizenship to all residents of the empire. In fact, Mary Beard argues that it was this openness, not military prowess, that made the Romans unique and successful.[4] The Ottoman Empire probably would not have survived for as long as it did if not for the toleration it offered Jews and Christians, often to a greater degree than neighboring Christian nations. None of these states even in their heydays matched today's standards of pluralism and tolerance, of course. Persian discrimination against the Egyptians may have been a glaring exception to their usual policy, the Romans could still be militantly parochial throughout their entire history, and Ottoman toleration had its highs and lows.

Still, a hardening of attitudes toward non-natives is quite often a facet of decline. Bigotry toward Germans, even once Germans began running what was left of the imperial armies, was a running theme in Rome's final decades. Athenian and Aztec exploitation of their "clients" and "partners" became a fatal liability for both empires once a serious, existential threat came. Nor could the British Empire long sustain its own myth of liberty and liberalism alongside its treatment of its non-British subjects. The total abandonment of even the pretense of religious pluralism and growing intolerance toward Hindus became a major and festering wound in the side of the Mughal Empire. Although the crusaders of the Fourth Crusade were undoubtedly to blame for triggering the chain of events that would finally fatally enfeeble the Byzantine Empire, religious intolerance on both sides made the disaster possible. And the Russian Empire did itself no favors by trying to force Russian supremacy on the empire's other populations, a lesson that went totally unlearned by the Russian Empire's successor, the Soviet Union. Even today, examples of xenophobia and isolation having negative and unintended economic and political con-sequences are not lacking in the cases of Brexit[5] or immigration crack-downs.[6]

Finally, besides empires becoming rigid toward non-native peoples, they also tend to grow stagnant when their policies become too in-flexible. In its relatively brief existence, Qin China could not abandon its brutal and hated ideology of Legalism until it was already much too late. Also evidence does suggest that it was the inability of the Khmers to adapt to the environmental challenges overwhelming them that doomed their great capital to ruin. Sometimes reform does come, but the reforms fail to solve all of the underlying crises facing the em-pire while at the same time expanding the possibilities of what is pos-sible in the minds of the people at large. Gorbachev's *glasnost* is a compelling example of reform that did come, but it did not serve its purpose of saving the Soviet government. True, if *glasnost* had not happened or if the Soviet hardliners had succeeded in reversing most of the reform program, the Soviet Union would have possibly dis-solved regardless. However, *glasnost* clearly did have unintended con-sequences that strengthened the gravity pulling at it.

As much as we may want to deny that the United States is a "true" empire or at least is only a "soft" kind of empire, there are parts of the story that are repeating today, especially in "the West." In the face of a global economic recession from which there was no clean recov-ery, environmental dilemmas that spark fears of the end of civilization, and growing disillusionment with the post-World War II political order, speaking of imperial decline is indeed very timely. Maybe it could be avoided by breaking the pattern of stagnation that Gore Vidal warned us about. Yet it was the Sumerians, the people who left behind the first written language starting around 4500 BCE, who be-lieved that the reason some of their city-states expanded and fell was because the gods, to prevent human civilization from becoming too brackish, withdrew their favor from one king and bestowed it on an-other on a regular basis. So far, their belief that empires are not made to last has not been proven wrong. In that respect, maybe the priority for the United States and "the West" in general should be to try to retire gracefully from hegemony and ease any hardships for their peo-ple.

However, if history has any lessons, it is that subtle yet far-reaching change is possible. While the legacies of the empires of the past still survive today with ugly political and economic consequences, especially for the parts of the world that had been subjugated and colonized for centuries, naked imperial conquest is still not an accepted part of the normal political lexicon. In fact, war is more rare today than at any other point in recorded human history. The international ideals of the recent past have been tarnished by the events of the twenty-first century so far, but the ideas of self-determination and human rights are still held up as axioms. Perhaps one day, too, it will no longer be taken for granted that the world has to be dominated by one or two superpowers or a clutch of rival "imperial" nations. In other words, maybe the very reality of empire will become as much a part of the past as the acceptance of empire.

NOTES

INTRODUCTION

1. William Skidelsky, "Niall Ferguson: 'Westerners don't understand how vulnerable freedom is,'" last accessed: 5/1/2015, http://www.theguardian.com/books/2011/feb/20/niall-ferguson-interview-civilization.
2. Deepak Lal, *In Praise of Empires: Globalization and Order* (New York: Palgrave, 2004), xix.
3. John A. Hobson, *Imperialism: A Study* (New York: James Pott and Co., 1902), 1.4.2.
4. Alexander J. Motyl, *Imperial Ends: The Decay, Collapse, and Revival of Empires* (New York: Columbia University Press, 2001), 7, 23-4.
5. Sir John Glubb, *The Fate of Empires and Search for Survival* (Edinburgh: William Blackwood & Sons, 1977).

CHAPTER ONE: THE ATHENIAN EMPIRE

1. Thucydides, 6.24 in *History of the Peloponessian War*, trans. Steven Lattimore (Indianapolis: Hackett, 1998).
2. Thucydides, 6.17.
3. Thucydides, 5.89.
4. Christian Meier, *Athens: A Portrait of the City in its Golden Age*, trans. Robert and Rita Kimber (New York: Metropolitan Books, 1998), 307.
5. Ibid., 520.
6. Plutarch, *Alkibiades*, trans. Bernadotte Perrin (Cambridge: Harvard University Press, 1916), 4.8.
7. Donald Kagan, *The Peace of Nicias and the Sicilian Expedition* (Ithaca: Cornell University Press, 1981), 210.
8. Thucydides, 6.32.
9. Peter Green, *Armada from Athens* (New York: Doubleday, 1970), 148.
10. Plutarch, Alkibiades, 22.2.
11. Kagan, 318.
12. Thucydides, 7.75.
13. Green, 335-6.
14. Ibid., 348.

CHAPTER TWO: THE PERSIAN EMPIRE

1. Michael Axworthy, *A History of Iran* (New York: Perseus Books, 2008), 22.
2. Xenophon, *Cyropaedia*, trans. Walter Miller (Cambridge: Harvard University Press, 1914), 8.8.15.
3. Herodotus, *Herodotus: The History*, trans. David Greene (Chicago: University of Chicago Press, 1998), 8.98.
4. Isaiah 45:1-3.
5. Josef Wiesehöfer, *Ancient Persia from 550 BCE to 650 AD*, trans. Azizeh Azodi (London: I.B. Tauris, 1996), 23.
6. A.T. Olmstead, *History of the Persian Empire* (Chicago: University of Chicago Press, 1970), 182.
7. Translated in Pierre Briant, *From Cyrus to Alexander: A History of the Persian Empire*, trans. Peter T. Daniels (Winona Lake, IN: Eisenbrauns, 2002), 168.
8. A.B. Boswrth, *Conquest and Empire: The Reign of Alexander the Great* (New York: Cambridge University Press, 1992), 92.
9. Diodorus Siculus, *Universal History*, trans. C. Bradford Welles (Cambridge: Harvard University Press, 1963), 17.37.36.
10. Arrian, *Anabasis of Alexander*, 3.18.
11. Plutarch, *Life of Alexander*, trans. Bernadotte Perrin (Cambridge: Harvard University Press, 1919), 38.1-8.
12. Michael Wood, *In the Footsteps of Alexander the Great: A Journey from Greece to Asia* (Berkeley: University of California Press, 1997), 117.

CHAPTER THREE: THE QIN EMPIRE

1. Sima Qian, *Records of the Grand Historian of China*, trans. Burton Watson (New York: Columbia University Press, 1961), 1.63.
2. Jane Portal and Qingbo Duan, *The First Emperor: China's Terracotta Army* (London: British Museum Press, 2007), 167.
3. Johh Keay, *China, A History* (New York: Basic Books, 2009), 54.
4. Quoted in Keay, 76.
5. Sima Qian, 1.37.
6. Jonathan Clemens, *The First Emperor of China* (Stroud, Gloucestershire: Sutton Publishing, 2006), 54-5.
7. *Annals of Lü Buwei*, trans. John Knoblock and Jeffrey Riegel (Stanford: Stanford University Press, 2000), 25.
8. Clements, 47-8.
9. Han Feizi in *Sources of Chinese Tradition*, trans. Burton Watson, eds. William Theodore de Bary and Irene Bloom (New York: Columbia University Press, 1999).
10. Quoted in Clements, 119.
11. Sima Qian, 1.43.
12. Clements, 106.
13. Sima Qian, 1.54-5.
14. Ibid., 1.48-9.
15. Ibid., 1.62.
16. Keay, 106.
17. Ibid., 109.
18. Sima Qian, 1.66.
19. Ibid., 1.206.

CHAPTER FOUR: THE CARTHAGINIAN EMPIRE

1. Livy, *A History of Rome,* trans. D. Spillan and Cyrus Edwards (London: G. Bell, 1989), 21.1.
2. Polybius, *The Histories,* trans. W.R. Paton (New York: Willian Heinemann, 1922-7), 6.13.
3. Richard Miles, *Carthage Must Be Destroyed: The Rise and Fall of an Ancient Civilization* (New York: Viking, 2011), 75-6.
4. Justin, *Epitome,* trans. Rev. John Selby Watson (London: Henry G. Bohn, 1853), 21.4.
5. Miles, 220-5.
6. Polybius, 3.22.
7. Livy, 43.6.
8. Pliny, *Natural History,* trans. William Heinneman (Cambridge: Harvard University Press, 1968), 15.20.
9. Diodorus, 35.33.5.
10. Miles, 334.
11. Quintillian, *The Orator's Education,* trans. Donald A. Robinson (Cambridge: Harvard University Press, 2002), 9.3.31.
12. Appian, *Roman History,* trans. Horace White (Cambridge: Harvard University Press, 1913), 8.19.127-31.
13. Appian, 8.19.132.
14. Sallust, *The Jugurthan War,* trans. J.C. Rolfe (Cambridge: Harvard University Press, 1921), 46.

CHAPTER FIVE: THE HAN EMPIRE

1. John Keay, *China: A History* (New York: Basic Books, 2011), 145.
2. Michael Loewe, *Everyday Life in Imperial China, During the Han Period 202 BCE–AD 220* (New York: G.P. Putna's Sons, 1968), 36-7, 98-100, 128-31.
3. Harold M. Tanner, *China: A History* (Indianapolis: Hackett, 2009), 124.
4. J.A.G. Roberts, *A Complete History of China* (Gloucestershire: Sutton Publishing, 2003), 60.
5. Ssu-ma Guang, *Last of the Han,* trans. Rafe de Crespigny (Canberra: Australian National University, 1969), xxvii.
6. Ibid., 7.
7. Roberts, 62.
8. Ssu-ma Guang, 28.
9. Ibid., 46.
10. Ibid., 56.

CHAPTER SIX: THE ROMAN EMPIRE

1. Edward Gibbon, *The Fall of the Roman Empire,* ed. Hans-Freidrich Mueller (New York: Random House, 2003), 23.
2. *Olympiodorus apud Photium,* 198.
3. Bertrand Lançon, *Rome in Late Antiquity,* trans. Antonia Nevill (New York: Routledge, 2000), 13.
4. Quoted in Michael Grant, *The Fall of the Roman Empire,* 3rd ed. (New York: Barnes & Noble, 2005), 82.
5. Ibid., 77-8.
6. Lançon, 93-4.
7. Giusto Traina, *428 AD: An Ordinary Year at the End of the Roman Empire,* trans. Allan Cameron (Princeton: Princeton University Press, 2009), 98.

8. Quoted in Grant, 162.
9. Traina, 76.
10. Grant, 134.
11. Hagith Sivan, *Galla Placidia* (Oxford: Oxford University Press, 2011), 85-7.
12. Wood, 105.
13. Quoted and translated in C.D. Gordon, *The Age of Attila: Fifth Century Byzantium and the Barbarians* (Ann Arbor, University of Michigan Press, 1960), 51.
14. Ibid., 200-1.

CHAPTER SEVEN: THE CAROLINGIAN EMPIRE

1. Einhard, *Life of Charlemagne*, trans. Sidney Painter (Ann Arbor: University of Michigan Press, 1960), 57.
2. Einhard, 1.
3. Pierre Riché, *The Carolingians: A Family Who Forged Europe*, trans. Michael Idomir Allen (Philadelphia: University of Pennsylvania Press, 1993), 125-30.
4. Rosamund McKitterick, *The Frankish Kingdoms Under the Carolingians* (London: Longman, 1983), 134.
5. Ibid., 56.
6. Ibid., 66.
7. Paul Edward Dutton, *A Carolingian Reader* (London: Broadview Press, 2004), 166.
8. Ibid., 167.
9. Roché, 152.
10. *Carolingian Chronicles*, 130.
11. Astronomer, *Son of Life: A Contemporary Life of Louis the Pious* (Syracuse: Syracuse University Press, 1961), 96.
12. Dutton, 170.
13. Roché, 156.
14. Dutton, 333, 9-11, 13.
15. Cabanis, 1961, 161; Roché, 1993, 163.
16. Janet Nelson, *Charles the Bald* (London: Longman, 1992), 132-3.
17. Roché, 166-8.
18. Ibid.
19. McKitterick, 1983, 173.
20. Quoted and translation in Roché, 168-9.

CHAPTER EIGHT: THE ABBASID CALIPHATE

1. Quoted in Gaston Wiet, *Baghdad: Metropolis of the Abbasid Caliphate*, trans. Seymour Feiler (Norman: University of Oklahoma Press, 1971), 9-10.
2. Hugh Kennedy, *When Baghdad Ruled the Muslim World: The Rise and Fall of Islam's Greatest Dynasty* (New York: Da Capo Press, 2005), 3.
3. Al-Suyuti, *History of the Caliphs*, trans. H.S. Jarrett (Calcutta: J.W. Thomas, 1881), 261.
4. G.E. von Grunebaum, *Classical Islam: A History, 600–1258* (Chicago: Aldine Publishing, 1970), 103.
5. Kennedy, 131-2.
6. Ibid., 258-60.
7. Wiet, 22.
8. Kennedy, 133-4.
9. Martin Sicker, *The Islamic World in Ascendancy: From the Arab Conquests to the Siege of Vienna* (Westport, CT: Praeger, 2000), 32-6.

10. Peter Brent, *The Mongol Empire, Genghis Khan: His Triumph and His Legacy* (London: Weidenfeld and Nicolson, 1976), 107.
11. *Mission to Asia*, ed. Christopher Dawson (Toronto: University of Toronto Press, 1940), 85.
12. Sicker, 110.
13. Quoted in Sicker, 111.
14. Stephen Turnbull, *Genghis Khan & the Mongol Conquests, 1190–1400* (London: Routledge, 2003), 58.
15. Quoted in Brent, 139.
16. Wiet, 166.
17. *The Travels of Marco Polo*, ed. and trans. Hugh Murray (Edinburgh: Oliver and Boyd, 1845), 211.
18. Al-Suyuti, 498. I have modernized the language of the translation.

CHAPTER NINE: THE BYZANTINE EMPIRE

1. "Pope sorrow over Constantinople," June 29, 2004, http://news.bbc.co.uk/2/hi/europe/3850789.stm.
2. Quoted in Louis Duchesne, *Early History of the Christian Church: From Its Foundation to the End of the Fifth Century* (New York: Longman, 1920), 2.456.
3. Niketas Choniates, *O City of Byzantium, Annals of Niketas Choniates*, trans. Harry J. Magoulias (Detroit: Wayne State University Press, 1984), 140-1.
4. Jonathan Phillips, *The Fourth Crusade and the Sack of Constantinople* (New York: Viking, 2004), 110.
5. Quoted in ibid., 124.
6. Niketas, 547-8.
7. Ibid., 296.
8. Geoffrey de Villehardouin, *Chronicle of the Fourth Crusade*, trans. Frank T. Marzials (London: J.M. Dent, 1908), 39.
9. Donald E. Queller and Thomas F. Madden, *The Fourth Crusade: The Conquest of Constantinople* (Philadelphia: University of Pennsylvania Press, 1997), 129-30.
10. Quoted in Philipps, 188.
11. Queller and Madden, 17.
12. Philipps, 208-9.
13. Quoted in ibid., 217.
14. "The Fourth Crusade" in *Translations and Reprints from the Original Sources in European History*, vol. 3, ed. and trans. Dana Carlton Munro (Philadelphia: University of Pennsylvania, 1907), 15-6.
15. Queller and Madden, 194.

CHAPTER 10: THE KHMER EMPIRE

1. Henri Mouhot, *Henri Mouhot's Diary*, ed. Christopher Pym (London: Oxford University Press, 1966).
2. Bruno Dagens, *Angkor: Heart of an Asian Empire* (London: Harry N. Abrams, 1995), 131.
3. Quoted in ibid., 23.
4. Mouhot, 92.
5. George Coedès, *Angkor: An Introduction*, trans. and ed. Emily Floyd Gardiner (Oxford: Oxford University Press, 1963), 96.
6. Karen J. Coates, *Cambodia Now: Life in the Wake of War* (Jefferson, NC: McFarland, 2005), 51.
7. Ian Mabbett and David Chandler, *The Khmers* (Oxford: Blackwell, 1995), 97.

8. Madeliene Gateau, *The Civilization of Angkor* (New York: Rizzoli, 1976), 80.
9. Mabbett and Chandler, 206-7.
10. Michael D. Coe, *Angkor and the Khmer Civilization* (London: Thames and Hudson, 2003), 142.
11. Mabbet and Chandler, 126.
12. Quoted and translated in Gateau, 38.
13. Ma Tuan-lin, *Ethnographie*, 484f., quoted in Mabbet and Chandler, 129.
14. Coe, 196-203; Mabbett and Chandler, 213-7.
15. B.-P. Groslier, "Agriculture et religion dans l'empire angkorien,"*Etudes rurales*, 53-6 (1974): 95-117.
16. "Did Climate Influence Angkor's Collapse?" March 29, 2010, https://www.ldeo. columbia.edu/news-events/did-climate-influence-angkors-collapse.
17. Richard Stone, "Divining Angkor," *National Geographic*, May 2014.

CHAPTER ELEVEN: THE AZTEC EMPIRE

1. Davíd Carrasco, *City of Sacrifice: The Aztec Empire and the Role of Violence in Civilization* (Boston: Beacon Press, 1999), 3.
2. Richard F. Townsend, *The Aztecs*, rev. ed. (London: Thames & Hudson, 2000), 166-8.
3. *Florentine Codex*, vol. 9, trans. Arthur J.O. Anderson and Charles E. Dibble, rev. ed. (Santa Fe: School of American Research, 1973), 73.
4. Quoted in Bernal Diaz del Castillo, *The Discovery and Conquest of Mexico*, trans. A.P. Maudslay (New York: Farrar, Straus, and Cudahy, 1956), 104-5.
5. Hernán Cortés, *Letters from Mexico*, trans. A.R. Pagden (New York: Orion Books, 1971), 67.
6. Townsend, 44-5.
7. Ibid., 58.
8. Eduardo Matos Moctezuma, *The Aztecs*, trans. Andrew Ellis (New York: Rizzoli, 1989), 31.
9. Ibid., 49-51.
10. Francisco López de Gómara, *Cortés: The Life of the Conqueror by His Secretary*, trans. Lesley Byrd Simpson (Berkeley: University of California Press, 1964), 162.
11. Cortés, 33, 35.
12. Townsend, 74.
13. C.A. Burland, *Montezuma, Lord of the Aztecs* (London: G.P. Putnam's Sons, 1973), 37.
14. George C. Vaillant, *Aztecs of Mexico: Origins, Rise, and Fall of the Aztec Nation*, rev. ed. (London: Allen Lane, 1962), 238.
15. Matthew Restall, *Seven Myths of the Spanish Conquest* (Oxford: Oxford University Press, 2003), 140-1.
16. *Florentine Codex*, vol. 12, 83.
17. Quoted in ibid., 87. Restall suggests that the quotation may be apocryphal.
18. Gómara, 33.
19. Burland, 39.
20. Susan Gillespie, *The Aztec Kings* (Tucson: University of Arizona Press, 1989), xvii-xli.
21. A thorough debunking of the Cortés-Quetzalcoatl story, and the idea that natives routinely mistook European explorers for gods, may be found in Restall, 108-20.
22. Restall, 142-3.
23. Cortés, 84.
24. Gómara, 185.

25. *Florentine Codex,* vol. 12, 55-6.
26. Cortés, 475n.

CHAPTER TWELVE: THE MUGHAL EMPIRE

1. Quoted in Pandit Sunderlal, *How India Lost Her Freedom* (Bombay: Popular Prakashan, 1970), xix.
2. Richard M. Eaton, "Temple desecration in pre-modern India," *Frontline* 17.25 (2000). http://www.frontline.in/static/html/fl1725/17250620.htm.
3. Denis Judd, *The Lion and the Tiger: The Rise and Fall of the British Raj, 1600–1947* (Oxford: Oxford University Press, 2004), 11.
4. S.M. Jaffar, *The Mughal Empire* (Delhi: Ess Ess Publications, 1974), 60-3.
5. Ashirbadi Lal Srivistava. *The Mughal Empire (1526–1803)* (Jaipur: Shiva Lal Agrawala & Co., 1964), 127-9.
6. Ibid., 294-6.
7. Quoted in John F. Richards, *The Mughal Empire* (New York: Cambridge University Press, 1993), 153.
8. Ibid., 175-7.
9. Quoted in Gopal Singh, *A History of the Sikh People, 1469-1978* (Delhi: World Sikh University Press, 1979), 290.
10. Richards, 213.
11. Sirivistava, 341-2, 350-1.
12. Jadunath Sarkar, *Shivaji and His Times* (London: Longman, 1920), 320-3.
13. Richards, 290-7.

CHAPTER THIRTEEN: THE OTTOMAN EMPIRE

1. Quoted and translated in *The Movement for Greek Independence, 1770-1821: A Collection of Documents,* ed. R. Cogg (New York: Macmillan, 1976), 59-60.
2. David Brewer, *The Greek War of Independence* (Woodstock, NY: Overlook Press, 2001), 12-3.
3. Caroline Finkel, *Osman's Dream: The History of the Ottoman Empire* (New York: Basic Books, 2004), 80.
4. Ibid., 191, 279-80.
5. Salih Gülen, *The Ottoman Sultans: Mighty Guests of the Throne* (New York: Blue Dome, 2010), 280.
6. Alan Palmer, *The Decline and Fall of the Ottoman Empire* (Cambridge: John Murray, 1992), 83.
7. George Waddington, *A Visit to Greece in 1823 and 1824* (London: John Murray, 1825), 23.
8. Brewer, 124, 129-30.
9. Ibid., 124-5.
10. Davide Rodogno, *Against Massacre: Humanitarian Interventions in the Ottoman Empire, 1815-1914* (Princeton: Princeton University Press, 2012), 68-9.
11. Brewer, 134-5.
12. Count Peter Gamba, *Lord Byron's Last Journey to Greece* (Paris: A. and W. Galignani, 1825), 117.
13. Roderick Beaton, *Byron's War: Romantic War, Greek Revolution* (New York: Cambridge University Press, 1991), 90-1.
14. Palmer, 85-8.
15. Ibid., 88-90.
16. Ibid., 98.

CHAPTER FOURTEEN: THE RUSSIAN EMPIRE

1. Nicholas V. Riasanovsky and Mark D. Steinberg, *A History of Russia*, 8th ed. (Oxford: Oxford University Press, 2011), 390.
2. Edvard Radzinsky, *The Last Tsar*, trans. Marian Schwartz (New York: Doubleday, 1992), 44.
3. Jerome Blum, *Lord and Peasant in Russia: From the Ninth to the Nineteenth Century* (Princeton: Princeton University Press, 1961), 420.
4. Hugh Seton-Watson, *The Decline of Imperial Russia, 1855—1914* (Strand: Methuen, 1952), 21.
5. Edvard Radzinsky, *Alexander II, The Last Great Tsar*, trans. Antonia W. Bouis (New York: Free Press, 2005), 115-8, 125-35.
6. Ibid., 229-30.
7. Seton-Watson, 68.
8. Ibid., 30.
9. Riasanovsky and Steinberg, *A History of Russia*, 8th ed. (Oxford: Oxford University Press, 2011), 393-4.
10. Walter Sablinsky, *The Road to Bloody Sunday: Father Gapon and the St. Petersburg Massacre of 1905* (Princeton: Princeton University Press, 1976), 38-40.
11. Quoted in ibid., 74.
12. Abraham Ascher, *The Revolution of 1905* (Stanford: Stanford University Press, 1988), 13-4.
13. Quoted in Sablinsky, 85.
14. Quoted and translated in Sablinsky, 188-9.
15. Ibid., 213-4.
16. Quoted in Sablinsky, 209.
17. Ibid., 238.
18. Quoted in Sablinsky, 243-4.
19. Ascher, 92.
20. Quoted in Ascher, 92.
21. Ascher, 102.
22. Sablinsky, 275.
23. Quoted in Ascher, 102.

CHAPTER FIFTEEN: THE EMPIRE OF JAPAN

1. John Toland, *The Rising Sun: The Decline and Fall of the Japanese Empire, 1936-1945* (New York: Random House, 1970), 181-2.
2. Herbert P. Bix, *Hirohito and the Making of Modern Japan* (New York: HarperCollins, 2000), 26-7.
3. Simon Stander, *Why War: Capitalism and the Nation State* (New York: Bloomsbury Academic, 2014), 90.
4. W.G. Beasley, *The Meiji Restoration* (Stanford: Stanford University Press, 1972), 350-1.
5. Quoted in ibid., 369-70.
6. Quoted in W.G. Beasley, *Japanese Imperialism, 1894-1945* (Oxford: Clarendon Press, 1987), 90.
7. Quoted in James Palmer, *The Bloody White Baron: The Extraordinary Story of the Russian Nobleman Who Became the Last Khan of Mongolia* (New York: Basic Books, 2009), 31.
8. Mark E. Caprio, *Japanese Assimilation Policies in Korea, 1910–1945* (Seattle: University of Washington Press, 1995), 49-81.

9. E. Taylor Atkins, *Primitive Selves: Korea in the Japanese Colonial Gaze, 1910-1945* (Berkeley: University of California Press, 2010).
10. Franz Lidz, "The Little-Known Legend of Jesus in Japan," *Smithsonian*, Last accessed: 3/4/2015, http://www.smithsonianmag.com/history/the-little-known-legend-of-jesus-in-japan.
11. Quoted in Bix, 200.
12. Bix, 191-4.
13. Ibid., 369-70.
14. "Conventional War Crimes (Atrocities)," *Judgment: International Military Tribunal for the Far East* (November 1948).
15. Quoted and translated in Toland, 812-3.
16. Emperor Shōwa, transmitted by Domei and recorded by the Federal Communications Commission, August 14, 1945.
17. Bix, 544.
18. Robert Harvey, *American Shogun: General MacArthur, Emperor Hirohito and the Drama of Modern Japan* (Woodstock, NY: Overlook Press, 2006), 14-8.
19. Quoted in Bix, 568.

CHAPTER SIXTEEN: THE BRITISH EMPIRE

1. Eric Hobsbawm, *The Age of Extremes: A History of the World, 1914–1991* (New York: Pantheon, 1994), 221.
2. Angus Maddison, *The World Economy: A Millennial Perspective* (Oxford: OECD, 2009), 242.
3. PBS NOW, Interview with Deborah Lessing, Last accessed: 4/1/2015, http://www.pbs.org/now/printable/transcript_lessing_print.html.
4. Quoted in Peter Clarke, *The Last Thousand Days of the British Empire* (New York: Penguin, 2008), 506.
5. Timothy Guinnane, *The Vanishing Irish: Households, Migration, and the Rural Economy in Ireland* (Princeton: Princeton University Press, 1997), 56-7.
6. Quoted in Mick Mulcrone, "The Famine and Collective Memory: The Role of the Irish-American Press in the Early Twentieth Century," *The Great Famine and the Irish Diaspora in America*, ed. Arthur Gribben (Boston: University of Massachusetts Press, 1999), 219.
7. Piers Brendon, *The Decline and Fall of the British Empire, 1781–1997* (New York: Alfred A. Knopf, 2008), 419.
8. Peter Hennessy, *Having It So Good: Britain in the Fifties* (London: Penguin, 2006), 245.
9. Hobsbawm, 216.
10. David Childs, *Britain Since 1939: Progress and Decline* (New York: St. Martin's Press, 1995), 111.
11. Brendon, 490-1.
12. Ibid., 494-5.
13. Quoted in Evelyn Shuckburgh, *Descent to Suez, Diaries 1951-56* (New York: W.W. Norton, 1987), 329.
14. Peter G. Boyle, *The Eden-Eisenhower Correspondence, 1955-1957* (Chapel Hill: University of North Carolina Press, 2005), Eden to Eisenhower, January 16, 1956.
15. Quoted in Brendon, 496.
16. Brendon, 497.
17. Quoted in Anthony Gorst and Lewis Johnman, *The Suez Crisis* (London: Routledge, 1997), 61-2.
18. Boyle, July 31, 1956.

19. Brendon, 497-8.
20. Quoted in ibid., 504.

CHAPTER SEVENTEEN: THE SOVIET UNION

1. "Khruschev-Nixon Debate," Last accessed: 4/27/2015, http://astro.temple.edu/~rimmerma/Khrushchev_Nixon_debate.htm.
2. Geoffrey Ponton, *The Soviet Union, Soviet Politics from Lenin to Yeltsin* (Oxford: Blackwell, 1994), 38.
3. Christopher Read, *The Making and Breaking of the Soviet System: An Interpretation* (Houndmills: Palgrave, 2001), 157-80.
4. Ibid., 37.
5. Simon Sebag Monteforte, *Stalin: The Court of the Red Tsar* (New York: Alfred A. Knopf, 2004), 120.
6. Hobsbawm, 96-7.
7. Riasanovsky and Steinberg, 527.
8. Quoted in Robert Conquest, *The Harvest of Sorrow: Soviet Collectivization and the Terror-Famine* (Oxford: Oxford University Press, 1986), 117.
9. Riasanovsky and Steinberg, 524.
10. Stephen Kotkin, *Armaggedon Averted: The Soviet Collapse, 1970–2000* (Oxford: Oxford University Press, 2001), 15-6, 19-20.
11. Ibid., 17.
12. Ibid., 62.
13. Quoted in ibid., 69.
14. Quoted in Riasanovsky and Steinberg, 632.
15. Ibid., 621-2.
16. Anatol Lieven, *The Baltic Revolution: Estonia, Latvia, Lithuania, and the Path to Independence* (New Haven: Yale University Press, 1993), 220.
17. Karina Petersone, "In the Face of a Great Adversary: Remembering the Baltic Way," Last accessed: 4/27/2015, http://www.latvia.eu/blog/face-great-adversary-remembering-baltic-way.
18. Lieven, 219.
19. Quoted in ibid., 223.
20. Lieven, 250-3.
21. Hobsbawm, 495.

CONCLUSION

1. Gore Vidal, "Requiem for the American Empire," *Nation*, Last accessed: 5/12/2019 https://www.thenation.com/article/requiem-american-empire/.
2. Walter Scheidel, *The Great Leveler: Violence and the History of Inequality from the Stone Age to the Twenty-First Century* (Princeton: Princeton University Press, 2017), 80.
3. For just one example, see Annie Lowrey, "The Hoarding of the American Dream," *Atlantic*, https://www.theatlantic.com/business/archive/2017/06/the-hoarding-of-the-american-dream/530481/.
4. Mary Beard, *SPQR: A History of Ancient Rome* (London: Liveright, 2015), 66-7.
5. Tom Belger, "Major UK firm to slash 'thousands of jobs' in Brexit move overseas," *Yahoo! Finance*, https://finance.yahoo.com/news/major-uk-firm-to-slash-thousands-of-jobs-in-brexit-move-overseas-102949823.html.
6. Mary Jo Dudley, "These U.S. Industries can't work without illegal immigrants," *CBS News*, https://www.cbsnews.com/news/illegal-immigrants-us-jobs-economy-farm-workers-taxes/.

FURTHER READING

INTRODUCTION

Burbank, Jane and Frederick Cooper. *Empires in World History: Power and Politics of Difference*. (Princeton: Princeton University Press, 2010).

Ferguson, Niall. *Empire: The Rise and Demise of the British World Order and the Lessons for Global Power*. (New York: Basic Books, 2003).

Glubb, Sir John. *The Fate of Empires and Search for Survival* (Edinburgh: William Blackwood & Sons, 1977).

Hobson, John A. *Imperialism: A Study* (New York: James Pott and Co., 1902).

Lal, Deepkak. *In Praise of Empires: Globalization and Order* (New York: Palgrave, 2004).

Motyl, Alexander J. *Imperial Ends: The Decay, Collapse, and Revival of Empires* (New York: Columbia University Press, 2001).

THE ATHENIAN EMPIRE

Green, Peter. *Armada from Athens* (New York: Doubleday, 1970).

Kagan, Donald. *The Peace of Nicias and the Sicilian Expedition* (Ithaca: Cornell University Press, 1981).

Meier, Christian. *Athens: A Portrait of the City in its Golden Age*, trans. Robert and Rita Kimber (New York: Metropolitan Books, 1998).

Plutarch. *Alkibiades*, trans. Bernadotte Perrin (Cambridge: Harvard University Press, 1916).

Thucydides. *History of the Peloponnessian War*, trans. Steven Lattimore (Indianapolis: Hackett, 1998).

THE PERSIAN EMPIRE

Arrian. *Anabasis of Alexander,* trans. P.A. Brunt (Cambridge: Harvard University Press, 1983).

Axworthy, Michael. *A History of Iran* (New York: Perseus Books, 2008).

Bosworth, A.B. *Conquest and Empire: The Reign of Alexander the Great* (New York: Cambridge University Press, 1992).

Briant, Pierre. *From Cyrus to Alexander: A History of the Persian Empire,* trans. Peter T. Daniels (Winona Lake, IN: Eisenbrauns, 2002).

Diodorus Siculus. *Universal History,* trans. C. Bradford Welles (Cambridge: Harvard University Press, 1963).

Green, Peter. *Armada from Athens* (New York: Doubleday, 1970).

Herodotus. *Herodotus: The History,* trans. David Green (Chicago: University of Chicago Press, 1998).

Olmstead, A.T. *History of the Persian Empire* (Chicago: University of Chicago Press, 1970).

Plutarch. *Life of Alexander,* trans. Bernadotte Perrin (Cambridge: Harvard University Press, 1919).

Wiesehöfer, Josef. *Ancient Persia from 550 BCE to 650 AD,* trans. Azizeh Azodi (London: I.B. Tauris, 1996).

Wood, Michael. *In the Footsteps of Alexander the Great: A Journey from Greece to Asia* (Berkeley: University of California Press, 1997).

Xenophon. *Cyropaedia,* trans. Walter Miller (Cambridge: Harvard University Press, 1914).

THE QIN EMPIRE

Annals of Lü Buwei, trans. John Knoblock and Jeffrey Riegel (Stanford: Stanford University Press, 2000).

Clemens, Jonathan. *The First Emperor of China* (Stroud, Gloucestershire: Sutton Publishing, 2006).

Portal, Jane and Duan, Quinbo. *The First Emperor: China's Terracotta Army* (London: British Museum Press, 2007).

Sima Qian. *Records of the Grand Historian of China,* trans. Burton Watson (New York: Columbia University Press, 1961).

Sources of Chinese Tradition, trans. Burton Watson, eds. William Theodore de Bary and Irene Bloom (New York: Columbia University Press, 1999).

THE CARTHAGINIAN EMPIRE

Appian. *Roman History*, trans. Horace White (Cambridge: Harvard University Press, 1913).
Justin. *Epitome*, trans. Rev. John Selby Watson (London: Henry G. Bohn, 1853).
Livy. *A History of Rome*, trans. D. Spillan and Cyrus Edwards (London: G. Bell, 1989).
Miles, Richard. *Carthage Must Be Destroyed: The Rise and Fall of an Ancient Civilization* (New York: Viking, 2011).
Pliny. *Natural History*, trans. William Heinemann (Cambridge: Harvard University Press, 1968).
Polybius, *The Histories*, trans. W.R. Paton (New York: Willian Heinemann, 1922-7).
Quintillian. *The Orator's Education*, trans. Donald A. Robinson (Cambridge: Harvard University Press, 2002).
Sallust. *The Jugurthan War*, trans. J.C. Rolfe (Cambridge: Harvard University Press, 1921).

THE HAN EMPIRE

Keay, John. *China: A History* (New York: Basic Books, 2011).
Loewe, Michael. *Everyday Life in Imperial China, During the Han Period 202 BCE–AD 220* (New York: G.P. Putnam's Sons, 1968).
Roberts, J.A.G. *A Complete History of China* (Gloucestershire: Sutton Publishing, 2003).
Ssu-ma Guang. *Last of the Han*, trans. Rafe de Crespigny (Canberra: Australian National University, 1969).
Tanner, Harold M. *China: A History* (Indianapolis: Hackett, 2009).

THE ROMAN EMPIRE

Gibbon, Edward. *The Fall of the Roman Empire*, ed. Hans-Freidrich Mueller (New York: Random House, 2003).
Gordon, C.D. *The Age of Attila: Fifth Century Byzantium and the Barbarians* (Ann Arbor: University of Michigan Press, 1960, 1993).
Grant, Michael. *The Fall of the Roman Empire*, 3rd ed. (New York: Barnes & Noble, 2005).
Lançon, Bertrand. *Rome in Late Antiquity*, trans. Antonia Nevill (New York: Routledge, 2000).
Photius, *Library*, trans. John Henry Freese (New York: Macmillan, 1920).

Sivan, Hagith. *Galla Placidia* (Oxford: Oxford University Press, 2011).
Traina, Giusto. *428 AD: An Ordinary Year at the End of the Roman Empire*, trans. Allan Cameron (Princeton: Princeton University Press, 2009).

THE CAROLINGIAN EMPIRE

Astronomer. *Son of Life: A Contemporary Life of Louis the Pious* (Syracuse: Syracuse University Press, 1961).
Dutton, Paul Edward. *A Carolingian Reader* (London: Broadview Press, 2004).
Einhard, *Life of Charlemagne*, trans. Sidney Painter (Ann Arbor: University of Michigan Press, 1960).
McKitterick, Rosamund. *The Frankish Kingdoms Under the Carolingians* (London: Longman, 1983).
Nelson, Janet. *Charles the Bald* (London: Longman, 1992).
Riché, Pierre. *The Carolingians: A Family Who Forged Europe*, trans. Michael Idomir Allen (Philadelphia: University of Pennsylvania Press, 1993).

THE ABBASID CALIPHATE

Al-Suyuti. *History of the Caliphs*, trans. H.S. Jarrett (Calcutta: J.W. Thomas, 1881).
Brent, Peter. *The Mongol Empire, Genghis Khan: His Triumph and His Legacy* (London: Weidenfeld and Nicolson, 1976).
Grunebaum, G.E. von. *Classical Islam: A History, 600–1258* (Chicago: Aldine Publishing, 1970).
Kennedy, Hugh. *When Baghdad Ruled the Muslim World: The Rise and Fall of Islam's Greatest Dynasty* (New York: Da Capo Press, 2005).
Marco Polo. *The Travels of Marco Polo*, ed. and trans. Hugh Murray (Edinburgh: Oliver and Boyd, 1845).
Mission to Asia, ed. and trans. Christopher Dawson (Toronto: University of Toronto Press, 1940).
Sicker, Martin. *The Islamic World in Ascendancy: From the Arab Conquests to the Siege of Vienna* (Westport, CT: Praeger, 2000).
Turnbull, Stephen. *Genghis Khan & the Mongol Conquests, 1190–1400* (London: Routledge, 2003).
Wiet, Gaston. *Baghdad: Metropolis of the Abbasid Caliphate*, trans. Seymour Feiler (Norman: University of Oklahoma Press, 1971).

THE BYZANTINE EMPIRE

Choniates, Niketas. *O City of Byzantium, Annals of Niketas Choniates*, trans. Harry J. Magoulias (Detroit: Wayne State University Press, 1984).

Duchesne, Louis. *Early History of the Christian Church: From Its Foundation to the End of the Fifth Century* (New York: Longman, 1920).

Oman, Charles W. C. *The Byzantine Empire*. 1892. Reprint. (Yardley, PA: Westholme, 2009).

Phillips, Jonathan. *The Fourth Crusade and the Sack of Constantinople* (New York: Viking, 2004).

Queller, Donald E. and Madden, Thomas F. *The Fourth Crusade: The Conquest of Constantinople* (Philadelphia: University of Pennsylvania Press, 1997).

Translations and Reprints from the Original Sources in European History, vol. 3, ed. and trans. Dana Carlton Munro (Philadelphia: University of Pennsylvania, 1907).

Villehardouin, Geoffrey de. *Chronicle of the Fourth Crusade*, trans. Frank T. Marzials (London: J.M. Dent, 1908).

THE KHMER EMPIRE

Coates, Karen J. *Cambodia Now: Life in the Wake of War* (Jefferson, NC: McFarland, 2005).

Coe, Michael D. *Angkor and the Khmer Civilization* (London: Thames and Hudson, 2003).

Coedès, George. *Angkor: An Introduction*, trans. and ed. Emily Floyd Gardiner (Oxford: Oxford University Press, 1963),

Dagens, Bruno. *Angkor: Heart of an Asian Empire* (London: Harry N. Abrams, 1995).

"Did Climate Influence Angkor's Collapse?" March 29, 2010. https://www.ldeo.columbia.edu/news-events/did-climate-influence-angkors-collapse.

Gateau, Madeleine. *The Civilization of Angkor* (New York: Rizzoli, 1976).

Groslier, B.P. "Agriculture et religion dans l'empire angkorien," *Etudes rurales*, 53-6 (1974): 95-117.

Mabbett, Ian and Chandler, David. *The Khmers* (Oxford: Blackwell, 1995).

Ma Tuan-lin. *Ethnographie* (Farnborough: Gregg, 1972).

Mouhot, Henri. *Diary*, ed. and trans. Christopher Pym (London: Oxford University Press, 1966).
Stone, Richard. "Divining Angkor," *National Geographic*, May 2014.

THE AZTEC EMPIRE

Burland, C.A. *Montezuma, Lord of the Aztecs* (London: G.P. Putnam's Sons, 1973).
Carrasco, David. *City of Sacrifice: The Aztec Empire and the Role of Violence in Civilization* (Boston: Beacon Press, 1999).
Cortés, Hernán. *Letters from Mexico*, trans. A.R. Pagden (New York: Orion Books, 1971).
del Castillo, Bernal Diaz. *The Discovery and Conquest of Mexico*, trans. A.P. Maudslay (New York: Farrar, Straus, and Cudahy, 1956).
Florentine Codex, vol. 9, trans. Arthur J.O. Anderson and Charles E. Dibble, rev. ed. (Santa Fe: School of American Research, 1973).
Gillespie, Susan. *The Aztec Kings* (Tucson: University of Arizona Press, 1989).
Gómara, Francisco López de. *Cortés: The Life of the Conqueror by His Secretary*, trans. Lesley Byrd Simpson (Berkeley: University of California Press, 1964).
Moctezuma, Eduardo Matos. *The Aztecs*, trans. Andrew Ellis (New York: Rizzoli, 1989).
Restall, Matthew. *Seven Myths of the Spanish Conquest* (Oxford: Oxford University Press, 2003).
Townsend, Richard F. *The Aztecs*, rev. ed. (London: Thames & Hudson, 2000).
Vaillant, George C. *Aztecs of Mexico: Origins, Rise, and Fall of the Aztec Nation*, rev. ed. (London: Allen Lane, 1962).

THE MUGHAL EMPIRE

Eaton, Richard M. "Temple desecration in pre-modern India," *Frontline* 17.25 (2000). http://www.frontline.in/static/html/fl1725/17250620.htm.
Lal Srivistava, Ashirbadi. *The Mughal Empire (1526–1803)* (Jaipur: Shiva Lal Agrawala & Co., 1964).
Richards, John F. *The Mughal Empire* (New York: Cambridge University Press, 1993).
Sarkar, Jadunath. *Shivaji and His Times* (London: Longman, 1920).
Singh, Gopal. *A History of the Sikh People, 1469-1978* (Delhi: World Sikh University Press, 1979).

Sunderlal, Pandit. *How India Lost Her Freedom* (Bombay: Popular Prakashan, 1970).

THE OTTOMAN EMPIRE

Beaton, Roderick. *Byron's War: Romantic War, Greek Revolution* (New York: Cambridge University Press, 1991).
Brewer, David. *The Greek War of Independence* (Woodstock, NY: Overlook Press, 2001).
Finkel, Caroline. *Osman's Dream: The History of the Ottoman Empire* (New York: Basic Books, 2004).
Gamba, Count Peter. *Lord Byron's Last Journey to Greece* (Paris: A. and W. Galignani, 1825).
Gülen, Salih. *The Ottoman Sultans: Mighty Guests of the Throne* (New York: Blue Dome, 2010).
The Movement for Greek Independence, 1770-1821: A Collection of Documents, ed. R. Cogg (New York: Macmillan, 1976).
Palmer, Alan. *The Decline and Fall of the Ottoman Empire* (Cambridge: John Murray, 1992).
Rodogno, Davide. *Against Massacre: Humanitarian Interventions in the Ottoman Empire, 1815-1914* (Princeton: Princeton University Press, 2012).
Waddington, George. *A Visit to Greece in 1823 and 1824* (London: John Murray, 1825).

THE RUSSIAN EMPIRE

Ascher, Abraham. *The Revolution of 1905* (Stanford: Stanford University Press, 1988).
Blum, Jerome. *Lord and Peasant in Russia: From the Ninth to the Nineteenth Century* (Princeton: Princeton University Press, 1961).
Burbank, Jane, Mark von Hagen, and Anatolyi Remnev, eds. *Russian Empire: Space, People, Power, 1700–1930.* (Bloomington: Indiana University Press, 2007).
Radzinsky, Edvard. *The Last Tsar*, trans. Marian Schwartz (New York: Doubleday, 1992).
_____. *Alexander II, The Last Great Tsar*, trans. Antonia W. Bouis (New York: Free Press, 2005).
Riasanovsky, Nicholas V. and Steinberg, Mark D. *A History of Russia*, 8th ed. (Oxford: Oxford University Press, 2011).
Sablinsky, Walter. *The Road to Bloody Sunday: Father Gapon and the St. Petersburg Massacre of 1905* (Princeton: Princeton University Press, 1976).

Seton-Watson, Hugh. *The Decline of Imperial Russia, 1855—1914* (Strand: Methuen, 1952).

THE EMPIRE OF JAPAN

Atkins, E. Taylor. *Primitive Selves: Korea in the Japanese Colonial Gaze, 1910-1945* (Berkeley: University of California Press, 2010).
Beasley, W.G. *Japanese Imperialism, 1894-1945* (Oxford: Oxford University Press, 1987).
_____. *The Meiji Restoration* (Stanford: Stanford University Press, 1972).
Bix, Herbert P. *Hirohito and the Making of Modern Japan* (New York: HarperCollins, 2000).
Caprio, Mark E. *Japanese Assimilation Policies in Korea, 1910–1945* (Seattle: University of Washington Press, 1995).
Emperor Shōwa, transmitted by Domei and recorded by the Federal Communications Commission, August 14, 1945.
Harvey, Robert. *American Shogun: General MacArthur, Emperor Hirohito and the Drama of Modern Japan* (Woodstock, NY: Overlook Press, 2006).
Hobsbawm, Eric. *The Age of Extremes: A History of the World, 1914–1991* (New York: Pantheon, 1994).
Judgment: International Military Tribunal for the Far East (November 1948).
Lidz, Franz. "The Little-Known Legend of Jesus in Japan" *Smithsonian* http://www.smithsonianmag.com/history/the-little-known-legend-of-jesus-in-japan Last accessed: 3/4/2015.
Palmer, James. *The Bloody White Baron: The Extraordinary Story of the Russian Nobleman Who Became the Last Khan of Mongolia* (New York: Basic Books, 2009).
Stander, Simon. *Why War: Capitalism and the Nation State* (New York: Bloomsbury Academic, 2014).
Toland, John. *The Rising Sun: The Decline and Fall of the Japanese Empire, 1936-1945* (New York: Random House, 1970).

THE BRITISH EMPIRE

Brendon, Piers. *The Decline and Fall of the British Empire, 1781–1997* (New York: Alfred A. Knopf, 2008).
Childs, David. *Britain Since 1939: Progress and Decline* (New York: St. Martin's Press, 1995).

Clarke, Peter. *The Last Thousand Days of the British Empire* (New York: Penguin, 2008).
The Eden-Eisenhower Correspondence, 1955-1957, ed. Peter G. Boyle (Chapel Hill: University of North Carolina Press, 2005).
Gorst, Anthony and Lewis Johnman. *The Suez Crisis* (London: Routledge, 1997).
Guinnane, Timothy. *The Vanishing Irish: Households, Migration, and the Rural Economy in Ireland* (Princeton: Princeton University Press, 1997).
Hennessy, Peter. *Having It So Good: Britain in the Fifties* (London: Penguin, 2006).
Hobsbawm, Eric. *The Age of Extremes: A History of the World, 1914–1991* (New York: Pantheon, 1994).
Maddison, Angus. *The World Economy: A Millennial Perspective* (Oxford: OECD, 2009).
Mulcrone, Mick. "The Famine and Collective Memory: The Role of the Irish-American Press in the Early Twentieth Century" in *The Great Famine and the Irish Diaspora in America*, ed. Arthur Gribben (Boston: University of Massachusetts Press, 1999).
PBS NOW. Interview with Deborah Lessing. Last accessed: 4/1/2015 http://www.pbs.org/now/printable/transcript_lessing_print.html.
Shuckburgh, Evelyn. *Descent to Suez, Diaries 1951-56* (New York: W.W. Norton, 1987).

THE SOVIET UNION

Conquest, Robert. *The Harvest of Sorrow: Soviet Collectivization and the Terror-Famine* (Oxford: Oxford University Press, 1986).
Kotkin, Stephen. *Armaggedon Averted: The Soviet Collapse, 1970–2000* (Oxford: Oxford University Press, 2001).
Lieven, Anatol. *The Baltic Revolution: Estonia, Latvia, Lithuania, and the Path to Independence* (New Haven: Yale University Press, 1993).
Monteforte, Simon Sebag. *Stalin: The Court of the Red Tsar* (New York: Alfred A. Knopf, 2004).
Petersone, Karina. "In the Face of a Great Adversary: Remembering the Baltic Way." Last accessed: 4/27/2015. http://www.latvia.eu/blog/face-great-adversary-remembering-baltic-way.
Poton, Geoffrey. *The Soviet Union, Soviet Politics from Lenin to Yeltsin* (Oxford: Blackwell, 1994).

Read, Christopher. *The Making and Breaking of the Soviet System: An Interpretation* (Houndmills: Palgrave, 2001).

CONCLUSION

Beard, Mary. *SPQR: A History of Ancient Rome* (London: Liveright, 2015).

Belger, Tom. "Major UK firm to slash 'thousands of jobs' in Brexit move overseas." *Yahoo! Finance.* https://finance.yahoo.com/news/major-uk-firm-to-slash-thousands-of-jobs-in-brexit-move-overseas-102949823.html.

Dudley, Mary Jo. "These U.S. Industries can't work without illegal immigrants." *CBS News.* https://www.cbsnews.com/news/illegal-immigrants-us-jobs-economy-farm-workers-taxes/.

Lowrey, Annie. "The Hoarding of the American Dream." *Atlantic.* https://www.theatlantic.com/business/archive/2017/06/the-hoarding-of-the-american-dream/530481/.

Scheidel, Walter. *The Great Leveler: Violence and the History of Inequality from the Stone Age to the Twenty-First Century* (Princeton: Princeton University Press, 2017).

Vidal, Gore. "Requiem for the American Empire." *Nation.* Last accessed: 5/12/2019. https://www.thenation.com/article/requiem-american-empire/.

ACKNOWLEDGMENTS

Many thanks to the excellent libraries at the University of Missouri, the University of Virginia, and Sweet Briar College for providing me with the resources to finish this book. Also, thanks to my friends and colleagues Josh Rice, Cassie Yacovazzi, Patrick Witt, Jonathan Root, and Chris Deutsch for providing valuable feedback and criticisms.

Lastly, I would like to thank my parents, Betty and Wayne, to whom I owe all my successes.

INDEX

Iwakura Mission, 163

Jahangir, 131-132
Jainists, 128, 130
Jalisco, 117
Janissary corps, 139
Japanese Empire, ix, 159-170, 194
Japan, ix, 33, 85, 110, 154, 156, 159-
170, 186, 194
Jayatataka, 108
Jayavarman II, 108
Jayavarman VII, 108
Jerusalem, 16, 89, 94, 99, 104, 136,
138
Jewel Voice Broadcast, 167
Jezebel, 40
Jianglü, 35
jizya, 128
Johanitza, 104
Johannes, 65
John of Antioch, 67
John Paul II, 89
John the Baptist, 102
Judith, 74-76
Jue, Zhang, 55-56
Julian "the Apostate", 64
Justin, 42
Justinian I, 103

Karkh, 84
Kazan, 148
Kennedy, Hugh, 81, 84
KGB, 188, 190
Khan, Genghis, 85-86, 130
Khan, Guyuk, 86
Khan, Hulagu, 87
Kharkov, 187
Khatun, Doquz, 87
Khmer Empire, 106-112
Khrushchev, Nikita, 181, 185, 187,
208n1
Kiev, 152
Kievan Rus', 148
King Ahab, 40
King Athaulf of the Visigoths, 64
King Farouk, 176
King Hussein of Jordan, 180
King Solomon, 106
Kirov, Sergei, 184
Kitchen Debate, 181-182
Komnenoi dynasty, 102

Korean Peninsula, 51
Krementski, Rittmeister, 153
Kuh-i Rahmat Mountain, 17
kulaks, 185
Kurush, 13-14, 16-17

Lake Texcoco, 117
Lal, Deepak, ix
Lamakhos, 2, 8
Laskaris, Theodoros, 102
Latvia, 186, 188-191
Latvian War of Independence, 188
Lebanon, 40, 175
Legend of Christ museum, 164
Lend-Lease program, 174
Lenin, Vladimir, 184, 187, 192
Leo III, 69
Lessing, Doris, 172
Libya, 6, 42, 85
The Life of Brian, x
Lincoln, Abraham, 6
Lincoln Memorial, 6
Lingsi, 55, 57
Lithuania, 186, 188-191
Lithuanian Communist Party, 189
Little Ice Age, 111
Livy, 39, 45
Lord Byron, 142
Lothar, 73-76, 78
Louis IX, 104
Louis the German, 76-78
Louis the Pious, 72-76, 78
Luoyang, 54, 56
Luxembourg, 69
Lysistrata (Aristophanes), 6

MacArthur, Douglas, 169-170
Macedonia, 17, 20, 26, 45
Mahmud II, 139-140, 142-145
Mamertines, 43-44
mamluks, 85
Manchukuo, 163
Mandate of Heaven, 37
Mang, Wang, 52, 54
Mani Peninsula, 135
Manuel I, 93
Marathas, 127, 134
Marduk, 16
Maria of Antioch, 93
Martel, Charles, 70, 76-77
Marxism, 182, 184-185, 190